BIRD'S DIARY

THE LIFE OF CHARLIE PARKER 1945-1955

To Dear Annie
with love + best wishes
on this very special
day!.
18 April 1997

D x x x

WRITTEN BY KEN VAIL

Published by Castle Communications plc,
A29 Barwell Business Park, Leatherhead Road,
Chessington, Surrey KT9 2NY.

ISBN 1 86074 132 0

Printed and bound in the UK by Staples Printers Rochester Limited

Acknowledgements

My grateful thanks to:
My children, Sam and Emily, for taking care of business so that I could write this book;
Eddie Bert for his recollections and photographs;
Dr Robert Bregman;
Rolf Dahlgren for his generosity in sharing his photographs;
Down Beat and *Metronome* magazines;
Ron Fritts for sharing his information and material of Charlie Parker in Washington D.C. and Baltimore M.D., especially in view of his forthcoming book on Parker in Washington;
Dave Green for sharing his collection of cuttings and photographs, and for his knowledge and enthusiasm;
Freddie Gruber for his recollections;
Jimmy Heath for a wonderful photograph and for his recollections;
Franz Hoffmann for his amazing series of books, *Jazz Advertised*;
Ken Jones of the National Jazz Foundation Archive at Loughton;
Melody Maker for permission to use extracts;
Mosaic Records for permission to use photographs from 'The Complete Dean Benedetti Recordings of Charlie Parker';
Phil Oldham, editor of the *IAJRC Journal*, for his help in trying to track down the itineraries of JATP tours;
Chan Parker for permission to use photographs, letters and other ephemera from her collection;
Doris Parker for her recollections;
Jim Patrick for sharing his material on the Buffalo area;
Brian Peerless for sharing his collection of *Metronomes* and *Down Beats* and much more besides;
Ross Russell for sharing his time and knowledge;
Norman Saks for sharing some of his vast collection of ephemera;
Dieter Salemann for his discographical observations;
Tony Shoppee for sharing his *Down Beat* collection;
Andrew Simons for access to the Chan & Charlie Parker Papers Collection at the British Museum National Sound Archive;
Malcolm Walker for copies of his *Discographical Forum* containing the Charlie Parker Chronology compiled by Gordon R. Davies;
Tony Williams of Spotlite Records, London Road, Sawbridgeworth for his generosity in sharing his vast collection of photographs;
and David Stonard, a Charlie Parker completist, for his diligent proof-reading and pertinent observations.

I would also like to acknowledge the kind assistance of
Ray Avery, John Chilton, Eddie Cook, Richard Cook, Allan Ganley, Dr Ernest Jackson, Nick Jones, Mark Miller, Hank O'Neal, Annie Ross, Duncan Schiedt, Joe Segal, Ernie Smith, Peter Vacher and Bob Weir.

I have also been grateful for the writings of Leonard Feather, Mark Gardner, Gary Giddins, Ira Gitler, Nat Hentoff, Mark Miller, Alun Morgan, Bob Porter, Brian Priestley, Robert Reisner, Ross Russell, Phil Schaap and Barry Ulanov.

Photographs from the collections of Ray Avery, Eddie Bert, Rolf Dahlgren, Frank Driggs, Arthur Granatstein, Dave Green, Max Jones, Mosaic Records, Redferns, Norman Saks, Duncan Schiedt, Huguette Rajotte Schwarz, Peter Vacher, Tony Williams and the author.

Preface

Bird's Diary sets out to provide a fascinating insight into the life and times of the most charismatic and influential saxophonist in jazz… Charlie 'Yardbird' Parker… Bird. Using contemporary photographs, newspaper reports, advertisements and reviews, I have attempted to chronicle his life month-by-month from the revolutionary bebop recordings he made with Dizzy Gillespie in February 1945 to his death on 12 March 1955, preceded by a brief resumé of his life up to February 1945. I have tried to include all known club, concert, television, film and jam session appearances as well as his recordings, although this is not intended to be a discography. For that, you should read *The Charlie Parker Discography* by Robert M. Bregman, Leonard Bukowski and Norman Saks.

I hope that you, the reader, will find this book an informative accompaniment when listening to Bird's records or reading any of his biographies. I am grateful to Penny Braybrooke of Castle Books for the faith she has shown in the project, and to Carolyn Begley for her dedication and energy in the exacting task of sourcing the photographs.

Ken Vail, Cambridge, March 1996

SUNDAY 29 AUGUST 1920
Charlie Parker is born in Kansas City, Kansas to Addie (née Boyley) and Charles Parker Sr. He has an older half-brother John, known as Ikey, the result of Charles Sr's liaison with an Italian woman.

1931
Charlie Parker graduates from Charles Sumner Elementary School in Kansas City, Kansas where he has been a model pupil. The family moves to Kansas City, Missouri. It is likely that Charles Sr has left for good, by this time, taking Ikey with him. When Charlie expresses an interest in music, his mother buys him a secondhand alto saxophone but his enthusiasm soon wanes and he loans it to a friend.
Charlie spends a year at Crispus Attucks Public School.

1932
Charlie enrols at Lincoln High School. By now, Charlie's days as a model pupil are over and he is an inveterate truant.

1933
Charlie begins studying music under Alonzo Lewis. Plays baritone horn and clarinet in the school band.

1934
Charlie grows tired of the baritone horn, retrieves his alto and begins practising along with fellow pupil, pianist Lawrence Keyes. He also spends much time sampling the Kansas City nightlife

TUESDAY 10 APRIL 1934
The Ruffin family move in with Charlie and Addie at 1516 Olive Street. The family consists of mother, five sisters and a brother. Charlie is immediately attracted to the pretty 14 year old Rebecca Ellen Ruffin.

1935
Charlie quits the Lincoln High School and plays his first professional engagement. He becomes a member of Lawrence Keyes' Deans of Swing. Also in the band are James Ross (trumpet), Vernon Walker and Freddie Culliver (saxes), Walter Brown(vocals) and Charlie's very close friend Robert Simpson (trombone). When Robert Simpson dies on the operating table at the age of twenty-one, Charlie is heartbroken.

SPRING 1936
Charlie is a regular at the Reno Club, listening to Lester Young with the Count Basie Band. One night, a jam session is organised after the last set and Charlie attempts to join in. He is out of his depth, and when drummer Jo Jones throws a cymbal at his feet, the humiliated Charlie leaves in tears.

SATURDAY 25 JULY 1936
Charlie Parker (16) marries Rebecca Ruffin (16) in the Kansas City Courthouse.

NOVEMBER 1936
Charlie is involved in a car accident on the way to a gig in Jefferson City. Bassist George Wilkerson is killed in the accident, drummer Ernie Daniels punctures a lung, and Charlie breaks three ribs and fractures his spine. He is confined to bed for two months.

JULY 1937
Rebecca catches Charlie using a needle.

SUMMER 1937
Charlie spends the summer with George Lee's Band at a summer resort in Eldon, Missouri. He studies and practises hard with pianist Carrie Powell and guitarist Efferge Ware during the long engagement and returns to Kansas City a much improved musician.

SEPTEMBER 1937
Charlie rehearses at the Reno with Buster Smith and Jay McShann. Charlie learns a lot from Buster and joins Jay McShann's Band for a three week engagement at a club called Martin's. By the end of the year Buster Smith decides to leave Kansas City and try his luck in New York.

MONDAY 10 JANUARY 1938
Rebecca gives birth to a son, Francis Leon Parker.

1938
Charlie is constantly away from home, and playing around with other women. One night, he has an altercation with a cab driver, cuts him with his knife, and ends up in jail. When he gets out, he pawns his alto and hops a freight train to Chicago. In Chicago, he visits the 65 Club where the King Kolax Band is working. He borrows Andrew 'Goon' Gardner's alto and sits in. Billy Eckstine and Budd Johnson are in the Kolax band and they are amazed by Charlie's prowess. Goon Gardner befriends Charlie, gives him clothes and a clarinet, and gets him jobs. But soon, Charlie pawns the clarinet and catches the bus to New York City.

1939
When he arrives in New York, Charlie looks up Buster Smith who takes him in. Charlie has no union card so music jobs are unavailable and he finds work as a dishwasher at Jimmy's Chicken Shack. At least he gets a nightly chance to hear Art Tatum who is featured at the Shack.
Charlie spends all his spare time jamming around Harlem, especially at Clark Monroe's Uptown House.
He recalls: *I remember one night I was jamming in a chili house on Seventh Avenue between 139th and 140th. It was December*

1939. Now, I'd been getting bored with the stereotyped changes that were being used all the time, at the time, and I kept thinking there's bound to be something else. I could hear it sometimes, but I couldn't play it. Well, that night, I was working over 'Cherokee' and, as I did, I found that by using the higher intervals of a chord as a melody line and backing them with appropriately related changes, I could play the thing I'd been hearing. I came alive.

1940

Charlie returns to Kansas City for his father's funeral after receiving a telegram and a train ticket from Addie.
He joins the Harlan Leonard Band where he becomes friends with the band's pianist/arranger Tadd Dameron. After four or five weeks Charlie is fired and joins the Jay McShann Orchestra where he is to stay on and off for the next three and a half years.
Charlie asks Rebecca for a divorce saying, *'If I were free, I think I could become a great musician.'*

FRIDAY 9 AUGUST 1940

Paper disc recordings of Jay McShann Orchestra playing at the Trocadero Ballroom in Wichita, Kansas.
BUDDY ANDERSON, ORVILLE MINOR (trumpet), BOB GOULD (trombone), CHARLIE PARKER, JOHN JACKSON (alto sax), BOB MABANE (tenor sax), JAY MCSHANN (piano), GENE RAMEY (bass), GUS JOHNSON (drums):
Jumping at the Woodside / I Got Rhythm

SATURDAY 30 NOVEMBER 1940

Recordings from a broadcast by the Jay McShann Octet on radio station KFBR, Wichita, Kansas.
BUDDY ANDERSON, ORVILLE MINOR (trumpet), BOB GOULD (trombone), CHARLIE PARKER (alto sax), WILLIAM J. SCOTT (tenor sax), JAY MCSHANN (piano), GENE RAMEY (bass), GUS JOHNSON (drums):
I Found a New Baby / Body and Soul
BUDDY ANDERSON, ORVILLE MINOR (trumpet), BOB GOULD (trombone/violin), CHARLIE PARKER (alto sax), BOB MABANE (tenor sax), JAY MCSHANN (piano), GENE RAMEY (bass), GUS JOHNSON (drums):
Honeysuckle Rose (vln BG) / Lady Be Good / Coquette / Moten Swing / Wichita Blues

WEDNESDAY 30 APRIL 1941

Recording session by Jay McShann Orchestra in Dallas, Texas.
BUDDY ANDERSON, ORVILLE MINOR (trumpet), JOE TASWELL BAIRD (trombone), CHARLIE PARKER, JOHN JACKSON (alto sax), HAROLD FERGUSON, BOB MABANE (tenor sax), JAY MCSHANN (piano), GENE RAMEY (bass), GUS JOHNSON (drums), WALTER BROWN (vocal):
Swingmatism / Hootie Blues (vWB) / Dexter Blues

Below: Jay McShann Orchestra at the Savoy Ballroom. Walter Brown sings and Charlie Parker is second saxophonist from the left.

TUESDAY 18 NOVEMBER 1941

Recordings from a broadcast by the Jay McShann Orchestra in Chicago, Illinois.

BUDDY ANDERSON, ORVILLE MINOR, BOB MERRILL (trumpet), LAWRENCE ANDERSON, JOE TASWELL BAIRD (trombone), CHARLIE PARKER or JOHN JACKSON (alto sax), FREDDIE CULLIVER, BOB MABANE (tenor sax), JAY MCSHANN (piano), LEONARD ENOIS (guitar), GENE RAMEY (bass), GUS JOHNSON (drums), WALTER BROWN (vocal):

One Woman Blues (vWB) / *'Fore Day Rider* (vWB) / *So You Won't Jump* / *New Confessin' the Blues* (vWB) / *Red River Blues* (vWB) / *Hootie's Ignorant Oil* (vWB)

JANUARY 1942

The Jay McShann Orchestra arrives in New York City and opens at the Savoy Ballroom opposite Lucky Millinder's Band. Dizzy Gillespie is playing trumpet with Lucky Millinder and he and Charlie spend their after-hours jamming at Monroe's Uptown House.

JANUARY – MARCH 1942

Recordings from a jam session at Clark Monroe's Uptown House in Harlem.

CHARLIE PARKER (alto sax), other musicians unknown:

Cherokee

FRIDAY 13 FEBRUARY 1942

Recordings from an NBC Blue Network broadcast by the Jay McShann Orchestra from the Savoy Ballroom in New York.

BUDDY ANDERSON, ORVILLE MINOR, BOB MERRILL (trumpet), LAWRENCE ANDERSON, JOE TASWELL BAIRD (trombone), CHARLIE PARKER, JOHN JACKSON (alto sax), FREDDIE CULLIVER, BOB MABANE (tenor sax), JAMES COE (baritone sax), JAY MCSHANN (piano), LEONARD ENOIS (guitar), GENE RAMEY (bass), GUS JOHNSON (drums), AL HIBBLER (vocal):

St Louis Mood / *I've Got it Bad* (vAH) / *I'm Forever Blowing Bubbles* / *Hootie Blues* / *Swingmatism* / *Love Don't Get You Nothing But The Blues*

THURSDAY 2 JULY 1942

Recording session by the Jay McShann Orchestra in New York City.

BUDDY ANDERSON, ORVILLE MINOR, BOB MERRILL (trumpet), LAWRENCE ANDERSON, JOE TASWELL BAIRD (trombone), CHARLIE PARKER, JOHN JACKSON (alto sax), FREDDIE CULLIVER, BOB MABANE (tenor sax), JAMES COE (baritone sax), JAY MCSHANN (piano), LEONARD ENOIS (guitar), GENE RAMEY (bass), HAROLD 'DOC' WEST (drums), WALTER BROWN, AL HIBBLER (vocal):

Lonely Boy Blues (vWB) / *Get Me On Your Mind* (vAH) / *The Jumpin' Blues* (vWB) / *Sepian Bounce*

SUMMER 1942

When the Jay McShann Orchestra heads back to Kansas City, Charlie decides to stay in New York.

DECEMBER 1942

Billy Eckstine and Benny Harris conspire to get Charlie a job in the Earl Hines Orchestra, replacing Budd Johnson on tenor sax. Dizzy Gillespie is already in the band.

FRIDAY 15 – THURSDAY 21 JANUARY 1943

The Earl Hines Orchestra, with Dizzy and Charlie, play the Apollo Theatre in Harlem.

Below: Charlie and Sarah Vaughan in Chicago.

Above: The Earl Hines Orchestra at the Apollo on 23 April 1943. Trumpets, l to r: Dizzy Gillespie, Benny Harris, Gail Brockman, Shorts McConnell; trombones: unknown, Gus Chappell, Benny Green; pianos: Earl Hines, Sarah Vaughan; drums: Shadow Wilson; bass: Jesse Simpkins; guitar: Connie Wainwright; accordion: Julie Gardner; saxophones: Thomas Crump, Andrew 'Goon' Gardner, Scoops Carry, John Williams, Charlie Parker.

FEBRUARY 1943

The Earl Hines Orchestra, with Dizzy and Charlie, are working in Chicago.

MONDAY 15 FEBRUARY 1943

Private recording by Bob Redcross in Room 305 of the Savoy Hotel, Chicago, Illinois.

CHARLIE PARKER (tenor sax), DIZZY GILLESPIE (trumpet), OSCAR PETTIFORD (bass):

Sweet Georgia Brown

CHARLIE PARKER (tenor sax), SHORTY MCCONNELL (trumpet), possibly HURLEY RAMEY (guitar):

Body And Soul / Shoe Shine Swing (Cottontail)

CHARLIE PARKER (tenor sax), BILLY ECKSTINE (trumpet), HURLEY RAMEY (guitar), BOB REDCROSS (brushes), UNKNOWN (tenor sax):

Boogie Woogie / Three Guesses

FRIDAY 2 – THURSDAY 8 APRIL 1943

The Earl Hines Orchestra, with Dizzy and Charlie, are at the Howard Theatre in Washington.

SATURDAY 10 APRIL 1943

Charlie marries Geraldine Marguerite Scott, a dancer, in Washington.

FRIDAY 23 – THURSDAY 29 APRIL 1943

The Earl Hines Orchestra, with Dizzy and Charlie, play the Apollo Theatre in Harlem.

FRIDAY 7 MAY 1943

The Earl Hines Orchestra embark on a Blue Ribbon Salute Tour with Louis Jordan and Ralph Cooper. The tour of army camps takes them through the South and Midwest. One night, a redneck hits Dizzy Gillespie on the head with a beer bottle. Charlie admonishes the assailant, *'You took advantage of my friend, you cur!'*

Arguments over money during the tour lead to several members of the band leaving, including Billy Eckstine, Sarah Vaughan and Dizzy Gillespie. Charlie leaves soon after and returns to his mother in Kansas City. He works intermittently with the bands of Tutty Clarkson and Noble Sissle.

APRIL 1944

Billy Eckstine gets backing to form a big band and asks Charlie to join and take charge of the reed section. The band includes Dizzy Gillespie, Wardell Gray, Oscar Pettiford and Shadow Wilson.

AUGUST 1944

Billy Eckstine Band, with Bird, Dizzy, Art Blakey and Sarah Vaughan, play a two-week engagement at the Riviera Club in St. Louis. The 18 year old Miles Davis sits in, replacing the ailing Buddy Anderson. During this engagement, Charlie gets Rebecca to join him and asks her to remarry him. She refuses.

FRIDAY 18 – THURSDAY 24 AUGUST 1944

Billy Eckstine Band, with Dizzy and Bird, play the Regal Theatre in Chicago.
When the band returns to New York City, Charlie quits.

SEPTEMBER 1944

Charlie makes his 52nd Street debut working with Ben Webster at the Onyx club. Around this time, Charlie meets Doris Sydnor, a hat check girl on 52nd Street, and they soon begin living together.

FRIDAY 15 SEPTEMBER 1944

Recording session as the Tiny Grimes Quintet for Savoy at the WOR Studios in New York City.
CHARLIE PARKER (alto sax), CLYDE HART (piano), TINY GRIMES (guitar), JIMMY BUTTS (bass), HAROLD 'DOC' WEST (drums):
Tiny's Tempo (3 takes) / *I'll Always Love You Just The Same* (3 takes) / *Romance Without Finance* (5 takes) / *Red Cross* (2 takes)

THURSDAY 4 JANUARY 1945

Recording session as Clyde Hart's All Stars in New York City.
CHARLIE PARKER (alto sax), DIZZY GILLESPIE (trumpet), TRUMMY YOUNG (trombone/vocal), DON BYAS (tenor sax), CLYDE HART (piano), MIKE BRYAN (guitar), AL HALL (bass), SPECS POWELL (drums), RUBBERLEGS WILLIAMS (vocal), :
What's The Matter Now (vRW) / *I Want Every Bit of It* (vRW) / *That's The Blues* (vRW) / *G.I. Blues* (vRW) / *4F Blues* (vRW) / *Dream of You* (vTY) / *Seventh Avenue* (vTY) / *Sorta Kinda* (vTY) / *Oh, Oh, My My, Oh, Oh* (vTY)

TUESDAY 13 FEBRUARY 1945

Recordings from a broadcast by the Cootie Williams Sextet/Orchestra from the Savoy Ballroom in New York City.
HAROLD JOHNSON, EMMIT PERRY, GEORGE TREADWELL, COOTIE WILLIAMS (trumpet), EDDIE BERT, BOB HORTON (trombone), CHARLIE PARKER, FRANK POWELL (alto sax), LEE POPE, SAM TAYLOR (tenor sax), EDDIE DE VERTEUIL (baritone sax), ARNOLD JARVIS (piano), LEROY KIRKLAND (guitar), CARL PRUITT (bass), SYLVESTER 'VESS' PAYNE (drums), TONY WARREN (vocal):
Round Midnight / Seven Eleven / Do Nothing Till You Hear From Me / Don't Blame Me / Perdido / Night Cap / Saturday Night Is The Loneliest Night Of The Week (vTW) / *Floogie Boo / St. Louis Blues*

THUR	**1**	THUR	**1**	SUN	**1**
FRI	**2**	FRI	**2**	MON	**2**
SAT	**3**	SAT	**3**	TUES	**3**
SUN	**4**	SUN	**4**	WED	**4**
MON	**5**	MON	**5**	THUR	**5**
TUES	**6**	TUES	**6**	FRI	**6**
WED	**7**	WED	**7**	SAT	**7**
THUR	**8**	THUR	**8**	SUN	**8**
FRI	**9**	FRI	**9**	MON	**9**
SAT	**10**	SAT	**10**	TUES	**10**
SUN	**11**	SUN	**11**	WED	**11**
MON	**12**	MON	**12**	THUR	**12**
TUES	**13**	TUES	**13**	FRI	**13**
WED	**14**	WED	**14**	SAT	**14**
THUR	**15**	THUR	**15**	SUN	**15**
FRI	**16**	FRI	**16**	MON	**16**
SAT	**17**	SAT	**17**	TUES	**17**
SUN	**18**	SUN	**18**	WED	**18**
MON	**19**	MON	**19**	THUR	**19**
TUES	**20**	TUES	**20**	FRI	**20**
WED	**21**	WED	**21**	SAT	**21**
THUR	**22**	THUR	**22**	SUN	**22**
FRI	**23**	FRI	**23**	MON	**23**
SAT	**24**	SAT	**24**	TUES	**24**
SUN	**25**	SUN	**25**	WED	**25**
MON	**26**	MON	**26**	THUR	**26**
TUES	**27**	TUES	**27**	FRI	**27**
WED	**28**	WED	**28**	SAT	**28**
		THUR	**29**	SUN	**29**
		FRI	**30**	MON	**30**
		SAT	**31**		

WEDNESDAY 28 FEBRUARY 1945

Recording session as Dizzy Gillespie Sextet for Guild in New York City.
DIZZY GILLESPIE (trumpet), CHARLIE PARKER (alto sax), CLYDE HART (piano), REMO PALMIERI (guitar), SLAM STEWART (bass), COZY COLE (drums)
Groovin' High / All The Things You Are / Dizzy Atmosphere

MARCH 1945

Dizzy Gillespie/Charlie Parker Combo open at the Three Deuces on 52nd Street opposite the Don Byas Band and the Erroll Garner Trio. They are to be resident at the Three Deuces until July.

MONDAY 19 MARCH 1945

Pianist Clyde Hart dies of tuberculosis aged 35.

Below: 52nd Street at this time features an impressive array of talent. Apart from the Dizzy Gillespie/Charlie Parker Combo at the Three Deuces, the Downbeat features Art Tatum, Benny Morton's Band and the Loumell Morgan Trio and the Spotlite has the Nat Jaffe/Charlie Shavers Combo.
Across the street, the Onyx features Ben Webster and the Stuff Smith Trio, while Mezz Mezzrow holds sway at Jimmy Ryans.

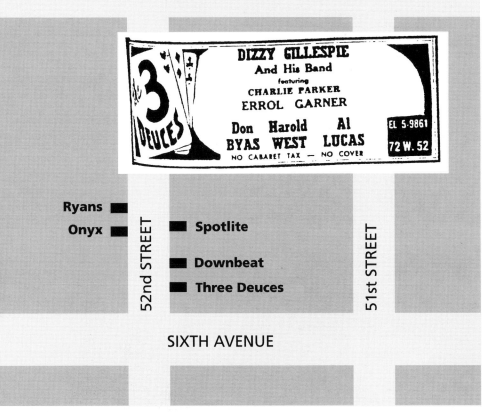

TUES	**1**
WED	**2**
THUR	**3**
FRI	**4**
SAT	**5**
SUN	**6**
MON	**7**
TUES	**8**
WED	**9**
THUR	**10**
FRI	**11**
SAT	**12**
SUN	**13**
MON	**14**
TUES	**15**
WED	**16**
THUR	**17**
FRI	**18**
SAT	**19**
SUN	**20**
MON	**21**
TUES	**22**
WED	**23**
THUR	**24**
FRI	**25**
SAT	**26**
SUN	**27**
MON	**28**
TUES	**29**
WED	**30**
THUR	**31**

Throughout May the Dizzy Gillespie/Charlie Parker Combo are resident at the Three Deuces opposite the Don Byas Band and the Erroll Garner Trio.

FRIDAY 11 MAY 1945
Recording session as Dizzy Gillespie and his All Stars for Musicraft in New York City.
DIZZY GILLESPIE (trumpet), CHARLIE PARKER (alto sax), AL HAIG (piano), CURLEY RUSSELL (bass), SIDNEY CATLETT (drums), SARAH VAUGHAN (vocal)
Salt Peanuts (vDG) / *Shaw 'Nuff* / *Lover Man* (vSV) / *Hot House*

WEDNESDAY 16 MAY 1945
Charlie Parker and Dizzy Gillespie appear at a Town Hall Concert for the New Jazz Foundation. Also billed to appear are Stuff Smith, Georgie Auld, Cozy Cole, Hot Lips Page, Slam Stewart, Dinah Washington, Skippy Williams, Teddy Wilson and the Leonard Feather Trio.

On stage at Town Hall: Dizzy, Harold West, Slam Stewart, Bird (right) and West, Curley Russell, Bird and Dizzy (below).

10

TUES	1
WED	2
THUR	3
FRI	4
SAT	5
SUN	6
MON	7
TUES	8
WED	9
THUR	10
FRI	11
SAT	12
SUN	13
MON	14
TUES	15
WED	16
THUR	17
FRI	18
SAT	19
SUN	20
MON	21
TUES	22
WED	23
THUR	24
FRI	25
SAT	26
SUN	27
MON	28
TUES	29
WED	30
THUR	31

Metronome's Barry Ulanov reviews the concert:

Dizzy Dazzles for an Hour; Rest of Concert Drags

THE NEW JAZZ FOUNDATION was well-served on Wednesday evening, May 17, [sic] at New York's Town Hall, when Dizzy Gillespie made his and the organization's concert debut. Dizzy was in magnificent form; I've never heard him play so well, muff so few notes, and reach such inspired heights. Though nineteenths of a concert is too much for a small band of the nature of Dizzy's, he and his associates acquitted themselves so well that the superfluity of chromatic runs, daring intervals and triplets, did not get on one's nerves.

The reason Dizzy and Charley Parker (on alto), Al Haig (piano), Curley Russell (bass) and Harold West (drums), had so much to play was that most of the announced guests didn't show. Dinah Washington sang Leonard Feather's *Evil Gal Blues* and *Blowtop Blues*, with Leonard at the piano. Dinah was, as usual, a brilliant shouter, at her best in the delightful lyrics of *Evil Gal*; she wasn't helped by the sordid analysis of the pathology of insanity which constitutes the story of the *Blowtop*. The Stuff Smith Trio appeared all too briefly to play *Desert Sands*, to play it with less than the conviction that usually attends its efforts. But the music is solidly constructed and Stuff and Jimmy Jones are always good to hear, and so their appearance was a great listening pleasure. I can't say as much for Slam Stewart's two contributions, *Play Fiddle Play* and *Lady Be Good*, both loused up with cheap chordal interpolations, uninspired cut-ins of such trivia as *Ridi, Pagliacci* and *The Volga Boatmen*. In *Play Fiddle Play* Slam indulged in another display of vaudeville jazz, playing all the way up the G string, until he hit his bow at the bridge; it was poor music and not impressive technically.

But poor Slam, fair Smith, fine Washington—these things were secondary to the performance of the Gillespie quintet. Dizzy's boys played through the first half of the concert unrelieved, and the effect was stunning. *Shaw 'Nuff* (named for booker Billy Shaw), *Night in Tunisia, Groovin' High, Be Bop, 'Round About Midnight*, and *Salt Peanuts*, were run played in programmed order, were run off magnificently by Dizzy and Charley and rhythm in that opening half. Dizzy and Charley played their unison passages with fabulous precision, no easy achievement when your lips and fingers are so tangled up in mad running-triplet figures. Charley's solos almost never failed to get a roar from the audience because of his habit of beginning them with four-bar introductions in which the rhythm was suspended (as in a cadenza), then slamming into tempo, giving his listeners a tremendous release, an excited relief. Al Haig played pleasant piano in Dizzy's groove and Curley and Harold played well; the former with an unusual regard for pitch and a big bass tone; the latter with a good feeling for Dizzy's style, all the more impressive when you realize that he is not his regular drummer.

The second half almost went to pieces. Guests didn't show and Symphony Sid, who was announcing the concert, became flustered and communicated his nervousness to Dizzy and the band. They did well with *Cherokee* and *Blue n' Boogie* and *Dizzy Atmosphere* and *Confirmation*, but not well enough to offset the obvious bewilderment on everybody's face and the long stage waits. And nothing could balance, for me, at least, the frantic jive of Symphony Sid, who is a creditable announcer on record shows, but much too anxious to knock you out with hip vocabulary. So sharp he was bleeding, he laid too much New Jazz Foundation hype on that audience. Somehow he didn't dig that we had our boots tightly laced; as a matter of fact, that audience seemed to me about the most hip I've ever seen or heard.

In spite of the limitations cited, this was an enjoyable concert, one which presented the right kind of music and musicians, one which justified the Foundation's claim that it is "not so much interested in the origin and historical background of jazz as … in its present status and its chance for growth in the future." Now, if Monte Kay and Mal Braveman, who are the NJF, will stop calling the art by that horrible name "jazz music," and will program their evenings with greater variety and more polish, we may look forward to the emergence of a society of real benefactors of jazz.

FRIDAY 25 MAY 1945
Recording session as Sarah Vaughan and her Octet for Musicraft in New York City.
DIZZY GILLESPIE (trumpet), CHARLIE PARKER (alto sax), FLIP PHILLIPS (tenor sax), NAT JAFFE (piano), TADD DAMERON (piano), BILL DE ARANGO (guitar), CURLEY RUSSELL (bass), MAX ROACH (drums), SARAH VAUGHAN (vocal)
What More Can A Woman Do? (p Nat Jaffe) / *I'd Rather Have A Memory Than A Dream* (p Tadd Dameron) / *Mean To Me* (p Nat Jaffe)

WEDNESDAY 30 MAY 1945
Charlie Parker and Dizzy Gillespie appear at a Town Hall Concert.

FRI	1
SAT	2
SUN	3
MON	4
TUES	5
WED	6
THUR	7
FRI	8
SAT	9
SUN	10
MON	11
TUES	12
WED	13
THUR	14
FRI	15
SAT	16
SUN	17
MON	18
TUES	19
WED	20
THUR	21
FRI	22
SAT	23
SUN	24
MON	25
TUES	26
WED	27
THUR	28
FRI	29
SAT	30

Throughout June the Dizzy Gillespie/Charlie Parker Combo are resident at the Three Deuces opposite the Don Byas Band and the Erroll Garner Trio.

TUESDAY 5 JUNE 1945

Charlie Parker and Dizzy Gillespie appear at a concert at the Academy of Music in Philadelphia. From a recording made at the concert, one number survives: DIZZY GILLESPIE (trumpet), CHARLIE PARKER (alto sax), AL HAIG (piano), CURLEY RUSSELL (bass), STAN LEVEY (drums)
Blue'n'Boogie

WEDNESDAY 6 JUNE 1945

Recording session as Red Norvo and his Selected Sextet in New York City
DIZZY GILLESPIE (trumpet), CHARLIE PARKER (alto sax), FLIP PHILLIPS (tenor sax), RED NORVO (vibes), TEDDY WILSON (piano), SLAM STEWART (bass), SPECS POWELL (drums)
Hallelujah (3 takes) / *Get Happy* (2 takes)
DIZZY GILLESPIE (trumpet), CHARLIE PARKER (alto sax), FLIP PHILLIPS (tenor sax), RED NORVO (vibes), TEDDY WILSON (piano), SLAM STEWART (bass), J. C. HEARD (drums)
Slam Slam Blues (2 takes) / *Congo Blues* (5 takes)

FRIDAY 15 JUNE 1945

Down Beat reviews Dizzy's latest record issue, one side of which features Charlie Parker, in **Diggin' the discs with Don**:

DIZZY GILLESPIE

Blue'n'Boogie / Groovin' High   Guild 1001
Neither side exhibits Dizzy's horn or style to the best advantage. Riffs are not new, except to one who has not dug Dizzy's work before; they're obvious but still interesting. Both sides, except during the ensemble parts, sound a little forced. *Boogie* has piano by Paparelli, under Dizzy's influence, then Dexter Gordon's tenor and Dizzy, typical but far from his best, playing ideas he's played innumerable times before. *Groovin'* showcases Charlie Parker's alto, Slam Stewart on bass and Remo Palmieri on guitar along with Diz's horn, both muted and open.

FRIDAY 22 JUNE 1945

The New Jazz Foundation hold their second and last concert at New York's Town Hall. Dizzy Gillespie Quintet (Dizzy, Charlie, Al Haig, Curley Russell, Max Roach) is featured and Coleman Hawkins plays with the Erroll Garner Trio (Al Lucas, Harold West). Also on hand are Slam Stewart, Buck Clayton, Don Byas, Sid Catlett and Pearl Bailey. Symphony Sid Torin is M.C.

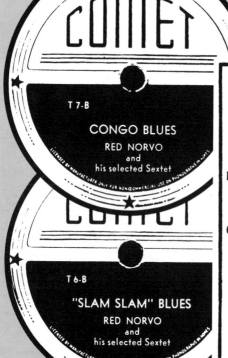

Jazz Stars Absence Drag Gillespie Bash

New York—The New Jazz Foundation is still shooting better-than-par. At its latest Town Hall soiree, two of the most widely-heralded stars, Coleman Hawkins and Slam Stewart, didn't show. Me, I'd like to know what goes on here.

If jazz promotors are going to run concerts and charge admission, then, like any other promotor, they must produce what they advertise and must plan their shows if they expect them to click. Several performers with heavy box-office appeal have failed to appear at both NJF shows and jazz fans who forked out good dough to attend the shows must be getting tired of the routine. Apparently contracts aren't made between the promotors and the artists or there wouldn't be such hit-or-miss attendance by announced jazzmen.

Concerts Badly Planned

Furthermore, the concerts are very badly planned. This is evident from the confusion existing on stage most of the time, from the meaningless program (rarely does any musician play in order or what he's listed to play), and especially from the stupid emceeing of a local radio announcer called Symphony Sid.

As for the music—well, lot of it was good but too much of it was repetitious and for that reason dull. Dizzy Gillespie's band and Don Byas certainly offered plenty of excitement but how great for how long can they be? Dizzy and alto-man Charlie Parker gave out with great music but it would have been a big help if their work was broken up by other acts instead of being presented in one

NEW JAZZ FOUNDATION TOWN HALL
123 W. 43rd St., N. Y. C.
Friday Eve., June 22, 8:15 P. M.
presenting
COLEMAN HAWKINS
DIZZY GILLESPIE
Charley Parker   Max Roach
Curley Russell   Al Haig
SLAM STEWART
Pearl   Buck
BAILEY   CLAYTON
Sidney   Don
CATLETT   BYAS
and introducing
ERROLL GARNER
Harold West   Al Lucas
Symphony Sid—Narrator
Tickets on sale at Town Hall and Rainbow Music Shop, 102 W. 125 St., N. Y. C. and Commodore Music Shop, 136 E. 42nd St.

SUN	**1**	WED	**1**
MON	**2**	THUR	**2**
TUES	**3**	FRI	**3**
WED	**4**	SAT	**4**
THUR	**5**	SUN	**5**
FRI	**6**	MON	**6**
SAT	**7**	TUES	**7**
SUN	**8**	WED	**8**
MON	**9**	THUR	**9**
TUES	**10**	FRI	**10**
WED	**11**	SAT	**11**
THUR	**12**	SUN	**12**
FRI	**13**	MON	**13**
SAT	**14**	TUES	**14**
SUN	**15**	WED	**15**
MON	**16**	THUR	**16**
TUES	**17**	FRI	**17**
WED	**18**	SAT	**18**
THUR	**19**	SUN	**19**
FRI	**20**	MON	**20**
SAT	**21**	TUES	**21**
SUN	**22**	WED	**22**
MON	**23**	THUR	**23**
TUES	**24**	FRI	**24**
WED	**25**	SAT	**25**
THUR	**26**	SUN	**26**
FRI	**27**	MON	**27**
SAT	**28**	TUES	**28**
SUN	**29**	WED	**29**
MON	**30**	THUR	**30**
TUES	**31**	FRI	**31**

THURSDAY 5 JULY 1945

Dizzy Gillespie/Charlie Parker Combo close at the Three Deuces. Dizzy forms a big band for an 8-week Southern tour with the Nicholas Brothers as 'Hepsations of 1945', beginning in Virginia on 8 July.

WEDNESDAY 1 AUGUST 1945

Down Beat reviews Dizzy's latest record issue, one side of which features Charlie Parker, in **Diggin' the discs with Don**:

DIZZY GILLESPIE

Be-Bop / Salted Peanuts Manor 5000

This could have been thrown out and swing fans would not have missed much. As it is it will undoubtedly give many listeners the wrong impression as to what Dizzy and Charlie Parker and their crew had been putting down on 52nd Street. In the first place, Don Byas, tenor, is on the sides and his horn doesn't blend with Dizzy's nearly as well as Parker's alto. Tone just isn't right for that kind of fast stuff. Then, too, the arrangements are too affected and overdone, so much that it's hardly good swing. Solos are by Dizzy, not too badly done as both solos are long enough to develop some ideas, Don Byas, Trummie Young on trombone, short and uninspired, and the late Clyde Hart on piano. Shelly Manne and Oscar Pettiford provide rhythm, though Shelly sounds a bit bewildered by all the nonsense. This is too frantic to be worthwhile, though noteworthy in being a bit of fresh air in the otherwise too stagnant swing music of today.

Above: Dizzy's Hepsations Band rehearsing at Nola's Studios. Back row, l to r: Lloyd Buchanan (bass), Max Roach (drums), John Smith (guitar), Al King, Ted Kelly (trombones). Middle row: Harry Proy, Kenny Dorham, Dizzy, Elmon Wright, Ed Lewis (trumpets). Front: Walter Fuller (arranger), Eddie de Verteuil, Charlie Rouse, Leo Williams, John Walker and Warren Lucky (saxes).

Charlie makes a few rehearsals with Dizzy's big band, but then sets about forming his own small combo. Early in August, the Charlie Parker Combo featuring Charlie (alto sax), Don Byas (tenor sax), Al Haig (piano), Curley Russell (bass) and Stan Levey (drums) open at the Three Deuces opposite the Erroll Garner Trio.

SAT	**1**
SUN	**2**
MON	**3**
TUES	**4**
WED	**5**
THUR	**6**
FRI	**7**
SAT	**8**
SUN	**9**
MON	**10**
TUES	**11**
WED	**12**
THUR	**13**
FRI	**14**
SAT	**15**
SUN	**16**
MON	**17**
TUES	**18**
WED	**19**
THUR	**20**
FRI	**21**
SAT	**22**
SUN	**23**
MON	**24**
TUES	**25**
WED	**26**
THUR	**27**
FRI	**28**
SAT	**29**
SUN	**30**

TUESDAY 4 SEPTEMBER 1945

Recording session as Sir Charles and his All Stars in New York City

BUCK CLAYTON (trumpet), CHARLIE PARKER (alto sax), DEXTER GORDON (tenor sax), SIR CHARLES THOMPSON (piano), DANNY BARKER (guitar), JIMMY BUTTS (bass), J. C. HEARD (drums)

Takin' Off / If I Had You / 20th Century Blues / The Street Beat

SATURDAY 8 SEPTEMBER 1945

Charlie takes part in a jam session at the Lincoln Square Center. Also appearing are Stuff Smith, Eddie Barefield, Don Byas, Erroll Garner, Dizzy Gillespie, Dexter Gordon, Ben Webster and the bands of John Kirby and Duke Ellington.

SATURDAY 22 SEPTEMBER 1945

Charlie takes part in a Symphony Sid Swing Session at the Fraternal Clubhouse.

SUNDAY 23 SEPTEMBER 1945

Charlie takes part in a Town Hall concert called Best in American Jazz. Also featured are Buster Bailey, Bill Coleman, J.C. Heard, Al Haig, Al Hall, Stuff Smith, Pete Glover (b), Freddie Jefferson (p), Teddy Wilson, Frankie Newton, George Wettling, Al Stein (16-yr-old saxophone virtuoso), Four Chicks and Chuck (vocal group) and Coker & Cimber (percussion duet).

MONDAY 24 SEPTEMBER 1945

Charlie turns up at the Downbeat Club ready to play, only to find another band working in his spot.

Down Beat prints this :
Sad Tale!
Downbeat Club, 52nd Street
Charlie Parker and his Combo.
Monday, September 24 –
Enters Charlie Parker, his alto and all.
Another band is on the stand!
Exit Charlie Parker, his alto and all.
Just a mute way of getting fired.

Below: The 4 September recording session of Sir Charles and his All Stars. L to r: Sir Charles Thompson (piano), Jimmy Butts (bass), Dexter Gordon (tenor sax), Buck Clayton (trumpet), J. C. Heard (drums), Danny Barker (guitar) and Charlie Parker (alto sax).

MONTE KAY presents

SYMPHONY SID'S SWING SESSION
AND DANCE

A WEEKLY NEW JAZZ FOUNDATION SHOW

-:- Starring -:-

"BIG SID" CATLETT
and a Sensational All-Star Orchestra

BUCK CLAYTON   TRUMMY YOUNG
CHARLEY PARKER   DEXTER GORDON
J. C. HEARD   TINY GRIMES
AL KILLIAN   TONY SCIACCA
BILLY TAYLOR   LEN GASKIN
LLOYD TROTTMAN   AL HAIG

Introducing ALLEN EAGER on Tenor Sax

SATURDAY EVE, SEPT. 22nd, from 8 to 2

at the FRATERNAL CLUBHOUSE
110 WEST 48th ST. [Between 6th & 7th Ave.] N. Y. C.
Tickets in Advance at MAIN STEM MUSIC SHOP
53rd Street & Broadway — Circle 5-9615
ADMISSION: $1.25 Plus Tax

MON	**1**	THUR	**1**
TUES	**2**	FRI	**2**
WED	**3**	SAT	**3**
THUR	**4**	SUN	**4**
FRI	**5**	MON	**5**
SAT	**6**	TUES	**6**
SUN	**7**	WED	**7**
MON	**8**	THUR	**8**
TUES	**9**	FRI	**9**
WED	**10**	SAT	**10**
THUR	**11**	SUN	**11**
FRI	**12**	MON	**12**
SAT	**13**	TUES	**13**
SUN	**14**	WED	**14**
MON	**15**	THUR	**15**
TUES	**16**	FRI	**16**
WED	**17**	SAT	**17**
THUR	**18**	SUN	**18**
FRI	**19**	MON	**19**
SAT	**20**	TUES	**20**
SUN	**21**	WED	**21**
MON	**22**	THUR	**22**
TUES	**23**	FRI	**23**
WED	**24**	SAT	**24**
THUR	**25**	SUN	**25**
FRI	**26**	MON	**26**
SAT	**27**	TUES	**27**
SUN	**28**	WED	**28**
MON	**29**	THUR	**29**
TUES	**30**	FRI	**30**
WED	**31**		

OCTOBER 1945

Sometime during October the Charlie Parker Combo (Charlie Parker, alto sax; Miles Davis, trumpet; Dexter Gordon, tenor sax; Sir Charles Thompson, piano; Leonard Gaskin, bass; Stan Levey, drums) opens at the Spotlite Club on 52nd Street (*above*).

THURSDAY 1 NOVEMBER 1945

Down Beat comments:

Highlight on 52nd street is Charlie Parker and his combo, which opened last month at the Spotlite club. Parker's great alto, complemented by drummer Stan Levy, Sir Charles on piano, bassist Leonard Gaskin, tenorman Dexter Gordon and Miles Davis on trumpet, cannot be outranked by the many other outstanding attractions on the street. The Buster Bailey Trio (William Smith, bass; Hank Jones, piano; Buster Bailey, clarinet) and singer Billy Daniels accompanied by pianist Kenny Wyatt alternate with Parker at the Spotlite.

During November, Charlie Parker and other stars from 52nd Street are in Toronto for a Massey Hall Concert. Charlie, Erroll Garner and Slam Stewart are photographed by *Down Beat* jamming at CKEY studios prior to the concert.

MONDAY 26 NOVEMBER 1945

Recording session as Charlie Parker's Reboppers for Savoy at the WOR Studios in New York City.
CHARLIE PARKER (alto sax), MILES DAVIS (trumpet), DIZZY GILLESPIE (trumpet/piano), ARGONNE THORNTON AKA SADIK HAKIM (piano), CURLEY RUSSELL (bass), MAX ROACH (drums)
Billie's Bounce (5 takes) / *Warming Up A Riff* / *Now's The Time* (4 takes) / *Thriving On A Riff* (3 takes) / *Meandering* / *Ko-Ko* (2 takes)
This is Charlie Parker's first record date as a leader.

SAT	**1**
SUN	**2**
MON	**3**
TUES	**4**
WED	**5**
THUR	**6**
FRI	**7**
SAT	**8**
SUN	**9**
MON	**10**
TUES	**11**
WED	**12**
THUR	**13**
FRI	**14**
SAT	**15**
SUN	**16**
MON	**17**
TUES	**18**
WED	**19**
THUR	**20**
FRI	**21**
SAT	**22**
SUN	**23**
MON	**24**
TUES	**25**
WED	**26**
THUR	**27**
FRI	**28**
SAT	**29**
SUN	**30**
MON	**31**

SATURDAY 1 DECEMBER 1945

Charlie signs a record contract with Savoy Records. This is thought to have been back-dated, and may come from 1947 when Savoy were in dispute with Ross Russell's Dial label.

MONDAY 10 DECEMBER 1945

Charlie and Dizzy Gillespie open at Billy Berg's on Vine Street in Hollywood.

Above and left: Charlie Parker on the stand at Billy Berg's club in Hollywood.

Diggin' Discs with DON

DIZZY GILLESPIE

Lover Man / Shaw 'Nuff   Guild 1002

Shaw 'Nuff is another of Dizzy Gillespie–Charlie Parker abandoned ensemble sides, with solos by both and pianist Al Haig in the now familiar and rather over-exhibitionistic style. There's a lot to this style – it's exciting and has plenty of musical worth, yet for lasting worth must rid itself of much that now clutters its true value. Dizzy's and Charlie's solos are both excellent in many ways, yet still too acrobatic and sensationalistic to be expressive in the true sense of good swing. *Lover Man* has a great Sarah Vaughan vocal, with wonderful backgrounds. Sarah's work, again, is clean and well-phrased, with nice feeling and understanding of the lyrics.

SATURDAY 29 DECEMBER 1945

Recording session as Slim Gaillard and his Orchestra for Savoy in Los Angeles.

CHARLIE PARKER (alto sax), DIZZY GILLESPIE (trumpet), JACK MCVEA (tenor sax), DODO MARMAROSA (piano), SLIM GAILLARD (guitar, vocal, piano on *Dizzy Boogie*), BAM BROWN (bass), ZUTTY SINGLETON (drums)

Dizzy Boogie (2 takes) / *Flat Foot Floogie* (2 takes) / *Popity Pop* / *Slim's Jam*

SATURDAY 29 DECEMBER 1945

Recording session as Dizzy Gillespie and his Rebop Six for the American Forces Radio Services (AFRS) show *Jubilee* which is broadcast weekly to military personnel overseas. The show is produced by Jimmy Lyons.

CHARLIE PARKER (alto sax), DIZZY GILLESPIE (trumpet), AL HAIG (piano), MILT JACKSON (vibes), RAY BROWN (bass), STAN LEVEY (drums), ERNIE WHITMAN (m.c.)

Dizzy Atmosphere / *Groovin' High* / *Shaw 'Nuff*

TUES	**1**	FRI	**1**
WED	**2**	SAT	**2**
THUR	**3**	SUN	**3**
FRI	**4**	MON	**4**
SAT	**5**	TUES	**5**
SUN	**6**	WED	**6**
MON	**7**	THUR	**7**
TUES	**8**	FRI	**8**
WED	**9**	SAT	**9**
THUR	**10**	SUN	**10**
FRI	**11**	MON	**11**
SAT	**12**	TUES	**12**
SUN	**13**	WED	**13**
MON	**14**	THUR	**14**
TUES	**15**	FRI	**15**
WED	**16**	SAT	**16**
THUR	**17**	SUN	**17**
FRI	**18**	MON	**18**
SAT	**19**	TUES	**19**
SUN	**20**	WED	**20**
MON	**21**	THUR	**21**
TUES	**22**	FRI	**22**
WED	**23**	SAT	**23**
THUR	**24**	SUN	**24**
FRI	**25**	MON	**25**
SAT	**26**	TUES	**26**
SUN	**27**	WED	**27**
MON	**28**	THUR	**28**
TUES	**29**		
WED	**30**		
THUR	**31**		

TUESDAY 22 JANUARY 1946

The first recording session for Dial Records, a new company set up by Ross Russell, is scheduled. Russell, owner of Tempo Music Shop at 5946 Hollywood Boulevard, hires pianist-arranger George Handy to supervise. The plan is to record the Dizzy Gillespie Sextet with Lester Young replacing Lucky Thompson and Handy playing piano. Tuesday is the band's off-night at Billy Berg's, but when Lester is discovered to have a gig in San Diego, the session is postponed for two weeks.

THURSDAY 24 JANUARY 1946

Dizzy Gillespie and his Rebop Six broadcast for WEAF from Billy Berg's Club.
CHARLIE PARKER (alto sax), DIZZY GILLESPIE (trumpet), LUCKY THOMPSON (tenor sax), AL HAIG (piano), MILT JACKSON (vibes), RAY BROWN (bass), STAN LEVEY (drums)
Salt Peanuts

MONDAY 28 JANUARY 1946

Charlie and Dizzy Gillespie take part in a *Down Beat* Award Winners Concert at the Philharmonic Hall in Los Angeles. Winners Charlie Ventura, Willie Smith, Mel Powell and Nat King Cole are featured along with Charlie, Dizzy, Lester Young (making his first major appearance after leaving the Army), Billy Hadnott, Howard McGhee, Al Killian and the Gene Krupa Trio. The concert is staged by Norman Granz. Some of the concert is recorded.
CHARLIE PARKER (alto sax), WILLIE SMITH (alto sax), HOWARD MCGHEE (trumpet), AL KILLIAN (trumpet), LESTER YOUNG (tenor sax), ARNOLD ROSS (piano), BILLY HADNOTT (bass), LEE YOUNG (drums)
Blues For Norman / I Can't Get Started / Lady Be Good / After You've Gone

CHARLIE PARKER (alto sax), WILLIE SMITH (alto sax), DIZZY GILLESPIE (trumpet), AL KILLIAN (trumpet), CHARLIE VENTURA (tenor sax), LESTER YOUNG (tenor sax), MEL POWELL (piano), BILLY HADNOTT (bass), LEE YOUNG (drums)
Sweet Georgia Brown

MONDAY 4 FEBRUARY 1946

Charlie and Dizzy Gillespie close at Billy Berg's on Vine Street in Hollywood.
Also on this date, Bird and Diz are privately recorded:
CHARLIE PARKER (alto sax), DIZZY GILLESPIE (trumpet), UNKNOWN (piano), RED CALLENDER (bass), possibly HAROLD 'DOC' WEST (drums)
Lover Come Back To Me

TUESDAY 5 FEBRUARY 1946

Recording session as Dizzy Gillespie Jazzmen for Dial at Electro Broadcasting Studios in Glendale. The first Dial recording date is a fiasco. Lester Young and Milt Jackson fail to show (Lucky Thompson and Arvin Garrison are drafted at the last minute) and the studio is filled with friends and hangers-on. Only one side is salvaged and another session is scheduled for Thursday 7th at 9 p.m.
CHARLIE PARKER (alto sax), DIZZY GILLESPIE (trumpet), LUCKY THOMPSON (tenor sax), GEORGE HANDY (piano), ARVIN GARRISON (guitar), RAY BROWN (bass), STAN LEVEY (drums)
Diggin' Diz

THURSDAY 7 FEBRUARY 1946

Charlie fails to show for the rescheduled session and the recording takes place without him.

SATURDAY 9 FEBRUARY 1946

Return airline tickets have been issued to the band but Charlie has traded his for cash, and as the rest of the band leave for New York Charlie is stranded in Los Angeles.

TUESDAY 26 FEBRUARY 1946

Charlie turns up at the Tempo Music Shop and signs a one-year exclusive recording contract with Dial Records.

FRI	**1**	MON	**1**	WED	**1**
SAT	**2**	TUES	**2**	THUR	**2**
SUN	**3**	WED	**3**	FRI	**3**
MON	**4**	THUR	**4**	SAT	**4**
TUES	**5**	FRI	**5**	SUN	**5**
WED	**6**	SAT	**6**	MON	**6**
THUR	**7**	SUN	**7**	TUES	**7**
FRI	**8**	MON	**8**	WED	**8**
SAT	**9**	TUES	**9**	THUR	**9**
SUN	**10**	WED	**10**	FRI	**10**
MON	**11**	THUR	**11**	SAT	**11**
TUES	**12**	FRI	**12**	SUN	**12**
WED	**13**	SAT	**13**	MON	**13**
THUR	**14**	SUN	**14**	TUES	**14**
FRI	**15**	MON	**15**	WED	**15**
SAT	**16**	TUES	**16**	THUR	**16**
SUN	**17**	WED	**17**	FRI	**17**
MON	**18**	THUR	**18**	SAT	**18**
TUES	**19**	FRI	**19**	SUN	**19**
WED	**20**	SAT	**20**	MON	**20**
THUR	**21**	SUN	**21**	TUES	**21**
FRI	**22**	MON	**22**	WED	**22**
SAT	**23**	TUES	**23**	THUR	**23**
SUN	**24**	WED	**24**	FRI	**24**
MON	**25**	THUR	**25**	SAT	**25**
TUES	**26**	FRI	**26**	SUN	**26**
WED	**27**	SAT	**27**	MON	**27**
THUR	**28**	SUN	**28**	TUES	**28**
FRI	**29**	MON	**29**	WED	**29**
SAT	**30**	TUES	**30**	THUR	**30**
SUN	**31**			FRI	**31**

Throughout March and April Charlie is resident at the Finale Club with Howard McGhee's Band. He also plays at Sunday afternoon jam sessions at Billy Berg's.

THURSDAY 28 MARCH 1946
Recording session as Charlie Parker Septet for Dial at Radio Recorders Studios in Glendale.
CHARLIE PARKER (alto sax), MILES DAVIS (trumpet), LUCKY THOMPSON (tenor sax), DODO MARMAROSA (piano), ARVIN GARRISON (guitar on *Moose The Mooche* only), VIC MCMILLAN (bass), ROY PORTER (drums)
Moose The Mooche (3 takes) / *Yardbird Suite* (2 takes) / *Ornithology* (3 takes) / *Famous Alto Break* / *Night In Tunisia* (3 takes)

Below: l to r: Bob Kesterson, Howard McGhee, Charlie Parker, Teddy Edwards and J.D.King.

WEDNESDAY 3 APRIL 1946
Charlie makes a handwritten contract to sign over half of his future royalties to Emery Byrd (Moose the Mooche), Charlie's supplier.

FRIDAY 12 APRIL 1946
Charlie takes part in a concert at the Carver Club on the UCLA campus. The concert stars Herb Jeffries, Kay Starr and the Nat Cole Trio. Also appearing are Benny Carter and Lester Young. Charlie opens the concert with an 8-piece group comprising: Charlie Parker (as), Miles Davis (t), Lucky Thompson (ts), Britt Woodman (tb), Dodo Marmarosa (g), Arv Garrison (g), Red Callender (b) and Perc White (d). After intermission, Charlie plays a set with Lester Young. The *Metronome* reviewer says: *This was by far the best number of the program.*

MONDAY 22 APRIL 1946
Charlie takes part in a Jazz at the Philharmonic concert at the Embassy Auditorium in Los Angeles. Part of Charlie's programme is recorded:
CHARLIE PARKER, WILLIE SMITH (as), COLEMAN HAWKINS, LESTER YOUNG (ts), BUCK CLAYTON (t), KENNY KERSEY (p), IRVING ASHBY (g), BILLY HADNOTT (b), BUDDY RICH (d)
I Got Rhythm / Norman Granz Introductions / JATP Blues

SAT	1	MON	1
SUN	2	TUES	2
MON	3	WED	3
TUES	4	THUR	4
WED	5	FRI	5
THUR	6	SAT	6
FRI	7	SUN	7
SAT	8	MON	8
SUN	9	TUES	9
MON	10	WED	10
TUES	11	THUR	11
WED	12	FRI	12
THUR	13	SAT	13
FRI	14	SUN	14
SAT	15	MON	15
SUN	16	TUES	16
MON	17	WED	17
TUES	18	THUR	18
WED	19	FRI	19
THUR	20	SAT	20
FRI	21	SUN	21
SAT	22	MON	22
SUN	23	TUES	23
MON	24	WED	24
TUES	25	THUR	25
WED	26	FRI	26
THUR	27	SAT	27
FRI	28	SUN	28
SAT	29	MON	29
SUN	30	TUES	30
		WED	31

MONDAY 15 JULY 1946

Down Beat's LA BAND BRIEFS reports: Howard McGhee Band to follow Benny Carter at Swing Club early in July: Howard (trumpet), Charlie Parker (alto sax), Sonny Criss (alto sax), Teddy Edwards (tenor sax), Gene Montgomery (tenor sax), Earl Echen (piano), Bob Kesterson (bass), Roy Porter (drums), Billy Renault (vocal).

Diggin' Discs with MIX

CHARLIE PARKER
Ornithology **
Night in Tunisia ***   Guild 1002

Ross Russell's latest experiment, this one arrived cracked, so there was a little difficulty reviewing it. *Ornithology* named for the Bird, is still the reigning fav *How High The Moon*, no matter what. Drummer Roy Porter bothers me a bit; there are times when his counter beats interfere with the pattern being played. Trumpet man Miles Davis follows in the dizzysteps admirably, and Lucky Thompson once again proves he has more than a big tone. Whole side is a little stiff for my dough, while I prefer *Tunisia* as made by Gillespie with the Raeburn band. Rhythm is much looser on this side tho, while Parker plays one fantastic four bar section crammed with notes and an idea that persists all the way through his chorus. This is some excellent jazz here, rebop or otherwise. (Dial 1002)

Above: the Howard McGhee Band. L to r: Earl Echen, Bob Kesterson, Gene Montgomery, Sonny Criss, Roy Porter, Howard McGhee, Charlie Parker and Teddy Edwards.

MONDAY 29 JULY 1946

Record session as Charlie Parker Quintet at the C.P. MacGregor Studios in Hollywood for Ross Russell's Dial.

CHARLIE PARKER(as), HOWARD MCGHEE (t), JIMMY BUNN (p), BOB KESTERSON (b), ROY PORTER (d)

Max is Making Wax / Lover Man / Gypsy / Bebop

Howard McGhee takes over the session when Charlie arrives in a desperate state and with nothing prepared. After three stumbling, hesitant pieces and a disastrous, fast *Bebop*, during which Charlie's sudden, uncoordinated movements become increasingly alarming, he collapses. He is sent home to the Civic Hotel and put to bed. Later in the evening, he twice wanders naked into the hotel lobby trying to use the pay phone. When he eventually is persuaded back to his room, he falls asleep smoking a cigarette and sets fire to his room. Charlie becomes abusive when manhandled from his room and is blackjacked and handcuffed by the police, and thrown into jail.

It takes Ross Russell ten days to finally locate Charlie in the Psychopathic Ward of the county jail. Russell and Howard McGhee find him in a strait jacket, chained to an iron cot in a small cell. Charlie pleads: 'For God's sake, man, get me out of this joint.'

Russell, McGhee and their associates appear before the judge on Charlie's behalf, and are relieved when Charlie is sentenced to be confined to Camarillo State Hospital for a minimum period of six months.

In September, Doris Sydnor moves out to California to be near him. She takes a job as a waitress and visits him three times a week throughout his period in Camarillo.

After a period of coming to terms with his new life and the withdrawal from drugs, Charlie volunteers for work in the hospital vegetable garden, and on Saturday nights he plays C-melody saxophone in the hospital band.

Ross Russell and Richard Freeman, the psychiatrist brother of Russell's partner, visit Camarillo once a month for consultations with Charlie's psychiatrist. They realise that he has little grasp of Charlie's character, and has quickly become the gullible victim of a Charlie Parker put on.

October sees the release of Charlie's Dial recordings. Ross Russell sells the Tempo Music Shop in order to become sole proprietor of Dial Records, and begins a heavy advertising campaign.

Charlie, meanwhile, is fitter and healthier than he has ever been and begins agitating to get out of Camarillo. Freeman discovers that it is possible for Charlie to be released into the custody of an approved Californian resident who would become legally responsible for him. Doris doesn't qualify, so Russell is elected, and forms are prepared requesting Charlie's release into the custody of Ross Russell.

A benefit concert is held to provide money for Charlie's rehabilitation, and eventually, at the end of January, it is announced that Charlie can be released.

SAT	**1**
SUN	**2**
MON	**3**
TUES	**4**
WED	**5**
THUR	**6**
FRI	**7**
SAT	**8**
SUN	**9**
MON	**10**
TUES	**11**
WED	**12**
THUR	**13**
FRI	**14**
SAT	**15**
SUN	**16**
MON	**17**
TUES	**18**
WED	**19**
THUR	**20**
FRI	**21**
SAT	**22**
SUN	**23**
MON	**24**
TUES	**25**
WED	**26**
THUR	**27**
FRI	**28**

At the end of January Charlie Parker is released from Camarillo State Hospital into the care of Ross Russell of Dial Records, who had been negotiating with night club operators in New York to find a regular job for Charlie in a night club.

SATURDAY 1 FEBRUARY
Ross Russell writes a letter to Chan Richardson.

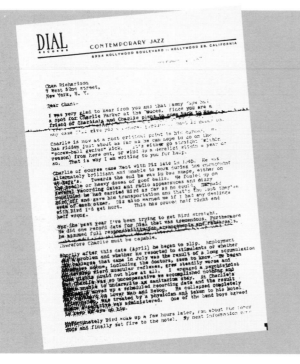

I was very glad to hear from you and that Sammy Kaye had a spot for Charlie Parker at the Deuces. Since you are a friend of Charlie's and Charlie plans to come back to New York very soon perhaps you can be of help to everyone. In any case I'll give you a general picture of what is going on...

Right now Charlie is determined to go straight. We were able to get him two sharp new suits, a complete wardrobe, and two airplane tickets to New York from the proceeds of the benefit last December. How long he can hold on to this determination is problematical. I am hopeful that he can take up his career and go ahead to become one of the important jazz names, musically and financially. He needs a lot of help and guidance. And he must make strong efforts himself.

The same evening a welcome home party is organised at the apartment of trumpeter Chuck Copeley. The party develops into a jam session which is recorded: Variously involved in the recordings are Charlie Parker (as), Melvin Broiles, Howard McGhee, Shorty Rogers (t), Russ Freeman (p), Arnold Fishkin (b), Jimmy Pratt (d):
Blues 1&2 / Lullaby in Rhythm / Yardbird Suite / Home Cookin'

SUNDAY 2 FEBRUARY
Bird is booked into Billy Berg's Club in North Hollywood for the first of four Sunday matinées. His quartet is completed by Erroll Garner (piano), Red Callender (bass) and Harold 'Doc' West (drums).

FRIDAY 7 FEBRUARY
Chan Richardson replies to Ross Russell, adding a handwritten postscript:

Just spoke to Sammy (Kaye). He offered $700 for the band. He said to let him know two weeks ahead and he can put them in any date. I'd advise you to ask for a two month guarantee at least, when you talk business. Sammy is a good guy. All you have to do is B.S. a little.

I don't know how good $700, but if you talk a little maybe you can raise it a little. $66 a man is scale here – and $90.75 for a leader. Hal West has always worked scale for Sammy. So I figured if you pay as follows it might work out all right.

Hal West	*70*
Red Callender	*75*
Wardell Gray	*75*
Erroll Garner	*100*
Howard McGhee	*190*
Bird	*190*
	700

But you can work that out – you know the earning capacity of these men better than I do.

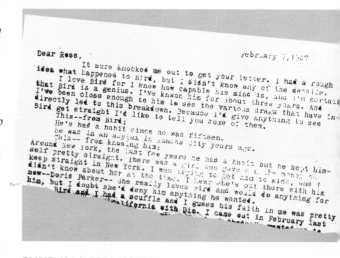

SUNDAY 9 FEBRUARY
The Charlie Parker Quartet play the second of their Sunday afternoon matinées at Billy Berg's.

SUNDAY 16 FEBRUARY
The Charlie Parker Quartet play the third of their Sunday afternoon matinées at Billy Berg's.

SAT	1
SUN	2
MON	3
TUES	4
WED	5
THUR	6
FRI	7
SAT	8
SUN	9
MON	10
TUES	11
WED	12
THUR	13
FRI	14
SAT	15
SUN	16
MON	17
TUES	18
WED	19
THUR	20
FRI	21
SAT	22
SUN	23
MON	24
TUES	25
WED	26
THUR	27
FRI	28

WEDNESDAY 19 FEBRUARY

Charlie Parker Quartet recording session for Dial at C.P. MacGregor Studios. Bird brings along vocalist Earl Coleman and insists that he is recorded.
CHARLIE PARKER (alto sax), ERROLL GARNER (piano), RED CALLENDER (bass), HAROLD 'DOC' WEST (drums), EARL COLEMAN (vocals)
Dark Shadows (vEC) / *This is always* (vEC) / *Bird's Nest* / *Cool Blues*
After the recording, Harold West prepares the food for a party at Lester Young's family home. A jam session ensues, which includes 20-yr-old John Coltrane.

These photographs taken at the 19 February recording session show (top, l to r) Harold 'Doc' West, Charlie Parker, Erroll Garner, Red Callender (bottom, l to r) Charlie Parker, Ross Russell, Doc West and Earl Coleman.

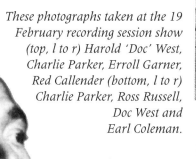

WEDNESDAY 26 FEBRUARY

Recording session for Dial at C.P. MacGregor Studios.
CHARLIE PARKER (alto sax), HOWARD McGHEE (trumpet), WARDELL GRAY (tenor sax), DODO MARMAROSA (piano), BARNEY KESSEL (guitar), RED CALLENDER (bass), DON LAMOND (drums)
Relaxin' at Camarillo (4 takes) / *Cheers* (4 takes) / *Carvin' the Bird* (4 takes) / *Stupendous* (4 takes)

C. P. MacGregor
Electrical Transcriptions
729 SOUTH WESTERN AVE
HOLLYWOOD, CALIFORNIA

SAT	**1**
SUN	**2**
MON	**3**
TUES	**4**
WED	**5**
THUR	**6**
FRI	**7**
SAT	**8**
SUN	**9**
MON	**10**
TUES	**11**
WED	**12**
THUR	**13**
FRI	**14**
SAT	**15**
SUN	**16**
MON	**17**
TUES	**18**
WED	**19**
THUR	**20**
FRI	**21**
SAT	**22**
SUN	**23**
MON	**24**
TUES	**25**
WED	**26**
THUR	**27**
FRI	**28**
SAT	**29**
SUN	**30**
MON	**31**

SATURDAY 1 MARCH 1947

Charlie and Howard McGhee's Band open at the Hi-de-Ho Club at 50th and Western. Local musician Dean Benedetti sets up his disc recording machine in a booth next to the bandstand and makes his first recordings of Bird.

CHARLIE PARKER (alto sax), HOWARD MCGHEE (trumpet), HAMPTON HAWES (piano), ADDISON FARMER (bass), ROY PORTER (drums) plus EARL COLEMAN (vocals)

September in the Rain / Rose Room / 52nd Street Theme / All the Things You Are / Blue 'n' Boogie / I Surrender Dear / Stardust (vocal)

SUNDAY 2 MARCH 1947

Dean Benedetti again records the band at the Hi-de-Ho Club.

CHARLIE PARKER (alto sax), HOWARD MCGHEE (trumpet), HAMPTON HAWES (piano), ADDISON FARMER (bass), ROY PORTER (drums) plus EARL COLEMAN (vocals)

Blues in F / The Man I Love / Cheers / Byas A Drink / Ornithology / Past Due (Relaxin' at Camarillo) / I'm In The Mood For Love (vocal) */ Yardbird Suite / September In The Rain / Sportsman's Hop / Night And Day / The Very Thought Of You* (vocal) */ Hot House / Cheers / I Don't Stand A Ghost Of A Chance* (vocal) */ Big Noise (Wee) / September In The Rain / Bean Soup / Big Noise (Wee) / I'm In The Mood For Love / 52nd Street Theme / Carvin' The Bird / Stardust* (vocal) */ Byas A Drink / Groovin' High / It's The Talk Of The Town / Body And Soul* (no Bird) */ Ornithology / Perdido / Sweet Georgia Brown / Night In Tunisia*

MONDAY 3 MARCH 1947

Off night at the Hi-de-Ho.

TUESDAY 4 MARCH 1947

Dean Benedetti again records the band at the Hi-de-Ho Club.

WEDNESDAY 5 MARCH 1947

Dean Benedetti again records the band at the Hi-de-Ho Club.

THURSDAY 6 MARCH 1947

Dean Benedetti again records the band at the Hi-de-Ho Club.

CHARLIE PARKER (alto sax), HOWARD MCGHEE (trumpet), HAMPTON HAWES (piano), ADDISON FARMER (bass), ROY PORTER (drums) plus EARL COLEMAN (vocals)

Sportsman's Hop / Night In Tunisia / The Very Thought Of You (vocal) */ Perdido / Now's The Time / Big Noise (Wee) / Hot House / Stuffy / Body And Soul / Ornithology / Sentimental Journey / 52nd Street Theme / Groovin' High / The Man I Love / I Don't Stand A Ghost Of A Chance* (vocal) */ Past Due (Relaxin' At Camarillo) / Night And Day / Moose The Mooche / Cheers*

FRIDAY 7 MARCH 1947

Benedetti learns more about disc cutting and begins dubbing. He is again at the Hi-de-Ho to record the band.

CHARLIE PARKER (alto sax), HOWARD MCGHEE (trumpet), HAMPTON HAWES (piano), ADDISON FARMER (bass), ROY PORTER (drums) plus EARL COLEMAN (vocals)

Hot House / The Man I Love / Past Due (Relaxin' at Camarillo) / S'Wonderful / Rose Room / Groovin' High / Big Noise (Wee) / Byas A Drink / Body And Soul (vocal) */ Hot House / Cheers / Night In Tunisia / Now's The Time / I'm In The Mood For Love* (vocal) */ September In The Rain / I Surrender Dear / Dee Dee's Dance / Stuffy / Perdido / Body And Soul* (vocal) */ Big Noise (Wee) / All The Things You Are* (vocal) */ Past Due (Relaxin' At Camarillo) / Sportsman's Hop / Dee Dee's Dance / Stardust* (vocal) */ I Don't Stand A Ghost Of A Chance / Ornithology / The Man I Love / Bean Soup*

SATURDAY 8 MARCH 1947

Dean Benedetti again records the band at the Hi-de-Ho Club.

CHARLIE PARKER (alto sax), HOWARD MCGHEE (trumpet), HAMPTON HAWES (piano), ADDISON FARMER (bass), ROY PORTER (drums) plus EARL COLEMAN (vocals)

Sportsman's Hop / Dee Dee's Dance / Stuffy / Hot House / Perdido / Disorder At The Border / I Surrender Dear / I'm In The Mood For Love / Night And Day / Bean Stalking / September In The Rain / Now's The Time / Wee / Bean Soup / Body And Soul / Night And Day / Prisoner Of Love / The Very Thought Of You / Byas A Drink / All The Things You Are / Stardust / Night In Tunisia / Ornithology / The Man I Love

SUNDAY 9 MARCH 1947

Dean Benedetti again records the band at the Hi-de-Ho Club.

CHARLIE PARKER (alto sax), HOWARD MCGHEE (trumpet), HAMPTON HAWES (piano), ADDISON FARMER (bass), ROY PORTER (drums) plus EARL COLEMAN (vocals)

Perdido / Indiana / Now's The Time / Night In Tunisia / Sweet And Lovely / Stardust / Bean Soup / Perdido / Moose The Mooche / Hot House / Dee Dee's Dance / Bird Lore / Past Due (Relaxin' At Camarillo) / Body And Soul / Ornithology / The Man I Love / Stuffy / Ornithology

MONDAY 10 MARCH 1947

Off night at the Hi-de-Ho.

SAT	1
SUN	2
MON	3
TUES	4
WED	5
THUR	6
FRI	7
SAT	8
SUN	9
MON	10
TUES	11
WED	12
THUR	13
FRI	14
SAT	15
SUN	16
MON	17
TUES	18
WED	19
THUR	20
FRI	21
SAT	22
SUN	23
MON	24
TUES	25
WED	26
THUR	27
FRI	28
SAT	29
SUN	30
MON	31

TUESDAY 11 MARCH 1947

Dean Benedetti again records the band at the Hi-de-Ho Club.
CHARLIE PARKER (alto sax), HOWARD MCGHEE (trumpet), HAMPTON HAWES (piano), ADDISON FARMER (bass), ROY PORTER (drums) plus EARL COLEMAN (vocals)
S'Wonderful (Stupendous) / Disorder At The Border / September In The Rain / Now's The Time / I'm In The Mood For Love (vocal) / Rifftide / Dee Dee's Dance / Ornithology / Cheers / Ballad / Perdido / Byas A Drink / Wee / The Very Thought Of You / Stardust / Bean Soup

WEDNESDAY 12 MARCH 1947

Dean Benedetti again records the band at the Hi-de-Ho Club.
CHARLIE PARKER (alto sax), HOWARD MCGHEE (trumpet), HAMPTON HAWES (piano), ADDISON FARMER (bass), ROY PORTER (drums) plus EARL COLEMAN (vocals)
Blues In B Flat / Unknown / Sweet And Lovely / Perdido / Cheers / Sportsman's Hop / Wee / Stuffy / Hot House / Ornithology / Dee Dee's Dance / The Man I Love / September In The Rain / I'm In The Mood For Love / Groovin' High / Cheers / Byas A Drink / Prisoner Of Love / Stardust / Now's The Time / Hot House / Wee / Moose The Mooche / Past Due (Relaxin' At Camarillo)

THURSDAY 13 MARCH 1947

Dean Benedetti again records the band on the last night of their engagement at the Hi-de-Ho Club.
CHARLIE PARKER (alto sax), HOWARD MCGHEE (trumpet), HAMPTON HAWES (piano), ADDISON FARMER (bass), ROY PORTER (drums) plus EARL COLEMAN (vocals)
Groovin' High / September In The Rain / Wee / Rifftide / Perdido / These Foolish Things / Body And Soul / Disorder At The Border / Hot House / Moose The Mooche / Sportsman's Hop / Blues In B Flat / Ornithology / Stuffy / Night In Tunisia / Byas A Drink / Indiana

Dean Benedetti

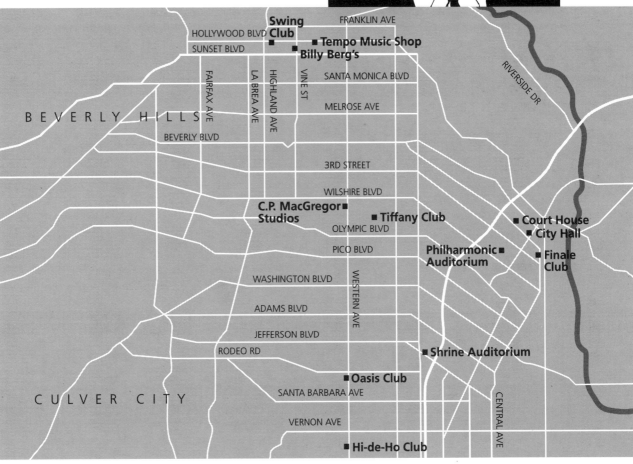

TUES	**1**
WED	**2**
THUR	**3**
FRI	**4**
SAT	**5**
SUN	**6**
MON	**7**
TUES	**8**
WED	**9**
THUR	**10**
FRI	**11**
SAT	**12**
SUN	**13**
MON	**14**
TUES	**15**
WED	**16**
THUR	**17**
FRI	**18**
SAT	**19**
SUN	**20**
MON	**21**
TUES	**22**
WED	**23**
THUR	**24**
FRI	**25**
SAT	**26**
SUN	**27**
MON	**28**
TUES	**29**
WED	**30**

FRIDAY 4 APRIL 1947
Charlie and Doris leave Los Angeles and fly to Chicago.

EASTER SUNDAY 6 APRIL 1947
Bird plays an Easter Sunday concert in Chicago with Howard McGhee.

EASTER MONDAY 7 APRIL 1947
Bird and Doris arrive in New York and move into the Dewey Square Hotel on W117th Street where they live for the next year. A party is held in Harlem at Smalls Paradise.

TUESDAY 8 APRIL 1947
Bird goes to the Savoy Ballroom and sits in with Dizzy Gillespie's Big Band.

TUES	**1**
WED	**2**
THUR	**3**
FRI	**4**
SAT	**5**
SUN	**6**
MON	**7**
TUES	**8**
WED	**9**
THUR	**10**
FRI	**11**
SAT	**12**
SUN	**13**
MON	**14**
TUES	**15**
WED	**16**
THUR	**17**
FRI	**18**
SAT	**19**
SUN	**20**
MON	**21**
TUES	**22**
WED	**23**
THUR	**24**
FRI	**25**
SAT	**26**
SUN	**27**
MON	**28**
TUES	**29**
WED	**30**

Charlie puts together a quintet with Miles Davis (trumpet), Duke Jordan (piano), Tommy Potter (bass) and Max Roach (drums). They begin rehearsing at the home of Teddy Reig, recording director for Savoy Records, and also at Max Roach's house in Brooklyn. According to Miles Davis, it is in April that they go into the Three Deuces club on 52nd Street for their first major gig. They share the bill with Lennie Tristano.

Although it is by no means certain at which point during the summer the Charlie Parker Quintet go into the Three Deuces, there is no doubt about the impact they create, especially with other musicians, on the Street. Below, l to r: Tommy Potter (bass), Bird, Miles Davis (trumpet) and Duke Jordan (piano). Max Roach (drums) is hidden but can be seen in the picture at the right.

THUR	**1**
FRI	**2**
SAT	**3**
SUN	**4**
MON	**5**
TUES	**6**
WED	**7**
THUR	**8**
FRI	**9**
SAT	**10**
SUN	**11**
MON	**12**
TUES	**13**
WED	**14**
THUR	**15**
FRI	**16**
SAT	**17**
SUN	**18**
MON	**19**
TUES	**20**
WED	**21**
THUR	**22**
FRI	**23**
SAT	**24**
SUN	**25**
MON	**26**
TUES	**27**
WED	**28**
THUR	**29**
FRI	**30**
SAT	**31**

Carnegie "POP" Concerts

presents

NORMAN GRANZ'

"JAZZ

AT THE

PHILHARMONIC"

FEATURING:

Coleman Hawkins — Benny Fonduille
Buddy Rich — Helen Humes
Willie Smith — Lennie Tristano
Buck Clayton — Hank Jones
Eddie Safranski — Harry Carney
Flip Phillips — Oscar Pettiford
Alvin Stoller — Theodore Navarro
Kenny Kersey

Monday, May 5th. 8:00 P.M.

BOX OFFICE NOW OPEN

Prices $1.50 to $3.60 (tax incl.)

CARNEGIE HALL 57th St. & 7th Ave. New York City

Granz N.Y. Bash Misses

New York—First of Norman Granz' Jazz at the Philharmonic Carnegie Hall Pops bashes was not a complete musical nor financial success. Principal reason was one of those nights when a lot of good musicians simply aren't playing up to their names. Secondary were Life photographer Gjon Mili, Carnegie Hall acoustics and the audience.

Mili, a friend of Granz', was there to take pictures. In his bumblings about the stage and flashings of pre-set lights, he not only disturbed the musicians, but gave the raucous section of the crowd a focal point for its bellicoseness. Result at the first intermission was a mass uproar which forced Mili to slacken his activities.

...Actual criticisms noted were that in the usual first set with Philharmonic standbys Buck Clayton, Willie Smith, Flip Phillips and trombonist Kai Winding working, there were too many tunes which had been heard before. Fast blues, Willie on Tea For Two, How High The Moon, Flip's Sweet And Lovely and Flying Home all came off—but they have been done here many times. A change of changes is in order.

...Second band with Buddy Rich, Ed Safranski, Hank Jones, Coleman Hawkins, Roy Eldridge and Charlie Parker sounded livelier, with Rich's fantastically technical yet swinging drums pacing the group. All the others hit occasional high spots, save Parker, who seemed too tired to play adequately.

MONDAY 5 MAY 1947

Charlie Parker takes part in the first of six Monday night concerts by Jazz At The Philharmonic at Carnegie Hall starting at 8.00 pm.

Later in the evening, Charlie is the star at Smalls' Paradise in Harlem for a Blue Monday Jam Session. The event is billed as Charlie's 2nd New York appearance in 2 years.

THURSDAY 8 MAY 1947

Recording session as Charlie Parker All Stars for Savoy at the Harris Smith Studios, New York City.
CHARLIE PARKER (alto sax), MILES DAVIS (trumpet), BUD POWELL (piano), TOMMY POTTER (bass), MAX ROACH (drums)
Donna Lee (5 takes) / *Chasing the Bird* (4 takes) / *Cheryl* (2 takes) / *Buzzy* (5 takes)

SATURDAY 31 MAY 1947

Bird and Dizzy Gillespie take part in the 'Salute to Negro Veterans' concert at Town Hall.

JOHNNY JACKSON PRESENTS HIS 10th

Blue Mon. Jazz Concert

(A Night of Musical Entertainment)

THIS MONDAY NIGHT, MAY 5th

At 9:30 P. M.

Bringing the Return Engagement of the World's Greatest Alto Saxophonist of Today's Modern Music

CHARLIE (YARDBIRD) PARKER

His 2nd New York appearance in 2 years

Playing for you some of his famous hit numbers that have influenced many of today's greatest musicians

– Plus –

A Dual Between Two Great Tenor Sax's

MORRIS LANE -vs- JAMES MOODY
Tenor direct from the / Tenor direct from the
"Cavalcade of Jazz" / D. Gillespie Band

Assisted by

JIMMY (The Face) BUTTS / TEDDY STEWART
On Bass / On Drums
GILLIE COGGINS, Piano / TONY SCOTT, Clarin.

KENNY DURHAN, Trumpet

Extra Added – Joe Livingston and His Quartet

SMALLS' PARADISE

135th St. & 7th Ave., N. Y. C.

Advance — $1.00   At Door — $1.25 (Tax In.

Yardbird Parker Is Blue Monday's Jam 'Sesh' Star

...This Monday night Johnny Jackson brings the saxophone moans and groans of "Yardbird" Parker pitted against John "Bad Man" Hardee, and Morris Lane—together with a terrific supporting cast of musicians which will include: George Jenkins, drums; Tony Scott, clarinet; Jimmy Butts, bass; Bill Durango, guitar; plus an array of celebs.

Town Hall Concert Salutes Negro Vets

New York—In a salute to 1,154,000 Negro war veterans, the United Negro and Allied veterans of America conducted a special program at Town Hall, May 31, that featured Dizzy Gillespie and Charlie (Yardbird) Parker in their first joint effort since Parker returned from the coast.

SUN	1	TUES	1
MON	2	WED	2
TUES	3	THUR	3
WED	4	FRI	4
THUR	5	SAT	5
FRI	6	SUN	6
SAT	7	MON	7
SUN	8	TUES	8
MON	9	WED	9
TUES	10	THUR	10
WED	11	FRI	11
THUR	12	SAT	12
FRI	13	SUN	13
SAT	14	MON	14
SUN	15	TUES	15
MON	16	WED	16
TUES	17	THUR	17
WED	18	FRI	18
THUR	19	SAT	19
FRI	20	SUN	20
SAT	21	MON	21
SUN	22	TUES	22
MON	23	WED	23
TUES	24	THUR	24
WED	25	FRI	25
THUR	26	SAT	26
FRI	27	SUN	27
SAT	28	MON	28
SUN	29	TUES	29
MON	30	WED	30
		THUR	31

The June issue of *Metronome* runs a piece on Charlie:

FRIDAY 18 JULY 1947
The Charlie Parker Quintet open at the New Bali in Washington for a two-week engagement.

THURSDAY 31 JULY 1947
The Charlie Parker Quintet close at the New Bali in Washington.

the bird

MOST INFLUENTIAL bebopper of them all is Yardbird Parker, christened Charlie, better known as Bird. The Bird's spectacular alto saxophone cadences have been the inspiration for one bop tyro after another, giving confidence, a range of ideas and a suggestion of form to kids who otherwise would be lost in their pursuit of the devious ins and outs of this most complex of jazz schools.

The Bird came back to new York in April, after more than a year on the West Coast, came back to a musicians' community wildly eager to see and hear him again. The night he arrived in town the word went around from one club to another, from one bar to another, "Bird's back in town!", whispered in sepulchral tones, usually reserved for religious leaders and revolutionaries. Every session he appeared at for the next few weeks was ballyhooed days in advance among the beboppers as another Bird-letter day and attendance was compulsory for those who wished to continue in the bebop school.

Happily, in spite of strong reports to the contrary, The Bird showed up in new York in good health, 40 pounds heavier than usual, still a brilliant musical thinker, still the most influential bebopper of them all if not yet in full possession of his technique, tone and taste.

Capital Nite Spots

By KNIGHT

Current arguments on the merits and demerits of the new trend in popular musical expression, "Be-Bop," will either be settled or intensified during the next two weeks while Charlie Parker, one of its foremost exponents (and, some say, one of its originators), is appearing at the New Bali Restaurant.

Parker is regarded as one of the greatest alto saxophone players in the country, and is said to have assisted Dizzy Gillespie in promoting "Be-Bop," a style that has the jitterbugs crazy. Parker and his orchestra open at the Bali tonight (Friday).

FRI	**1**
SAT	**2**
SUN	**3**
MON	**4**
TUES	**5**
WED	**6**
THUR	**7**
FRI	**8**
SAT	**9**
SUN	**10**
MON	**11**
TUES	**12**
WED	**13**
THUR	**14**
FRI	**15**
SAT	**16**
SUN	**17**
MON	**18**
TUES	**19**
WED	**20**
THUR	**21**
FRI	**22**
SAT	**23**
SUN	**24**
MON	**25**
TUES	**26**
WED	**27**
THUR	**28**
FRI	**29**
SAT	**30**
SUN	**31**

THURSDAY 7 AUGUST 1947
Charlie Parker Quintet open at the Three Deuces opposite Coleman Hawkins.

TUESDAY 12 & WEDNESDAY 13 AUGUST 1947
Rehearsals for the Miles Davis recording session on 14th. Charlie is persuaded to play tenor sax.

THURSDAY 14 AUGUST 1947
Recording session as Miles Davis All Stars for Savoy at the Harris Smith Studios, New YorkCity.
MILES DAVIS (trumpet), CHARLIE PARKER (tenor sax), JOHN LEWIS (piano), NELSON BOYD (bass), MAX ROACH (drums)
Milestones (3 takes) / *Little Willie Leaps* (3 takes) / *Half Nelson* (2 takes) / *Sippin' at Bells* (4 takes)

WEDNESDAY 20 AUGUST 1947
Charlie Parker Quintet close at the Three Deuces.

FRIDAY 29 AUGUST 1947
Bird's 27th birthday

FRI **1**

SAT **2**

SUN **3**

MON **4**

TUES **5**

WED **6**

THUR **7**

FRI **8**

SAT **9**

SUN **10**

MON **11**

TUES **12**

WED **13**

THUR **14**

FRI **15**

SAT **16**

SUN **17**

MON **18**

TUES **19**

WED **20**

THUR **21**

FRI **22**

SAT **23**

SUN **24**

MON **25**

TUES **26**

WED **27**

THUR **28**

FRI **29**

SAT **30**

SUN **31**

Left: Charlie drops into the Downbeat between sets at the Three Deuces to hear Dizzy Gillespie. Sitting next to him is Red Rodney who is working nearby at the Troubadour with Georgie Auld's Band.

Below: 52nd Street at this time. Coleman Hawkins gets top billing at the Three Deuces, Dizzy is at the Downbeat, Earle Warren down the street at the Famous Door, Billy Eckstine across the street at the Onyx and Jack Teagarden at Jimmy Ryan's.

MON	**1**
TUES	**2**
WED	**3**
THUR	**4**
FRI	**5**
SAT	**6**
SUN	**7**
MON	**8**
TUES	**9**
WED	**10**
THUR	**11**
FRI	**12**
SAT	**13**
SUN	**14**
MON	**15**
TUES	**16**
WED	**17**
THUR	**18**
FRI	**19**
SAT	**20**
SUN	**21**
MON	**22**
TUES	**23**
WED	**24**
THUR	**25**
FRI	**26**
SAT	**27**
SUN	**28**
MON	**29**
TUES	**30**

SATURDAY 13 SEPTEMBER 1947

Bird plays with Barry Ulanov's All Star Modern Jazz Musicians on the 'Bands for Bonds' radio broadcast via station WOR from the Mutual Studios in New York. The show is compered by Barry Ulanov, Bruce Elliot and Rudy Blesh.

CHARLIE PARKER (alto sax), DIZZY GILLESPIE (trumpet), JOHN LA PORTA (clarinet), LENNIE TRISTANO (piano), BILLY BAUER (guitar), RAY BROWN (bass), MAX ROACH (drums).

Koko (theme) / *Hot House / Fine and Dandy / I Surrender Dear* (without Charlie Parker)

SATURDAY 20 SEPTEMBER 1947

Bird again plays with Barry Ulanov's All Star Modern Jazz Musicians on the 'Bands for Bonds' radio broadcast via station WOR from the Mutual Studios in New York. The show is compered by Barry Ulanov, Carl Caruso and Rudy Blesh.

CHARLIE PARKER (alto sax), DIZZY GILLESPIE (trumpet), JOHN LA PORTA (clarinet), LENNIE TRISTANO (piano), BILLY BAUER (guitar), RAY BROWN (bass), MAX ROACH (drums).

Koko (theme) / *On the Sunny Side of the Street / 52nd Street Theme / Tiger Rag – Dizzy Atmosphere / How Deep is the Ocean?*

MONDAY 29 SEPTEMBER 1947

Dizzy Gillespie Big Band with Ella Fitzgerald star in a concert at Carnegie Hall in New York. Charlie Parker appears as a guest star.

CHARLIE PARKER (alto sax), DIZZY GILLESPIE (trumpet), JOHN LEWIS (piano), AL MCKIBBON (bass), JOE HARRIS (drums)

A Night in Tunisia / Dizzy Atmosphere / Groovin' High / Confirmation / Koko

WED	1	SAT	1
THUR	2	SUN	2
FRI	3	MON	3
SAT	4	TUES	4
SUN	5	WED	5
MON	6	THUR	6
TUES	7	FRI	7
WED	8	SAT	8
THUR	9	SUN	9
FRI	10	MON	10
SAT	11	TUES	11
SUN	12	WED	12
MON	13	THUR	13
TUES	14	FRI	14
WED	15	SAT	15
THUR	16	SUN	16
FRI	17	MON	17
SAT	18	TUES	18
SUN	19	WED	19
MON	20	THUR	20
TUES	21	FRI	21
WED	22	SAT	22
THUR	23	SUN	23
FRI	24	MON	24
SAT	25	TUES	25
SUN	26	WED	26
MON	27	THUR	27
TUES	28	FRI	28
WED	29	SAT	29
THUR	30	SUN	30
FRI	31		

The American Federation of Musicians announce that a second recording ban will commence on 1 January 1948. Both Dial and Savoy urge Charlie Parker into the recording studios.

TUESDAY 28 OCTOBER 1947

Recording session for Dial at WOR Studios, 1440 Broadway, New York under the supervision of Ross Russell. This is the first recording by the working Quintet.
CHARLIE PARKER (alto sax), MILES DAVIS (trumpet), DUKE JORDAN (piano), TOMMY POTTER (bass), MAX ROACH (drums)
Dexterity (2 takes) / *Bongo Bop* (2 takes) / *Dewey Square* (3 takes) / *The Hymn* / *Superman (The Hymn)* / *Bird of Paradise* (3 takes) / *Embraceable You* (2 takes)

TUESDAY 4 NOVEMBER 1947

Second recording session for Dial at WOR Studios, 1440 Broadway, New York under the supervision of Ross Russell.
CHARLIE PARKER (alto sax), MILES DAVIS (trumpet), DUKE JORDAN (piano), TOMMY POTTER (bass), MAX ROACH (drums)
Bird Feathers / *Klact-oveeseds-tene* (2 takes) / *Scrapple from the Apple* (2 takes) / *My Old Flame* / *Out of Nowhere* (3 takes) / *Don't Blame Me*

Bird rarely bothered to name his compositions, but when Ross Russell later pressed for titles for this session Bird came up with an unexplained title for the second number which he wrote out on the back of a Three Deuces $2 mimimum charge card – Klact-oveeseds-tene. Red Rodney maintains that Bird was dabbling with German, Klatschen – *clap, applause*; Auf wiedersehn – *goodbye*.

SATURDAY 8 NOVEMBER 1947

Bird again plays with Barry Ulanov's All Star Modern Jazz Musicians on the 'Bands for Bonds' radio broadcast via station WOR from the Mutual Studios in New York. The show is compered by Barry Ulanov and Bruce Elliot.
CHARLIE PARKER (alto sax), FATS NAVARRO (trumpet), JOHN LA PORTA (clarinet), ALLEN EAGER (tenor sax), LENNIE TRISTANO (piano), BILLY BAUER (guitar), TOMMY POTTER (bass), BUDDY RICH (drums), SARAH VAUGHAN (vocals):
52nd Street Theme (theme) / *Donna Lee* / *Everything I Have is Yours* (vSV, CP out) / *Fats Flats* / *Tea For Two* (CP out) / *Don't Blame Me* (CP out) / *Groovin' High* / *Koko* / *Anthropology*

TUESDAY 11 NOVEMBER 1947

The Quintet open at the Argyle Lounge in Chicago for a two-week engagement. During the engagement some private recordings are made:
My Old Flame / *How High The Moon* / *Big Foot* / *Slow Boat to China* / *All of Me* / *Cheryl* / *Home Sweet Home* / *Wee* / *Unknown title* / *Little Willie Leaps* / *The Way You Look Tonight* / *A Night In Tunisia* / *The Way You Look Tonight*

SUNDAY 23 NOVEMBER 1947

The Quintet close at the Argyle Lounge in Chicago.

SATURDAY 29 NOVEMBER 1947

Charlie and the Quintet appear in a One-Nite Stand Concert at Town Hall in New York with Pearl Bailey and Babs Gonzales, 3 Bips & a Bop.

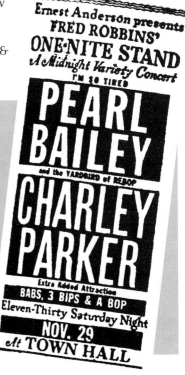

MON	**1**
TUES	**2**
WED	**3**
THUR	**4**
FRI	**5**
SAT	**6**
SUN	**7**
MON	**8**
TUES	**9**
WED	**10**
THUR	**11**
FRI	**12**
SAT	**13**
SUN	**14**
MON	**15**
TUES	**16**
WED	**17**
THUR	**18**
FRI	**19**
SAT	**20**
SUN	**21**
MON	**22**
TUES	**23**
WED	**24**
THUR	**25**
FRI	**26**
SAT	**27**
SUN	**28**
MON	**29**
TUES	**30**
WED	**31**

BIRD BORROWED MY HORN DURING HIS PHILLY ENGAGEMENT. I BROUGHT IT TO HIM EVERY NIGHT. WHEN MY BAND PLAYED A BENEFIT CONCERT FOR A YOUNG GIRL WHO HAD HER LEG SEVERED BY A STREET CAR, BIRD AGREED TO PLAY WITH MY BAND. THIS OCCASION WAS ONE OF THE HIGHLIGHTS OF MY LIFE. TRANE WAS PLAYING IN THE BAND AND HIS EXPRESSION CONVEYS ALL OF OUR AMAZEMENT.

TUESDAY 2 DECEMBER 1947
Quintet open at the Downbeat, Philadelphia.

SATURDAY 6 DECEMBER 1947
Quintet close at the Downbeat, Philadelphia.

MONDAY 15 DECEMBER 1947
Rehearsal by the Quintet plus trombonist J.J. Johnson for the forthcoming record session.

WEDNESDAY 17 DECEMBER 1947
Final recording session for Dial as the Charlie Parker Sextet at the WOR Studios in New York City. Ross Russell has flu and cannot attend.
CHARLIE PARKER (alto sax), MILES DAVIS (trumpet), J.J. JOHNSON (trombone), DUKE JORDAN (piano), TOMMY POTTER (bass), MAX ROACH (drums)
Drifting on a Reed (3 takes) / *Quasimodo* (2 takes) / *Charlie's Wig* (3 takes) / *Bongo Beep* (2 takes) / *Crazeology* (4 takes) / *How Deep Is The Ocean* (2 takes)

For this date Charlie has a brand new French Selmer saxophone.

Above: Charlie solos in front of the Jimmy Heath Band at a benefit concert in Philadelphia. Between Bird and Jimmy, John Coltrane sits in wonderment, his cigarette burning his fingers. Max Roach also sits in but is not visible in the photograph.

Jimmy Heath remembers:

FRIDAY 19 DECEMBER 1947
Charlie Parker Quintet open at El Sino in Detroit opposite Sarah Vaughan for a two-week engagement. The engagement is a great success and they sell-out.

SUNDAY 21 DECEMBER 1947
Recording session as Charlie Parker AllStars at the United Sound Studios, Detroit, for Savoy.
CHARLIE PARKER (alto sax), MILES DAVIS (trumpet), DUKE JORDAN (piano), TOMMY POTTER (bass), MAX ROACH (drums)
Another Hairdo (4 takes) / *Bluebird* (3 takes) / *Klaunstance* / *Bird Gets The Worm* (3 takes)

THUR	1	SUN	1
FRI	2	MON	2
SAT	3	TUES	3
SUN	4	WED	4
MON	5	THUR	5
TUES	6	FRI	6
WED	7	SAT	7
THUR	8	SUN	8
FRI	9	MON	9
SAT	10	TUES	10
SUN	11	WED	11
MON	12	THUR	12
TUES	13	FRI	13
WED	14	SAT	14
THUR	15	SUN	15
FRI	16	MON	16
SAT	17	TUES	17
SUN	18	WED	18
MON	19	THUR	19
TUES	20	FRI	20
WED	21	SAT	21
THUR	22	SUN	22
FRI	23	MON	23
SAT	24	TUES	24
SUN	25	WED	25
MON	26	THUR	26
TUES	27	FRI	27
WED	28	SAT	28
THUR	29	SUN	29
FRI	30		
SAT	31		

THURSDAY 1 JANUARY 1948
The Quintet close at the El Sino in Detroit. The AFM recording ban begins.

SATURDAY 3 JANUARY 1948
The Quintet open at the Pershing Ballroom in Chicago for a 4-night engagement. They double at a Saturday night dance at the New Savoy opposite Claude McLin and his Combo. During the engagement some private recordings are made:
CHARLIE PARKER (alto sax), MILES DAVIS (trumpet), DUKE JORDAN (piano), TOMMY POTTER (bass), MAX ROACH (drums)
The Chase / Drifting on a Reed

TUESDAY 6 JANUARY 1948
Quintet close at the Pershing Ballroom.

WEDNESDAY 18 FEBRUARY 1948
Red Rodney is divorced from Norma.

SUNDAY 29 FEBRUARY 1948
Charlie and the Quintet battle with Gene Ammons and his Band at the New Savoy in Chicago.

MON	1
TUES	2
WED	3
THUR	4
FRI	5
SAT	6
SUN	7
MON	8
TUES	9
WED	10
THUR	11
FRI	12
SAT	13
SUN	14
MON	15
TUES	16
WED	17
THUR	18
FRI	19
SAT	20
SUN	21
MON	22
TUES	23
WED	24
THUR	25
FRI	26
SAT	27
SUN	28
MON	29
TUES	30
WED	31

FRIDAY 26 MARCH 1948
Bird in concert at the Hotel Diplomat in New York where he is presented with two Metronome plaques – one for top alto sax and the other for top jazz influence.

TUESDAY 30 MARCH 1948
Charlie Parker Quintet opens at the Three Deuces on 52nd Street for a two-week engagement opposite Margie Hyams' group.

Harris, Parker Get Beat Plaques

New York — Bill Harris and Charlie Parker were presented their **Down Beat** poll awards as a highlight of the initial Bob Feldman jazz club dance session at the Hotel Diplomat. Presentations were made to the trombonist and alto saxist by jazz critic and master of ceremonies of the evening, Leonard Feather.

Musically, the evening was regarded a success though it fell a little short on finances. Particularly heavy competition in the local jazz concert field that weekend may explain this situation. Feldman, the sponsor, is an English clarinetist who ran a similar series, familiar to many former GIs, in London.

Feldman, with Feather again in as emcee, was slated to give a second whirl at the Diplomat last Friday night with Teddy Wilson, Cozy Cole, Alkan Eager and Linda Keene as headliners.

Right: Pincus, the 'unofficial mayor of 52nd Street' salutes the opening of the Charlie Parker Quintet at the Three Deuces.
Opposite page: The changing face of 52nd Street. The Spotlite and Downbeat clubs are gone, replaced by the Famous Door and the Carousel.

WEDNESDAY 31 MARCH 1948
Dean Benedetti is at the Three Deuces with his new recording equipment, a Brush Sound Mirror paper-based tape recorder. The Deuces management allow him to tape two sets but when they realise he is not going to spend any money, he is thrown out.
CHARLIE PARKER (alto sax), MILES DAVIS (trumpet), DUKE JORDAN (piano), TOMMY POTTER (bass), MAX ROACH (drums), plus KENNY 'PANCHO' HAGOOD (vocal)
52nd Street Theme / Big Foot / Dizzy Atmosphere / My Old Flame / 52nd Street Theme / Half Nelson / All The Things You Are (vocal) / *52nd Street Theme*

MON **1**

TUES **2**

WED **3**

THUR **4**

FRI **5**

SAT **6**

SUN **7**

MON **8**

TUES **9**

WED **10**

THUR **11**

FRI **12**

SAT **13**

SUN **14**

MON **15**

TUES **16**

WED **17**

THUR **18**

FRI **19**

SAT **20**

SUN **21**

MON **22**

TUES **23**

WED **24**

THUR **25**

FRI **26**

SAT **27**

SUN **28**

MON **29**

TUES **30**

WED **31**

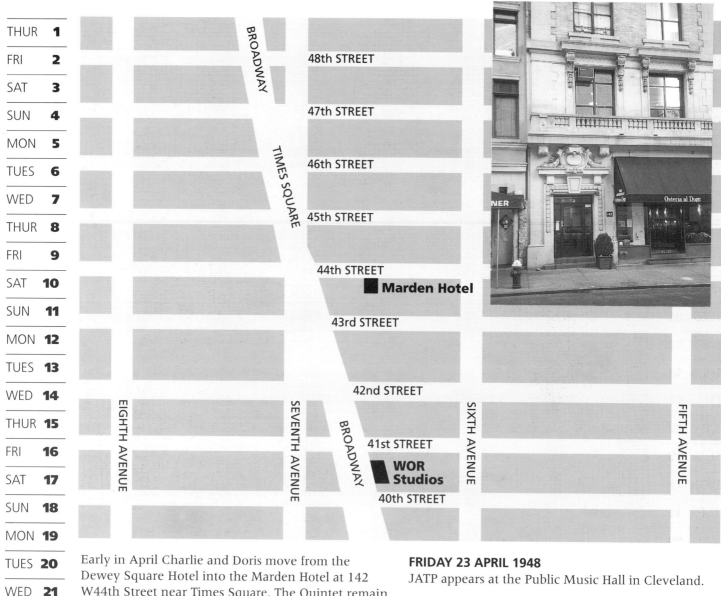

THUR	**1**
FRI	**2**
SAT	**3**
SUN	**4**
MON	**5**
TUES	**6**
WED	**7**
THUR	**8**
FRI	**9**
SAT	**10**
SUN	**11**
MON	**12**
TUES	**13**
WED	**14**
THUR	**15**
FRI	**16**
SAT	**17**
SUN	**18**
MON	**19**
TUES	**20**
WED	**21**
THUR	**22**
FRI	**23**
SAT	**24**
SUN	**25**
MON	**26**
TUES	**27**
WED	**28**
THUR	**29**
FRI	**30**

Early in April Charlie and Doris move from the Dewey Square Hotel into the Marden Hotel at 142 W44th Street near Times Square. The Quintet remain at the Three Deuces until 11 April.

SUNDAY 11 APRIL 1948
The Quintet close at the Three Deuces

SUNDAY 18 APRIL 1948
Charlie Parker Quintet plus Sarah Vaughan join a 26-day JATP tour in Cincinnati.
CHARLIE PARKER (alto sax), MILES DAVIS (trumpet), DUKE JORDAN (piano), TOMMY POTTER (bass), MAX ROACH (drums), plus Sarah's husband and manager George Treadwell.

TUESDAY 20 APRIL 1948
JATP appears at Kleinhan's Music Hall in Buffalo, N.Y.

THURSDAY 22 APRIL 1948
JATP appears in Pittsburgh.

FRIDAY 23 APRIL 1948
JATP appears at the Public Music Hall in Cleveland.

SATURDAY 24 APRIL 1948
JATP appears at the Masonic Auditorium in Detroit.

SUNDAY 25 APRIL 1948
JATP appears in Indianapolis.

MONDAY 26 APRIL 1948
JATP appears in Milwaukee.

TUESDAY 27 APRIL 1948
JATP appears in Kansas City.

WEDNESDAY 28 APRIL 1948
JATP appears in Des Moines.

FRIDAY 30 APRIL 1948
JATP appears in St Louis.

SAT	1	
SUN	2	
MON	3	
TUES	4	
WED	5	
THUR	6	
FRI	7	
SAT	8	
SUN	9	
MON	10	
TUES	11	
WED	12	
THUR	13	
FRI	14	
SAT	15	
SUN	16	
MON	17	
TUES	18	
WED	19	
THUR	20	
FRI	21	
SAT	22	
SUN	23	
MON	24	
TUES	25	
WED	26	
THUR	27	
FRI	28	
SAT	29	
SUN	30	
MON	31	

SATURDAY 1 MAY 1948
JATP appears at the Civic Opera House in Chicago.

SUNDAY 2 MAY 1948
JATP appears in Minneapolis.

TUESDAY 4 MAY 1948
Stan Levey (on JATP tour with Sarah?) borrows $70 from Bird and gives him an IOU promising to pay him back by 18th May but no sooner than 13 May.

FRIDAY 7 MAY 1948
JATP begin a one-week engagement at the Paradise Theatre, Detroit.

THURSDAY 13 MAY 1948
JATP closes at the Paradise Theatre, Detroit.

FRIDAY 14 MAY 1948
JATP appears in Philadelphia.

SATURDAY 15 MAY 1948
JATP appears in Newark, NJ at 8.30 followed by a midnight concert at Carnegie Hall, NYC.

SUNDAY 16 MAY 1948
JATP appears in Boston.

WEDNESDAY 19 MAY 1948
Down Beat reports:
Red Rodney, trumpet, and Stan Levey, drums, joining up with Charlie Parker's outfit for theatre tour, replacing Miles Davis and Max Roach.

Bop vs. Boogie Show

New York—A package called Be Bop Vs. Boogie Woogie is being sent out on the road by the Gale agency, featuring Freddie Slack and a seven-piece unit for the boogie, Charlie Parker and five others for bop. Tour is moving westward.

Feldman Gives Up

New York—After two financially unsuccessful attempts to corner local jazz enthusiasts for weekly sessions of his hot club, Bob Feldman called it quits, with plans to return to his native England for a brief vacation. Though fine social successes, the sessions, held at the Hotel Diplomat, failed to bring out sufficient patrons to meet the overhead. Feldman did not conduct concerts, rather dances, and it is questionable whether the real jazz addicts, accustomed to just sitting and listening to their idols, care for the dance format. Name talent, such as Teddy Wilson, Bill Harris, Cozy Cole, Charlie Parker, Pete Brown, Linda Keene, was used.

TUES	**1**	THUR	**1**
WED	**2**	FRI	**2**
THUR	**3**	SAT	**3**
FRI	**4**	SUN	**4**
SAT	**5**	MON	**5**
SUN	**6**	TUES	**6**
MON	**7**	WED	**7**
TUES	**8**	THUR	**8**
WED	**9**	FRI	**9**
THUR	**10**	SAT	**10**
FRI	**11**	SUN	**11**
SAT	**12**	MON	**12**
SUN	**13**	TUES	**13**
MON	**14**	WED	**14**
TUES	**15**	THUR	**15**
WED	**16**	FRI	**16**
THUR	**17**	SAT	**17**
FRI	**18**	SUN	**18**
SAT	**19**	MON	**19**
SUN	**20**	TUES	**20**
MON	**21**	WED	**21**
TUES	**22**	THUR	**22**
WED	**23**	FRI	**23**
THUR	**24**	SAT	**24**
FRI	**25**	SUN	**25**
SAT	**26**	MON	**26**
SUN	**27**	TUES	**27**
MON	**28**	WED	**28**
TUES	**29**	THUR	**29**
WED	**30**	FRI	**30**
		SAT	**31**

TUESDAY 6 JULY 1948

Charlie Parker Quintet open at the Onyx Club in New York for one week.

Dean Benedetti is on hand with his tape recorder and records on at least 4 nights. The sequence for opening night is guesswork by Phil Schaap.

CHARLIE PARKER (alto sax), MILES DAVIS (trumpet), DUKE JORDAN (piano), TOMMY POTTER (bass), MAX ROACH (drums)

52nd Street Theme / Out of Nowhere / My Old Flame / Chasin' the Bird / The Way You Look Tonight / This Time The Dream's On Me / Shaw Nuff / 52nd Street Theme / 52nd Street Theme / Cheryl / Bird Lore / These Foolish Things / Groovin' High / Little Willie Leaps / Night And Day / This Time The Dream's On Me / 52nd Street Theme / The Way You Look Tonight / Out Of Nowhere / My Old Flame / Blues

WEDNESDAY 7 JULY 1948

CHARLIE PARKER (alto sax), MILES DAVIS (trumpet), DUKE JORDAN (piano), TOMMY POTTER (bass), MAX ROACH (drums)

Out of Nowhere / How High The Moon / 52nd Street Theme

SATURDAY 10 JULY 1948

Benedetti is present at an afternoon rehearsal in the Onyx.

CHARLIE PARKER (alto sax), MILES DAVIS (trumpet), DUKE JORDAN (piano), TOMMY POTTER (bass), MAX ROACH (drums)

Chasin' The Bird / Don't Blame Me / Tico Tico / Out Of Nowhere / Medley: Indiana, Donna Lee

Benedetti returns to the club for the evening performance.

CHARLIE PARKER (alto sax), MILES DAVIS (trumpet), DUKE JORDAN (piano), TOMMY POTTER (bass), MAX ROACH (drums) plus CARMEN MCRAE (vocal) and an unidentified tenor saxist sits in on *Groovin' High*

52nd Street Theme / How High The Moon / I'm In The Mood For Love / This Time The Dream's On Me / Yesterdays / 52nd Street Theme / 52nd Street Theme / How High The Moon / Groovin' High / What Price Love (Yardbird Suite) (Carmen McRae vocal, followed by an encore as Bird scolds the audience for not listening) */ 52nd Street Theme / Cheryl*

SUNDAY 11 JULY 1948

Closing night at the Onyx. Benedetti is again present with his tape recorder.

CHARLIE PARKER (alto sax), MILES DAVIS (trumpet), DUKE JORDAN (piano), TOMMY POTTER (bass), MAX ROACH (drums) plus THELONIOUS MONK (piano) on *Well, You Needn't* and PANCHO HAGOOD (vocal) on *All The Things You Are, Spotlite* and *September Song*, and either Pancho or EARL COLEMAN (vocal) on *My Old Flame:*

All The Things You Are / Well You Needn't / Big Foot / I Can't Get Started / Dizzy Atmosphere / Spotlite / 52nd Street Theme / How High The Moon / September Song / Hot House / 52nd Street Theme / Night In Tunisia / My Old Flame / The Hymn

Bird is not present on the final two numbers on Benedetti's tape and it is possible that he left early.

Half Nelson / Little Willie Leaps

FRIDAY 23 JULY 1948

Charlie Parker Quintet begin a week at the Apollo Theatre, Harlem. Also on the bill is the Buddy Johnson Band.

WEDNESDAY 28 JULY 1948

Amateur Nite at the Apollo.

THURSDAY 29 JULY 1948

Bird and the Quintet close at the Apollo.

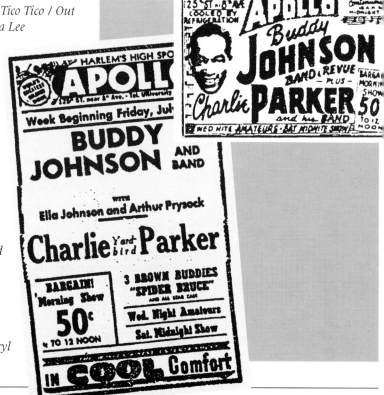

SUN	**1**	WED	**1**
MON	**2**	THUR	**2**
TUES	**3**	FRI	**3**
WED	**4**	SAT	**4**
THUR	**5**	SUN	**5**
FRI	**6**	MON	**6**
SAT	**7**	TUES	**7**
SUN	**8**	WED	**8**
MON	**9**	THUR	**9**
TUES	**10**	FRI	**10**
WED	**11**	SAT	**11**
THUR	**12**	SUN	**12**
FRI	**13**	MON	**13**
SAT	**14**	TUES	**14**
SUN	**15**	WED	**15**
MON	**16**	THUR	**16**
TUES	**17**	FRI	**17**
WED	**18**	SAT	**18**
THUR	**19**	SUN	**19**
FRI	**20**	MON	**20**
SAT	**21**	TUES	**21**
SUN	**22**	WED	**22**
MON	**23**	THUR	**23**
TUES	**24**	FRI	**24**
WED	**25**	SAT	**25**
THUR	**26**	SUN	**26**
FRI	**27**	MON	**27**
SAT	**28**	TUES	**28**
SUN	**29**	WED	**29**
MON	**30**	THUR	**30**
TUES	**31**		

SUNDAY 29 AUGUST 1948
Bird's 28th birthday

FRIDAY 3 SEPTEMBER 1948
Charlie Parker appears for the first time at the Royal Roost. He is an added star attraction over the Labor Day weekend.

SATURDAY 4 SEPTEMBER 1948
Charlie Parker broadcasts from the Royal Roost on Broadway between 47th and 48th Street.
CHARLIE PARKER (alto sax), MILES DAVIS (trumpet), TADD DAMERON (piano), CURLEY RUSSELL (bass), MAX ROACH (drums), SYMPHONY SID TORIN (mc)
52nd Street Theme / Koko / 52nd Street Theme

SYMPHONY SID:

> AND AS OUR SURPRISE FOR THIS MORNING HERE ON THE ALL NIGHT ALL FRANTIC ONE WITH OUR MICROPHONES DOWN HERE AT THE ROYAL ROOST, WE BRING YOU ONCE AGAIN THE WONDERFUL AND OUTSTANDING CHARLIE PARKER AND HIS WONDERFUL ORGANISATION. THAT'S RIGHT... FOR THE WEEKEND, LADIES AND GENTLEMEN, WE'RE BRINGING YOU THE GREAT CHARLIE PARKER AND HIS WONDERFUL ORGANISATION FEATURING MILES DAVIS ON TRUMPET, MAX ROACH ON DRUMS, TADD DAMERON ON PIANO AND CURLEY RUSSELL ON BASS. I KNOW YOU'LL HAVE A LOT OF FUN OVER THE WEEKEND ... C'MON ON DOWN AND DIG THE GREAT CHARLIE PARKER, THE ONE AND ONLY ... THE MAN OF JAZZ!

SATURDAY 18 SEPTEMBER 1948
Recording session as the Charlie Parker All Stars for Savoy at the Harris Smith Studios.
CHARLIE PARKER (alto sax), MILES DAVIS (trumpet), JOHN LEWIS (piano), CURLEY RUSSELL (bass), MAX ROACH (drums)
Barbados (4 takes) / *Ah Leu Cha* (2 takes) / *Constellation* (5 takes) / *Parker's Mood* (5 takes)

FRIDAY 24 SEPTEMBER 1948
Recording session as the Charlie Parker All Stars for Savoy at the Harris Smith Studios.
CHARLIE PARKER (alto sax), MILES DAVIS (trumpet), JOHN LEWIS (piano), CURLEY RUSSELL (bass), MAX ROACH (drums)
Perhaps (7 takes) / *Marmaduke* (12 takes) / *Steeplechase* (2 takes) / *Merry-Go-Round* (2 takes)

SUNDAY 26 SEPTEMBER 1948
Charlie Parker guests with Dizzy Gillespie Orchestra at the Pershing Ballroom, Chicago
CHARLIE PARKER (alto sax), DIZZY GILLESPIE, DAVE BURNS, WILLIE COOK, ELMON WRIGHT (trumpets), JESSE TARRANT, ANDY DURYEA (trombones), JOHN BROWN, ERNIE HENRY (alto sax), JOE GAYLES, JAMES MOODY (tenor sax), CECIL PAYNE (baritone sax), JAMES FOREMAN JR (piano), NELSON BOYD (bass), TEDDY STEWART (drums), CHANO POZO (conga)
Private recording
Things To Come / Oo-Bop-Sh-Bam / Yesterdays / Night In Tunisia / Round Midnight / Good Bait / What Is This Thing Called Love? / Manteca / Algo Bueno / Lover Man / Unknown Blues / Don't Blame Me / I Can't Get Started / Groovin' High / Ool Ya Koo / Ool Ya Koo / All The Things You Are

Above: Bird solos in front of Dizzy's band at the Pershing. The saxophonists are Ernie Henry (l) and James Moody (r).

Charlie Parker Quintet end the month at Ciro's in Philadelphia.

FRI	1	MON	1
SAT	2	TUES	2
SUN	3	WED	3
MON	4	THUR	4
TUES	5	FRI	5
WED	6	SAT	6
THUR	7	SUN	7
FRI	8	MON	8
SAT	9	TUES	9
SUN	10	WED	10
MON	11	THUR	11
TUES	12	FRI	12
WED	13	SAT	13
THUR	14	SUN	14
FRI	15	MON	15
SAT	16	TUES	16
SUN	17	WED	17
MON	18	THUR	18
TUES	19	FRI	19
WED	20	SAT	20
THUR	21	SUN	21
FRI	22	MON	22
SAT	23	TUES	23
SUN	24	WED	24
MON	25	THUR	25
TUES	26	FRI	26
WED	27	SAT	27
THUR	28	SUN	28
FRI	29	MON	29
SAT	30	TUES	30
SUN	31		

SUNDAY 10 OCTOBER 1948

Sunday afternoon Bop Concert at Royal Roost features Fats Navarro, James Moody and Al Haig, Tommy Potter and Max Roach from Bird's Quintet.

Below: Howard McGhee, Flip Phillips and Bird pose in front of the aircraft during the JATP tour.
Inset: Doris and Bird on the tarmac.

SATURDAY 6 NOVEMBER 1948

Bird joins the JATP party with Howard McGhee, Tommy Turk, Sonny Criss, Coleman Hawkins, Flip Phillips, Al Haig, Tommy Potter, J.C. Heard and Kenny 'Pancho' Hagood for the 1st of 35 concerts in nearly as many cities. The opening concert is at Carnegie Hall, New York

He also signs a recording contract with Mercury Records under the supervision of Norman Granz.

MON	**1**
TUES	**2**
WED	**3**
THUR	**4**
FRI	**5**
SAT	**6**
SUN	**7**
MON	**8**
TUES	**9**
WED	**10**
THUR	**11**
FRI	**12**
SAT	**13**
SUN	**14**
MON	**15**
TUES	**16**
WED	**17**
THUR	**18**
FRI	**19**
SAT	**20**
SUN	**21**
MON	**22**
TUES	**23**
WED	**24**
THUR	**25**
FRI	**26**
SAT	**27**
SUN	**28**
MON	**29**
TUES	**30**

SATURDAY 13 NOVEMBER 1948
JATP at the Masonic Temple in Detroit.

TUESDAY 16 NOVEMBER 1948
JATP at the Denman Auditorium in Vancouver. Bird doesn't appear at this show.

TUESDAY 16 NOVEMBER 1948
JATP at the Moore Theatre in Seattle.

In Salt Lake City, Bird is interviewed by Al 'Jazzbo' Collins.

FRIDAY 19 NOVEMBER 1948
JATP at the Portland Auditorium in Portland.

SATURDAY 20 NOVEMBER 1948
JATP at the Municipal Auditorium in Long Beach, CA. Charlie and Doris drive down to Tia Juana to get married returning for the evening concert.

MONDAY 22 NOVEMBER 1948
JATP at the Shrine Auditorium in Los Angeles.

TUESDAY 23 NOVEMBER 1948
JATP at the Oakland Auditorium in Oakland.

WEDNESDAY 24 NOVEMBER 1948
JATP at the Opera House in San Francisco.

FRIDAY 26 NOVEMBER 1948
JATP at Chicago's Civic Opera House, 8.30 pm.

NORMAN GRANZ
JAZZ AT THE PHILHARMONIC

Featuring

Charlie Parker	Flip "Perdido" Phillips
Coleman Hawkins	Howard McGhee
J. C. Heard	Sonny Criss
Tommy Turk	Al Haig
Tommy Potter	Kenny "Pancho" Hagood

FRIDAY NIGHT – 8:30 P.M.
NOVEMBER 26

CIVIC OPERA
HOUSE

TICKETS NOW ON SALE AT
OPERA HOUSE BOX OFFICE
$1.25, $1.85, $2.50, $3.10
(Tax included)

Fans Sore; Bird Fails To Show Up

Vancouver, B. C.—Protests are being voiced by music fans here against the recent *Jazz at the Philharmonic* concert at the Park auditorium.

Main complaint is that altoist Charlie Parker was billed but failed to appear.

One of Vancouver's most popular disc jockeys has retired, temporarily at least. Al Reusch recently completed a three-year stint on the request record show *Name It, Play It* over CKMO.

The airing rates some 2,000 letters a week, with an estimated 15,000 listeners. During the last year, regular listeners formed an International Al Reusch Fan club of more than 1,000 members.

Next year will start off with Hazel Scott due in for a concert on January 12, the Louis Armstrong All-Stars arriving that same month. Tex Beneke and band come for a one-niter about February 6.

—Marke Paise

Salt Lake City Jockey Gives JATP Assist

Salt Lake City—With invaluable assistance from local disc jockey Al (Jazzbo) Collins, Norman Granz' *Jazz at the Philharmonic* came to town. Show time at the South Hi auditorium was 9 p.m., and by 8:30 p.m. the house was sold out. The city was about to accept, for the first time, with overwhelming enthusiasm, some jazz greats of the land.

Show opener was *How High the Moon*, with all the boys blowing great, especially Tommy Turk on trombone. Next was Howard McGhee's trumpet on *I Can't Get Started*. Special mention should be given here for the rhythm section—J. C. Heard, drums; Al Haig, piano, and Tommy Potter, bass—played some wonderful chord progressions and breaks.

Jazzbo And JATP Give SLC Kicks

Salt Lake City—According to disc jockey Al (Jazzbo) Collins, who helped promote it, the JATP concert there recently was the Utah town's first JAZZ concert, and "a start." Showing one of the reasons why the audience got their kicks is tenor star Flip Phillips, right, above. From the left are Collins, altoist Charlie Parker, and singer Kenny (Pancho) Hagood.

WED	**1**
THUR	**2**
FRI	**3**
SAT	**4**
SUN	**5**
MON	**6**
TUES	**7**
WED	**8**
THUR	**9**
FRI	**10**
SAT	**11**
SUN	**12**
MON	**13**
TUES	**14**
WED	**15**
THUR	**16**
FRI	**17**
SAT	**18**
SUN	**19**
MON	**20**
TUES	**21**
WED	**22**
THUR	**23**
FRI	**24**
SAT	**25**
SUN	**26**
MON	**27**
TUES	**28**
WED	**29**
THUR	**30**
FRI	**31**

THURSDAY 9 DECEMBER 1948

Charlie Parker Quintet with Al Haig on piano in place of Duke Jordan open at the Royal Roost for an extended engagement which lasts four months. Also on the bill is Billy Eckstine and the Charlie Ventura Group.

SYMPHONY SID:

> AND SO, LADIES AND GENTLEMEN, ONCE AGAIN HERE AT THE **METROPOLITAN BOPERA HOUSE**, THE ORIGINAL HOUSE THAT BOP BUILT, ON BROADWAY BETWEEN 47TH AND 48TH, WE'RE PRESENTING TO YOU, OVER THE CHRISTMAS HOLIDAY, RIGHT UP INTO THE NEW YEAR... THE **GREAT CHARLIE PARKER AND THE ALL-STARS**, MISTER B – **BILLY ECKSTINE**, AND THE **WONDERFUL CHARLIE VENTURA** AND THE BOP GROUP. WE INVITE YOU TO COME DOWN, SIT BACK AND RELAX AND HAVE A WONDERFUL TIME.

SATURDAY 11 DECEMBER 1948

In the early hours of Saturday, Charlie Parker and the Quintet broadcast from the Royal Roost.
CHARLIE PARKER (alto sax), MILES DAVIS (trumpet), AL HAIG (piano), TOMMY POTTER (bass), MAX ROACH (drums), SYMPHONY SID TORIN (announcer)
Groovin' High / Big Foot / Ornithology / Slow Boat to China

After the show at the Roost, the whole company move up to the ApolloTheatre on 125th Street.

> AND DON'T BE SURPRISED IF WE *GO* OFF THE AIR AND GO BACK TO THE APOLLO THEATRE. I'D LIKE TO REMIND YOU THAT IT'S DONE FOR A WONDERFUL CAUSE, AND I ALSO WOULD LIKE TO REMIND YOU THAT WE'RE GONNA TAKE THE SAME GROUP AROUND 4.15 ... AND WE'RE GONNA TAKE **CHARLIE PARKER AND THE ALL-STARS**, THE GREAT MISTER B – BILLY ECKSTINE, AND THE WONDERFUL CHARLIE VENTURA AND THE BOP GROUP, AND TAKE THEM RIGHT UP TO THE **APOLLO THEATRE** WHERE WE'LL DO EXACTLY THE SAME THING AS WE'RE HAVING DOWN HERE AT THE ROOST. SO STAND BY, AND HAVE A LOT OF FUN. I KNOW THAT YOU WILL ... DIGGIN' THE GREAT BIRD AND THE ALL-STARS.'

BROADWAY

SEVENTH AVENUE

W 51st STREET

W 50th STREET

W 49th STREET

W 48th STREET

■ **Royal Roost**

W 47th STREET

W 46th STREET

WED	1
THUR	2
FRI	3
SAT	4
SUN	5
MON	6
TUES	7
WED	8
THUR	9
FRI	10
SAT	11
SUN	12
MON	13
TUES	14
WED	15
THUR	16
FRI	17
SAT	18
SUN	19
MON	20
TUES	21
WED	22
THUR	23
FRI	24
SAT	25
SUN	26
MON	27
TUES	28
WED	29
THUR	30
FRI	31

SUNDAY 12 DECEMBER 1948

In the early hours of Sunday, Charlie Parker and the Quintet broadcast from the Royal Roost.
CHARLIE PARKER (alto sax), MILES DAVIS (trumpet), AL HAIG (piano), TOMMY POTTER (bass), MAX ROACH (drums), ART FORD (announcer)
Hot House / Salt Peanuts

WEDNESDAY 15 DECEMBER 1948

Downbeat magazine announces that Charlie has come second to Johnny Hodges in the alto sax poll.

SATURDAY 18 DECEMBER 1948

In the early hours of Saturday, Charlie Parker and the Quintet broadcast from the Royal Roost.
CHARLIE PARKER (alto sax), MILES DAVIS (trumpet), AL HAIG (piano), TOMMY POTTER (bass), MAX ROACH (drums), SYMPHONY SID TORIN (announcer)
Chasin' The Bird / Out Of Nowhere / How High The Moon

Below: The building that housed the Royal Roost, pictured in 1990 shortly before being demolished to make way for a hotel. Pictured from the corner of Broadway and 48th Street.

MONDAY 20 DECEMBER 1948

Recording session as Charlie Parker with Machito and his Orchestra in New York City.
CHARLIE PARKER (alto sax), MARIO BAUZA, FRANK 'PAQUITO' DAVILLA, BOB WOODLEN (trumpets), GENE JOHNSON, FRED SKERRITT (alto sax), JOSE MADERA (tenor sax), LESLIE JOHNAKINS (baritone sax), RENE HERNANDEZ (piano), ROBERTO RODRIGUEZ (bass), JOSE MANGUEL (bongo), LUIS MIRANDA (conga), UMBALDO NIETO (timbales), MACHITO (maraccas)
No Noise Pt 1 / No Noise Pt 2 / Mango Mangue

Royal Roost

WED	**1**
THUR	**2**
FRI	**3**
SAT	**4**
SUN	**5**
MON	**6**
TUES	**7**
WED	**8**
THUR	**9**
FRI	**10**
SAT	**11**
SUN	**12**
MON	**13**
TUES	**14**
WED	**15**
THUR	**16**
FRI	**17**
SAT	**18**
SUN	**19**
MON	**20**
TUES	**21**
WED	**22**
THUR	**23**
FRI	**24**
SAT	**25**
SUN	**26**
MON	**27**
TUES	**28**
WED	**29**
THUR	**30**
FRI	**31**

WED **1**
THUR **2**
FRI **3**
SAT **4**
SUN **5**
MON **6**
TUES **7**
WED **8**
THUR **9**
FRI **10**
SAT **11**
SUN **12**
MON **13**
TUES **14**
WED **15**
THUR **16**
FRI **17**
SAT **18**
SUN **19**
MON **20**
TUES **21**
WED **22**
THUR **23**
FRI **24**
SAT **25**
SUN **26**
MON **27**
TUES **28**
WED **29**
THUR **30**
FRI **31**

THURSDAY 23 DECEMBER 1948
Miles Davis storms off the stand at the Royal Roost complaining: 'Bird makes you feel about one foot high'. Max Roach also quits but agrees to stay two more nights until Joe Harris can take over on drums.

FRIDAY 24 DECEMBER 1948
Kenny Dorham joins the Quintet at the Royal Roost to replace Miles.

SATURDAY 25 DECEMBER 1948
In the early hours of Saturday, Charlie Parker and the Quintet broadcast from the Royal Roost.
CHARLIE PARKER (alto sax), KENNY DORHAM (trumpet), AL HAIG (piano), TOMMY POTTER (bass), MAX ROACH (drums), SYMPHONY SID TORIN (announcer)
Half Nelson / White Christmas / Little Willie Leaps

On Saturday evening Charlie appears at a Christmas Night Concert at Carnegie Hall.

Opposite page: Bird at the Royal Roost.

SAT	1
SUN	2
MON	3
TUES	4
WED	5
THUR	6
FRI	7
SAT	8
SUN	9
MON	10
TUES	11
WED	12
THUR	13
FRI	14
SAT	15
SUN	16
MON	17
TUES	18
WED	19
THUR	20
FRI	21
SAT	22
SUN	23
MON	24
TUES	25
WED	26
THUR	27
FRI	28
SAT	29
SUN	30
MON	31

Throughout January, the Charlie Parker Quintet and the Charlie Ventura Group are resident at the Royal Roost. Flip Phillips shares the bill for the first half of the month and is replaced by Dinah Washington on Wednesday 19th.

SATURDAY 1 JANUARY 1949

In the early hours of Saturday, Charlie Parker and the Quintet broadcast from the Royal Roost.

CHARLIE PARKER (alto sax), KENNY DORHAM (trumpet), AL HAIG (piano), TOMMY POTTER (bass), JOE HARRIS (drums), SYMPHONY SID TORIN (announcer)

Be-Bop / Slow Boat To China / Ornithology / Groovin' High / East Of The Sun / Cheryl

The broadcast ends with a jam session featuring CHARLIE PARKER (alto sax), FLIP PHILLIPS, CHARLIE VENTURA (tenor sax), CONTE CANDOLI (trumpet), BENNIE GREEN (trombone), AL HAIG (piano), CURLEY RUSSELL, TOMMY POTTER (bass), JOE HARRIS, SHELLY MANNE, ED SHAUGHNESSY (drums)

How High The Moon

MONDAY 3 JANUARY 1949

Charlie takes part in the Metronome All Stars recording session in New York City.

MILES DAVIS, DIZZY GILLESPIE, FATS NAVARRO (trumpet), J. J. JOHNSON, KAI WINDING (trombone), BUDDY DEFRANCO (clarinet), CHARLIE PARKER (alto sax), CHARLIE VENTURA (tenor sax), ERNIE CACERES (baritone sax), LENNIE TRISTANO (piano), BILLY BAUER (guitar), EDDIE SAFRANSKI (bass), SHELLY MANNE (drums), PETE RUGOLO (director)

Overtime (2 takes) / *Victory Ball* (3 takes)

SAT	1
SUN	2
MON	3
TUES	4
WED	5
THUR	6
FRI	7
SAT	8
SUN	9
MON	10
TUES	11
WED	12
THUR	13
FRI	14
SAT	15
SUN	16
MON	17
TUES	18
WED	19
THUR	20
FRI	21
SAT	22
SUN	23
MON	24
TUES	25
WED	26
THUR	27
FRI	28
SAT	29
SUN	30
MON	31

FRIDAY 14 JANUARY 1949

Charlie takes out a driving licence. His address is Hotel Marden, 142 W44th Street, New York

SATURDAY 15 JANUARY 1949

In the early hours of Saturday, Charlie Parker and the Quintet broadcast from the Royal Roost.
CHARLIE PARKER (alto sax), KENNY DORHAM (trumpet), AL HAIG (piano), TOMMY POTTER (bass), JOE HARRIS (drums), SYMPHONY SID TORIN (announcer)
Scrapple From The Apple / Be-Bop / Hot House

SATURDAY 22 JANUARY 1949

In the early hours of Saturday, Charlie Parker and the Quintet broadcast from the Royal Roost.
CHARLIE PARKER (alto sax), KENNY DORHAM (trumpet), AL HAIG (piano), TOMMY POTTER (bass), MAX ROACH (drums), SYMPHONY SID TORIN (announcer)
Oop Bop Sh'Bam / Scrapple From The Apple / Salt Peanuts

FRIDAY 28 JANUARY 1949

Down Beat reviews Charlie's latest record release:

> **CHARLIE PARKER**
> ***** Embraceable You**
> **** Bongo Bop**
> *You* is a prime example of the heights of originality that the Bird can soar to when he's in the mood. He plays impeccably with a richness of ideas and change of pace that at once astounds you and then enables you to coast a bit while assimilating what went before. *Bop* is bop, but the *Bongo* part is a misnomer, for it is merely a riff tune with conventional rhythm. Miles Davis is on the No.2 side on trumpet, and Max Roach is on both. (**Dial 1024**)

SATURDAY 29 JANUARY 1949

In the early hours of Saturday, Charlie Parker and the Quintet broadcast from the Royal Roost.
CHARLIE PARKER (alto sax), KENNY DORHAM (trumpet), AL HAIG (piano), TOMMY POTTER (bass), MAX ROACH (drums), SYMPHONY SID TORIN (announcer)
Jumpin' With Symphony Sid (theme) / *Groovin' High*

Below: The queues start to form outside the Royal Roost.

TUES	**1**
WED	**2**
THUR	**3**
FRI	**4**
SAT	**5**
SUN	**6**
MON	**7**
TUES	**8**
WED	**9**
THUR	**10**
FRI	**11**
SAT	**12**
SUN	**13**
MON	**14**
TUES	**15**
WED	**16**
THUR	**17**
FRI	**18**
SAT	**19**
SUN	**20**
MON	**21**
TUES	**22**
WED	**23**
THUR	**24**
FRI	**25**
SAT	**26**
SUN	**27**
MON	**28**

Throughout February, the Charlie Parker Quintet are resident at the Royal Roost.

SATURDAY 5 FEBRUARY 1949

In the early hours of Saturday, Charlie Parker and the Quintet broadcast from the Royal Roost.
CHARLIE PARKER (alto sax), KENNY DORHAM (trumpet), AL HAIG (piano), TOMMY POTTER (bass), MAX ROACH (drums), SYMPHONY SID TORIN (announcer)
Jumpin' With Symphony Sid (theme) / *Scrapple From The Apple / Barbados / Salt Peanuts / Jumpin' With Symphony Sid* (theme)

FRIDAY 11 FEBRUARY 1949

JATP concert in Carnegie Hall, NYC. Charlie Parker and Machito's Orchestra guest with the troupe which includes Coleman Hawkins, Flip Phillips, Sonny Criss, Tommy Turk, Fats Navarro, Hank Jones, Ray Brown, Shelly Manne and Ella Fitzgerald.

SATURDAY 12 FEBRUARY 1949

In the early hours of Saturday, Charlie Parker and the Quintet broadcast from the Royal Roost.
CHARLIE PARKER (alto sax), KENNY DORHAM (trumpet), AL HAIG (piano), TOMMY POTTER (bass), MAX ROACH (drums), SYMPHONY SID TORIN (announcer)
Scrapple From The Apple / Barbados / Be-Bop / Jumpin' With Symphony Sid (theme)

THURSDAY 17 FEBRUARY 1949

The Tadd Dameron Big Ten replace Charlie Ventura and Dinah Washington at the Royal Roost.

Below: A happy group at the bar of the Royal Roost. L to r: Milt Jackson, Al Haig, unknown, Charlie Parker, Nicole Barclay, Max Roach and Mr & Mrs Kenny Dorham.

TUES	1
WED	2
THUR	3
FRI	4
SAT	5
SUN	6
MON	7
TUES	8
WED	9
THUR	10
FRI	11
SAT	12
SUN	13
MON	14
TUES	15
WED	16
THUR	17
FRI	18
SAT	19
SUN	20
MON	21
TUES	22
WED	23
THUR	24
FRI	25
SAT	26
SUN	27
MON	28

SATURDAY 19 FEBRUARY 1949

In the early hours of Saturday, Charlie Parker and the Quintet broadcast from the Royal Roost.
CHARLIE PARKER (alto sax), KENNY DORHAM (trumpet), AL HAIG (piano), TOMMY POTTER (bass), MAX ROACH (drums), SYMPHONY SID TORIN (announcer)
Groovin' High / Confirmation / Salt Peanuts / Jumpin' With Symphony Sid (theme)

Tadd Dameron's Big Ten also broadcast from the Royal Roost.

SUNDAY 20 FEBRUARY 1949

Charlie appears at a matinee benefit concert for baritone saxist Leo Parker at the Royal Roost. Also taking part are Babs Gonzales 3 Bips and a Bop, Tadd Dameron, Wynton Kelly, Miles Davis, Cecil Payne, Jack the Bear, Max Roach, Kenny Clarke, Sonny Rollins, Pee Wee Tinney, Dave Burns, Arturo Phipps and Tommy Potter.

MONDAY 21 FEBRUARY 1949

Charlie appears on a television show on WPIX, New York – The Metronome Award Show of 1949. Charles Delaunay presents Charlie with an award.
CHARLIE PARKER (alto sax), GEORGE BUSHKIN (piano), CHUBBY JACKSON (bass), GEORGE WETTLING (drums)
Now's The Time / Lover (TEDDY HALE tap dances)
SHORTY SHEROCK (trumpet) joins the group
I Can't Get Started
SIDNEY BECHET (soprano saxophone) and a trombonist join in the jam session finale.

SATURDAY 26 FEBRUARY 1949

In the early hours of Saturday, Charlie Parker and the Quintet broadcast from the Royal Roost with some guests.
CHARLIE PARKER (alto sax), KENNY DORHAM (trumpet), LUCKY THOMPSON (tenor sax), MILT JACKSON (vibes), AL HAIG (piano), TOMMY POTTER (bass), MAX ROACH (drums), SYMPHONY SID TORIN (announcer)
Half Nelson / Night In Tunisia / Scrapple From The Apple / Deedle (vocals DAVE LAMBERT, BUDDY STEWART) / *What's This* (vocals DAVE LAMBERT, BUDDY STEWART) / *Jumpin' With Symphony Sid* (theme)

Tadd Dameron's Big Ten also broadcast from the Royal Roost.

Granz Overseer Of Mercury Bop

Chicago—Norman Granz, bereted and booted guardian of the *Jazz at the Philharmonic* concert troupes, will supervise all of Mercury records' bop jazz cuttings, under a new program planned to consolidate and enlarge Mercury's hot jazz recordings.

Emphasis, Granz says, will be on Afro-Cuban bop. First record, scheduled for immediate release, is *No Noise*, Parts I and II. Soloist on the first side is Flip Phillips, with Charlie Parker featured on the second. Both will be backed by Machito's eight rhythm, four saxes, and three trumpets.

Other records featuring Machito, Parker, Phillips, and Howard McGhee will be issued soon.

Mercury's plans include a new label design and color for its complete jazz line.

Among the first Mercury cuttings since the recording ban was lifted were four sides by Big Bill Broonzy, of which *Watercoast Blues* is the first release. With blues-shouting guitarist Broonzy on the date were Carl (Pieface) Sharp, piano; Ransom Knowling, bass, and Alfred Wallace, drums.

Chicago, February 25, 1949

JATP Tour Snares Vets

New York—The *Jazz at the Philharmonic* tour which starts at Carnegie Hall February 11, will include JATP veterans Coleman Hawkins, Flip Phillips, Sonny Criss, and Tommy Turk, plus newcomers Ella Fitzgerald, Hank Jones, Ray Brown, Shelly Manne, and Fats Navarro.

The Carnegie date will also find Machito's band and altoist Charlie Parker on the stage, although they will not tour with the group. Show goes to the Academy of Music, Philadelphia, on February 12; Symphony hall, Boston, 13; Kleinhans', Buffalo, 20; Massey hall, Toronto, 21; University of Michigan, Ann Arbor, Mich., 25; Masonic hall, Detroit, 26; Memorial hall, Columbus, Ohio, 27, and dates through March taking the unit to California and back to the east coast.

A new JATP album, the ninth, was to be released by Mercury this week. It consists of six sides of *Jammin' the Blues*, with the same personnel as Volume 8 of the JATP album series. Both albums were recorded at the November, 1947, concert in Carnegie hall. A third album from that concert has yet to be released.

Billy Shaw Agency Working With Bird

New York—Billy Shaw lost no time in opening his own booking agency following his retirement from the Gale setup.

Located in the RCA building, he opened operations with the Charlie Parker combo, Buddy De Franco, Miles Davis, and Milt Buckner, Lionel Hampton's former pianist who left a few months ago to form his own band.

*To D. Dah
My Man
Best Wishes
Your friend forever
Charlie Parker*

TUES	1
WED	2
THUR	3
FRI	4
SAT	5
SUN	6
MON	7
TUES	8
WED	9
THUR	10
FRI	11
SAT	12
SUN	13
MON	14
TUES	15
WED	16
THUR	17
FRI	18
SAT	19
SUN	20
MON	21
TUES	22
WED	23
THUR	24
FRI	25
SAT	26
SUN	27
MON	28
TUES	29
WED	30
THUR	31

FRIDAY 4 MARCH 1949

Charlie appears on a CBS television show 'Adventures in Jazz'

CHARLIE PARKER (alto sax), MILES DAVIS (trumpet), MAX KAMINSKY (trumpet), KAI WINDING (trombone), JOE MARSALA (clarinet), MIKE CALUCCIO (piano), SPECS POWELL, MAX ROACH (drums), WILLIAM B. WILLIAMS (MC)

Anthropology (JOE SULLIVAN plays piano) / *Bop City* / *I Get A Kick Out Of You* (vocal: ANN HATHAWAY) / *Big Foot* (Finale jam session)

SATURDAY 5 MARCH 1949

In the early hours of Saturday, Charlie Parker and the Quintet broadcast from the Royal Roost with some guests.

CHARLIE PARKER (alto sax), KENNY DORHAM (trumpet), LUCKY THOMPSON (tenor sax), MILT JACKSON (vibes), AL HAIG (piano), TOMMY POTTER (bass), MAX ROACH (drums), SYMPHONY SID TORIN (announcer)

Jumpin' With Symphony Sid (theme) / *Cheryl* / *Anthropology* / *Hurry Home* (vocal BUDDY STEWART) / *Deedle* (vocals DAVE LAMBERT, BUDDY STEWART) / *What's This* (vocals DAVE LAMBERT, BUDDY STEWART) / *Royal Roost Bop*

Tadd Dameron's Big Ten also broadcast from the Royal Roost

Saturday morning: Bird appears at a Youth Forum at the Waldorf Astoria Hotel, organised by the *NY Herald Tribune* as part of a presentation by Rudi Blesh entitled 'Battle of the Bands' – a dixieland band led by Sidney Bechet and a bop band led by Bird (his regular quintet)

CHARLIE PARKER (alto sax), KENNY DORHAM (trumpet), AL HAIG (piano), TOMMY POTTER (bass), MAX ROACH (drums), MILT JACKSON (vibes)

How High The Moon / *Barbados* / *Anthropology*

SIDNEY BECHET (soprano sax), BUSTER BAILEY (clarinet), WILBUR DE PARIS (trombone), RALPH SUTTON (piano), WALTER PAGE (bass), GEORGE WETTLING (drums)

I Found A New Baby / *Ad Lib Blues* / *Dear Old Southland*

SATURDAY 12 MARCH 1949

In the early hours of Saturday, Charlie Parker and the Quintet broadcast from the Royal Roost with some guests.

CHARLIE PARKER (alto sax), KENNY DORHAM (trumpet), LUCKY THOMPSON (tenor sax), MILT JACKSON (vibes), AL HAIG (piano), TOMMY POTTER (bass), MAX ROACH (drums), SYMPHONY SID TORIN (announcer)

Cheryl / *Slow Boat to China* / *Chasin' The Bird* / *Jumpin' With Symphony Sid* (theme)

SUNDAY 13 MARCH 1949

Charlie stars in a Sunday afternoon 'Bop in the Bronx Concert at the Bronx Winter Garden at Washington and Tremont Avenues. Also taking part are Miles Davis, Tadd Dameron, Ike Quebec, Kai Winding, Milt Jackson, Curley Russell and Max Roach.

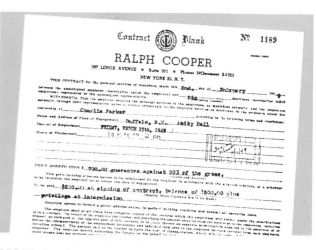

Around this time there is a Charlie Parker Septet recording session in New York for Mercury/Verve.

CHARLIE PARKER (alto sax), KENNY DORHAM (trumpet), TOMMY TURK (trombone), AL HAIG (piano), TOMMY POTTER (bass), MAX ROACH (drums), CARLOS VIDAL (bongo)

Cardboard / *Visa*

FRIDAY 25 MARCH 1949

Charlie Parker Quintet with Kenny Dorham, Al Haig, Tommy Potter and Max Roach play a one-nighter at Amity Hall, Buffalo, N.Y.

MONDAY 28 MARCH 1949

Charlie Parker Quintet with Kenny Dorham, Al Haig, Tommy Potter and Max Roach plus vocalist Arthur Daniels open at the Beige Room of the Pershing Hotel in Chicago for a two-week engagement.

FRI **1**
SAT **2**
SUN **3**
MON **4**
TUES **5**
WED **6**
THUR **7**
FRI **8**
SAT **9**
SUN **10**
MON **11**
TUES **12**
WED **13**
THUR **14**
FRI **15**
SAT **16**
SUN **17**
MON **18**
TUES **19**
WED **20**
THUR **21**
FRI **22**
SAT **23**
SUN **24**
MON **25**
TUES **26**
WED **27**
THUR **28**
FRI **29**
SAT **30**

SUNDAY 10 APRIL 1949
Charlie Parker Quintet closes at the Beige Room of the Pershing Hotel in Chicago.

TUESDAY 12 APRIL 1949
Charlie Parker Quintet open at the Music Bowl in Chicago for a two-week engagement.

THURSDAY 14 APRIL 1949
Bop City opens in New York City at Broadway and 49th Street, just a block away from the Royal Roost.

MONDAY 18 APRIL 1949
On the off-night at the Music Bowl, the quintet guest star at another Chicago venue (*see photograph*).

SUNDAY 24 APRIL 1949
Charlie Parker Quintet close at the Music Bowl, Chicago. Then play a dance date in Gary, Indiana before a series of one-nighters to take them back east.

Below: A Monday night crowd cram into a Chicago hall to see the Charlie Parker Quintet. Visible are Tommy Potter (bass), Max Roach (drums), Kenny Dorham (trumpet) and Bird.

SUN	**1**
MON	**2**
TUES	**3**
WED	**4**
THUR	**5**
FRI	**6**
SAT	**7**
SUN	**8**
MON	**9**
TUES	**10**
WED	**11**
THUR	**12**
FRI	**13**
SAT	**14**
SUN	**15**
MON	**16**
TUES	**17**
WED	**18**
THUR	**19**
FRI	**20**
SAT	**21**
SUN	**22**
MON	**23**
TUES	**24**
WED	**25**
THUR	**26**
FRI	**27**
SAT	**28**
SUN	**29**
MON	**30**
TUES	**31**

THURSDAY 5 MAY 1949

Charlie Parker Quintet recording session in New York for Mercury/Verve
CHARLIE PARKER (alto sax), KENNY DORHAM (trumpet), AL HAIG (piano), TOMMY POTTER (bass), MAX ROACH (drums)
Segment / Diverse / Passport / Passport

SATURDAY 7 MAY 1949

Charlie Parker flies to Paris with Doris, the Quintet, Howard McGhee, Hot Lips Page, Flip Phillips and Tadd Dameron to appear at the Paris Jazz Festival.

Below: After touching down in Paris. L to r: Hot Lips Page, Tommy Potter, unknown, Big Chief Russell Moore, Sidney Bechet, Al Haig, Charlie Parker, Max Roach, Miles Davis and Kenny Dorham.

SUN	1
MON	2
TUES	3
WED	4
THUR	5
FRI	6
SAT	7
SUN	8
MON	9
TUES	10
WED	11
THUR	12
FRI	13
SAT	14
SUN	15
MON	16
TUES	17
WED	18
THUR	19
FRI	20
SAT	21
SUN	22
MON	23
TUES	24
WED	25
THUR	26
FRI	27
SAT	28
SUN	29
MON	30
TUES	31

OUVERTURE DU FESTIVAL
*
SYDNEY BECHET
*
PETE JOHNSON
*
Oran « HOT LIPS » PAGE - « Big Chief » RUSSEL MOORE DON BYAS, GEORGE JOHNSON, etc...
*
MILES DAVIS, TAD DAMERON Quintet,
featuring : James MOODY,
Kenny CLARKE - « bass » SPIELER

CHARLIE PARKER'S Quintet
featuring : Kenny DORHAM, AL. HAIG,
Tommy POTTER et Max ROACH

SUNDAY 8 MAY 1949
Charlie Parker Quintet play at a Salle Pleyel Concert in Paris.

MONDAY 9 MAY 1949
Charlie Parker Quintet play at a Salle Pleyel Concert in Paris.

TUESDAY 10 MAY 1949
Charlie Parker Quintet play in Marseilles.

WEDNESDAY 11 MAY 1949
Charlie Parker Quintet play in Marseilles at the Rex movie theatre and afterwards at the Martinez & Christera club.

THURSDAY 12 MAY 1949
Charlie Parker Quintet play in Roubaix at the Colisee Movie Theatre where a private recording is made
CHARLIE PARKER (alto sax), KENNY DORHAM (trumpet), AL HAIG (piano), TOMMY POTTER (bass), MAX ROACH (drums)
Ornithology / Out Of Nowhere / Cheryl / 52nd Street Theme / Lover Man / Groovin' High / Half Nelson / 52nd Street Theme

Below: The Charlie Parker Quintet on stage at the Salle Pleyel. L to r: Al Haig (piano), Kenny Dorham (trumpet), Charlie Parker (alto sax), Tommy Potter (bass), Max Roach (drums).

SUN	1
MON	2
TUES	3
WED	4
THUR	5
FRI	6
SAT	7
SUN	8
MON	9
TUES	10
WED	11
THUR	12
FRI	13
SAT	14
SUN	15
MON	16
TUES	17
WED	18
THUR	19
FRI	20
SAT	21
SUN	22
MON	23
TUES	24
WED	25
THUR	26
FRI	27
SAT	28
SUN	29
MON	30
TUES	31

Drummer/composer/arranger Allan Ganley is one of an army of young British musicians who travel to Paris to hear Charlie Parker. He recalls:

I was 18 and it was a couple of months before I went into the Air Force, and I decided to take the bull by the horns and go to the Paris Jazz Festival. It was the first time I had been out of England, actually, and on the boat over I met another young musician called Jack Sharpe. Also on the boat were members of the Club Eleven… John Dankworth, Ronnie Scott, Pete Chilvers… we didn't know them at that time… they were already stars in our eyes. We got to Paris, and followed John Dankworth and the other guys and booked into the same hotel, the Sphinx…quite a seedy place. Jack and I went out to look around… we walked by a café with a large plate glass window and I just happened to look inside and saw a whole bunch of black musicians… I knew they were musicians because they had their instrument cases down at the side… sitting in a corner. We went in, stood at the bar, and had a coffee. Suddenly, one got up to leave, and I said to Jack, 'That's Charlie Parker!' He said, 'Nah…' So anyway, as he came by, I stood in front of him and said, 'Are you Charlie Parker?' and he said, 'Yeah.' I shook his hand and said we were musicians from England and had come to hear him. He was very friendly, and introduced us to the other guys, Big Chief Russell Moore and, I seem to remember, Hot Lips Page… Miles wasn't there. He was really pleased that we had come from London to hear him play, and said he was going to be at the Club St Germain

des Pres later and to come on by. So we went down there, and Bird came in, and borrowed John Dankworth's horn… and Joe Muddel from Club Eleven played bass with him. Next night we went to the concerts and I heard Bird with Kenny Dorham, Al Haig, Tommy Potter and Max Roach. What a wonderful experience!

SUN 1
MON 2
TUES 3
WED 4
THUR 5
FRI 6
SAT 7
SUN 8
MON 9
TUES 10
WED 11
THUR 12
FRI 13
SAT 14
SUN 15
MON 16
TUES 17
WED 18
THUR 19
FRI 20
SAT 21
SUN 22
MON 23
TUES 24
WED 25
THUR 26
FRI 27
SAT 28
SUN 29
MON 30
TUES 31

This page: The Quintet in action in Paris.
Opposite page, below: Bird at the Paris Lido with, l to r:
Jean Berdin, unknown lady, Tadd and Mrs Dameron,
Eddy and Nicole Barclay.

SUN	**1**
MON	**2**
TUES	**3**
WED	**4**
THUR	**5**
FRI	**6**
SAT	**7**
SUN	**8**
MON	**9**
TUES	**10**
WED	**11**
THUR	**12**
FRI	**13**
SAT	**14**
SUN	**15**
MON	**16**
TUES	**17**
WED	**18**
THUR	**19**
FRI	**20**
SAT	**21**
SUN	**22**
MON	**23**
TUES	**24**
WED	**25**
THUR	**26**
FRI	**27**
SAT	**28**
SUN	**29**
MON	**30**
TUES	**31**

NEWS   DOWN BEAT   3

Chicago, July 1, 1949

Crowds Jam Paris Jazz Festival

Paris—Chummy photos, above, indicate the fine, gemutlich feeling that prevailed during the International Jazz festival here recently. American and European musicians, playing all styles of jazz, gathered under the sponsorship of French jazz enthusiast Charles Delaunay for a week of music. First photo shows trumpeter Gosta Turner of Sweden and Oran (Lips) Page of the United States, comparing notes. Swedish drummer Sven Bollhem, left, relaxes with Max Roach, center, and Charlie Parker, right, in the second picture. Last photo, taken at a pre-concert rehearsal, shows, from the left, Aime Barelli, Don Byas, Jack Dieval (standing), James Moody, Claude Luter, Pierre Braslavsky, and Rene Leroux. All except Americans Byas and Moody are French. The concert was a huge success. Acme photos.

By MARIAN McPARTLAND

Paris—Backstage at the Salle Pleyel, an excited crowd shuffled back and forth. Musicians were warming up, stage technicians barked last minute directions, critics and kibitzers chattered excitedly and craned their necks as, 15 minutes late, a French emcee sidled in front of the curtain and announced "Le Festival Internationale de Jazz est ouvert."

And for a whole week the 25,000-capacity auditorium was jammed. Devotees of New Orleans music rubbed shoulders with bop disciples. When, on opening night, the first notes of Vic Lewis bop-styled 15-piece British band were heard, purists in the audience booed and hissed!

...er to find the groove.

Bird Slays 'Em

Bringing the boppers to the edges of their seats was the Charlie Parker quintet, with Kenny Dorham, trumpet; Al Haig, piano; Tommy Potter, bass, and Max ... brought the audience to yelling for more.

Sid Great

Sidney Bechet, backed by Pierre Braslavsky band, ... mendous ovation. When t... takable sound of his sop... cut through the closed... there were bursts of che... applause. It would be ... for anyone who professe... musician, in the broades... ...ot to have e... of Su...

Bird Slays 'Em

Bringing the boppers to the edges of their seats was the Charlie Parker quintet, with Kenny Dorham, trumpet; Al Haig, piano; Tommy Potter, bass, and Max Roach, drums. The band had a tremendous beat, and Parker, displaying his prodigious technique and originality of ideas, wove in and out of the rhythmic patterns laid down by Roach to the accompaniment of ecstatic cries of "Formidable!" from the fanatics.

But whether their tastes were Bechet or Parker, for a whole week 25,000 jazz fans were in their glory nightly.

Vive le jazz!

LONDON LARGO

Palladium SRO Sign Out

Right: Bird jams with Big Chief Russell Moore

SUN	1
MON	2
TUES	3
WED	4
THUR	5
FRI	6
SAT	7
SUN	8
MON	9
TUES	10
WED	11
THUR	12
FRI	13
SAT	14
SUN	15
MON	16
TUES	17
WED	18
THUR	19
FRI	20
SAT	21
SUN	22
MON	23
TUES	24
WED	25
THUR	26
FRI	27
SAT	28
SUN	29
MON	30
TUES	31

FRIDAY 13 MAY 1949
The Quintet have a day off.

SATURDAY 14 MAY 1949
Charlie Parker Quintet play at a Salle Pleyel Concert in Paris.

SUNDAY 15 MAY 1949
Charlie Parker Quintet play two concerts at the Salle Pleyel. In the final concert (8.45pm) Bird jams with Sidney Bechet and Don Byas in the finale session
KENNY DORHAM, AIME BARELLI, BILL COLEMAN, MILES DAVIS, HOT LIPS PAGE (trumpets), BIG CHIEF RUSSELL MOORE (trombone), HUBERT ROSTAING (clarinet), PIERRE BRASLAVSKY, SIDNEY BECHET (soprano sax), CHARLIE PARKER (alto sax), DON BYAS, JAMES MOODY (tenor sax), AL HAIG, BERNARD PEIFFER (piano), HAZY OSTERWALD (vibes), TOOTS THIELEMANS (guitar), TOMMY POTTER (bass), MAX ROACH (drums)
Farewell Blues

After the concert Bird jams at the Club St Germain where he meets Jean-Paul Sartre.

Right: On the bus to the airport, Bird, Bechet and Kenny Clarke.
Below: Waiting to board, l to r: Max Roach, Bird, Miles Davis (hidden), Kenny Clarke.

MONDAY 16 MAY 1949
Bird meets with Charles Delaunay and Andre Hodeir before returning to the States.
Back in New York, the Quintet go into the Onyx on 52nd Street for a two-week engagement.

FRIDAY 20 MAY 1949
Down Beat reviews Charlie's new Mercury release:

CHARLIE PARKER with MACHITO
*** Mango Mangue
*** Okey Dokie
A very fertile combination this, even better than Flip Phillips with the Afro-Cuban bop styled ensemble of Machito. Parker's hard, pert tone bites through without weighting down the rhythm. His solo on the second chorus of Mango is worthy of almost bar for bar study. For construction and ease of creation under the complexities of the sections in back of him, this one takes the small gold kazoo. (**Mercury 11017**)

WED	1
THUR	2
FRI	3
SAT	4
SUN	5
MON	6
TUES	7
WED	8
THUR	9
FRI	10
SAT	11
SUN	12
MON	13
TUES	14
WED	15
THUR	16
FRI	17
SAT	18
SUN	19
MON	20
TUES	21
WED	22
THUR	23
FRI	24
SAT	25
SUN	26
MON	27
TUES	28
WED	29
THUR	30

Bird, Ventura Leave Milwaukee; Louis In

Milwaukee—There was much rejoicing when Bob Paliafito, Continental owner, brought Charlie Parker to his club June 6 for a week. Continuing to operate on a no minimum or cover charge basis, despite high price attractions, Paliafito remains one of the most popular guys in town. Parker, newly returned from the Paris jazz festival, spoke highly of the congeniality of the French people.

Bird described the language as being beautiful, with interesting rhythms and musical sounds. "You know, some of the French cats sounded better than the guys in New York," he remarked.

Following Parker were the Charlie Ventura and Louis Armstrong units for a week each. Billie Holiday will be back July 25.

When Does It Happen?

"You sing on a television show, Charlie Parker says you sound great, but," asks Connie Milan, "when do things start happening?"

Equipped with a rich, well-controlled voice, plus the ability to please an audience, Milan has

one of the deals he's contemplating will be it.

Off to Michigan

Off to Hancock, Mich., for a three-week engagement is Kenny Powers, rated one of the best local tenorists. With him goes Jerry King, drummer, and Louie Hammer, pianist.

Norm Ebron, who, a few years ago, was getting praise in and out of town for his fine trio, has formed the Town House booking agency.

His trio, consisting of Ebron, piano; George Lott, trumpet, and Leroy Dixon, bass, broke up when Ebron became ill last year. He has no desire, at present, to reorganize, but his reluctance to leave the music business after so many years prompted him to venture into booking.

MONDAY 6 JUNE 1949
Charlie Parker Quintet open at the Continental Club in Milwaukee for a one-week engagement.

SUNDAY 12 JUNE 1949
Charlie Parker Quintet close at the Continental Club in Milwaukee.

Below: the Charlie Parker Quintet at the Blue Note in Chicago. The singer may be Junior Daniels, Tommy Potter is on bass, Kenny Dorham on trumpet and Max Roach is on drums.

Yardbird Singer Inks Pact With Discovery

New York—Junior Daniels, 18-year-old baritone currently under the wing of Billy Shaw, has signed a five-year disc pact with Discovery records. Deal followed a guest appearance by Daniels at Cafe Society.

Shaw has set Junior with Charlie Parker's band as vocalist. On his solo discs, however, he will probably be backed by Discovery's Phil Moore and a studio crew.

WED	**1**
THUR	**2**
FRI	**3**
SAT	**4**
SUN	**5**
MON	**6**
TUES	**7**
WED	**8**
THUR	**9**
FRI	**10**
SAT	**11**
SUN	**12**
MON	**13**
TUES	**14**
WED	**15**
THUR	**16**
FRI	**17**
SAT	**18**
SUN	**19**
MON	**20**
TUES	**21**
WED	**22**
THUR	**23**
FRI	**24**
SAT	**25**
SUN	**26**
MON	**27**
TUES	**28**
WED	**29**
THUR	**30**

Above: Symphony Sid begins a new radio show on station WJZ, Crazy for JZ. Wishing him luck at the opening broadcast are, l to r: George Simon, Pete Rugolo, Alvino Rey, Leonard Feather, Buddy Johnson, Illinois Jacquet, Norman Granz, Chubby Jackson, Sarah Vaughan, George Shearing and Charlie Parker.

TUESDAY 14 JUNE 1949
Charlie Parker Quintet open at the Blue Note, Chicago for a one-week engagement.

SUNDAY 19 JUNE 1949
Charlie Parker Quintet close at the Blue Note

Charlie appears with Jazz At The Philharmonic in Carnegie Hall, New York.
Radio broadcast:
CHARLIE PARKER (alto sax), ROY ELDRIDGE (trumpet), COLEMAN HAWKINS (tenor sax), HANK JONES (piano), EDDIE SAFRANSKI (bass), BUDDY RICH (drums)
Lover Come Back To Me / Stuffy

FRI	1	MON	1
SAT	2	TUES	2
SUN	3	WED	3
MON	4	THUR	4
TUES	5	FRI	5
WED	6	SAT	6
THUR	7	SUN	7
FRI	8	MON	8
SAT	9	TUES	9
SUN	10	WED	10
MON	11	THUR	11
TUES	12	FRI	12
WED	13	SAT	13
THUR	14	SUN	14
FRI	15	MON	15
SAT	16	TUES	16
SUN	17	WED	17
MON	18	THUR	18
TUES	19	FRI	19
WED	20	SAT	20
THUR	21	SUN	21
FRI	22	MON	22
SAT	23	TUES	23
SUN	24	WED	24
MON	25	THUR	25
TUES	26	FRI	26
WED	27	SAT	27
THUR	28	SUN	28
FRI	29	MON	29
SAT	30	TUES	30
SUN	31	WED	31

FRIDAY 29 JULY 1949
Down Beat reviews Charlie's first LP released on the Dial label:

CHARLIE PARKER
Relaxing at Camarillo
Carvin' the Bird
Dark Shadows
Blowtop Blues
Bongo Bop
Cool Blues
Album Rating—***

This is Dial records' first LP side, with 13 tracks by Bird (3 of *Relaxing*, two each of the others). All of these records have been previously issued, and, while with the additional takes it is interesting stuff for students of Parker, it still is an expensive buy for the music involved. Then, too, Ross Russell has annoyingly coupled these so that there is no complete previous record on the LP platter. Thus, you can't replace present records in your collection with the LP, and if you want the other side of a disc with one dubbed on this platter, you have to shell out a buck for a record, one side of which you already have. This may be smart salesmanship, but I think in the long run it will diminish, rather than increase, Dial's sales. **(Dial LP 1.)**

THURSDAY 4 AUGUST 1949
Charlie Parker Quintet open at Bop City, New York. Also on the bill are Count Basie and his Orchestra: Emmett Berry, Harry Edison, Jimmy Nottingham, Clark Terry (trumpet), Dickie Wells, George Matthews, Ted Donnelly (trombone), Earl Warren, Charles Price (alto sax), Paul Gonsalves, Willie Parker (tenor sax), Singleton Palmer (bass), Freddie Green (guitar), Butch Ballard (drums), Jimmy Rushing (vocal)

MONDAY 29 AUGUST 1949
Charlie Parker's 29th birthday.

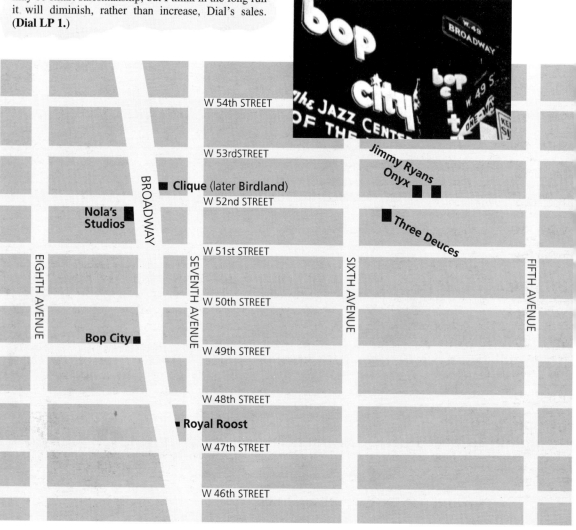

THUR	**1**
FRI	**2**
SAT	**3**
SUN	**4**
MON	**5**
TUES	**6**
WED	**7**
THUR	**8**
FRI	**9**
SAT	**10**
SUN	**11**
MON	**12**
TUES	**13**
WED	**14**
THUR	**15**
FRI	**16**
SAT	**17**
SUN	**18**
MON	**19**
TUES	**20**
WED	**21**
THUR	**22**
FRI	**23**
SAT	**24**
SUN	**25**
MON	**26**
TUES	**27**
WED	**28**
THUR	**29**
FRI	**30**

City Halts Birdland Debut

New York—Birdland, new bop spot on the site of the old Clique, failed to open as scheduled Sept. 8. The alcohol beverage commission refused to give the spot a license. Although a sign on the door on opening night said the opening had been postponed, chances are it won't open at all.

Spot was to have been operated by Monte Kay, formerly of the Royal Roost, and his brothers, Joe and Sol Kaplan. Turndown from the liquor board came at noon of the scheduled opening day. Decorations had been completed and ads were running in that day's papers announcing the opening.

Came Too Late

Hundreds of people who planned to attend the opening turned up at the closed doors that night since the liquor license refusal came too late to cancel the ads or get the word out to the papers that the opening was off.

The Kaplans and Kay are said to have spent some $8,000 fixing the room up. Opening show was to have been the Charlie Parker and Lennie Tristano combos, plus Harry Belafonte, Stan Getz, and himself to blame."

Short Explanation

Turndown by the liquor board was explained only by the customary notation that it was "not in the best interests of the commission."

The Kaplans and Kay, who have a six-year lease on the room, are now trying to peddle the place.

Getz, who had been scheduled to leave J. J. Johnson's group at the Three Deuces to take the Birdland job, immediately retrieved his job with Johnson and was playing at the Deuces the night he was supposed to be opening at Birdland.

The Orchid room, 52nd St. spot which had been using the Jackie Paris trio and singer Peggy Payne, picked up other remnants of the Birdland show at the end of September, moving in the Lennie Tristano sextet, Harry Belafonte and Bud Powell. Only element of Birdland show not work month's end was the Parker group.

Sells Roost Records

Following the Birdland Kay sold his Roost rec Sammy Kaye, one of the o of the Three Deuces. a

London Adds More American-Cut Wax

New York—London records, building up a catalog of American-cut wax, has bought four masters from Sharp records, Chicago outfit, and signed a new singer, 19-year-old Teresa Brewer.

Masters bought from Sharp are by the Jack Teter trio and Lee Monti's Tu-Tones. Miss Brewer, who recently appeared at the Village Vanguard in New York hasn't recorded before.

But, Baby, It's Cold

New York — Elliot Law band got caught with their clothes on in September ing one-niters in Mont

TUESDAY 6 SEPTEMBER 1949

Charlie Parker appears at a Town Hall Concert which also features Erroll Garner, Lennie Tristano, Bud Powell, Miles Davis & Harry Belafonte

THURSDAY 8 SEPTEMBER 1949

A new jazz club, to be called Birdland, is scheduled to open on Broadway with Bird, Lennie Tristano, Stan Getz, Bud Powell and Harry Belafonte. The opening is postponed when the club fails to get a liquor licence.

FRIDAY 16 SEPTEMBER 1949

Bird joins JATP for the fall tour, beginning at the Bushnell Memorial Auditorium, Hartford, Connecticut.

SATURDAY 17 SEPTEMBER 1949

Bird with JATP at a midnight concert in Carnegie Hall
CHARLIE PARKER (alto sax), FLIP PHILLIPS (tenor sax), LESTER YOUNG (tenor sax), ROY ELDRIDGE (trumpet), TOMMY TURK (trombone), HANK JONES (piano), RAY BROWN (bass), BUDDY RICH (drums), ELLA FITZGERALD (vocal)
The Opener / Lester Leaps In / Embraceable You / The Closer / Flying Home (Vocal: Ella) / *How High The Moon* (vocal: Ella) / *Perdido* (vocal: Ella)

SUNDAY 18 SEPTEMBER 1949

Bird with JATP at the Uline Arena in Washington D.C.

MONDAY 19 SEPTEMBER 1949

Charlie Parker signs a contract to appear at the Three Deuces in October with his Quintet.

FRIDAY 30 SEPTEMBER 1949

Bird with JATP at the Public Music Hall in Cleveland.

THUR	**1**
FRI	**2**
SAT	**3**
SUN	**4**
MON	**5**
TUES	**6**
WED	**7**
THUR	**8**
FRI	**9**
SAT	**10**
SUN	**11**
MON	**12**
TUES	**13**
WED	**14**
THUR	**15**
FRI	**16**
SAT	**17**
SUN	**18**
MON	**19**
TUES	**20**
WED	**21**
THUR	**22**
FRI	**23**
SAT	**24**
SUN	**25**
MON	**26**
TUES	**27**
WED	**28**
THUR	**29**
FRI	**30**

Charlie is featured heavily in the 9 September issue of *Down Beat*:

No Bop Roots In Jazz: Parker

By MICHAEL LEVIN and JOHN S. WILSON

DOWN BEAT

VOL. 16—NO. 17   CHICAGO, SEPTEMBER 9, 1949

(Copyright, 1949, Down Beat, Inc.)

Kaye Blasts Krupa For 'Insulting Biz'

Dinah Harks To Her Master's Voice

New York—"Bop is no love-child of jazz," says Charlie Parker. The creator of bop, in a series of interviews that took more than two weeks, told us he felt that "bop is something entirely separate and apart" from the older tradition; that it drew little from jazz, has no roots in it. The chubby little alto man, who has made himself an international music name in the last five years, added that bop, for the most part, had to be played by small bands.

"Gillespie's playing has changed from being stuck in front of a big band. Anybody's does. He's a fine musician. The leopard coats and the wild hats are just another part of the managers' routines to make him box office. The same thing happened a couple of years ago when they stuck his name on some tunes of mine to give him a better commercial reputation."

Asked to define bop, after several evenings of a r g u i n g, Charlie still was not precise in his definition.

"It's just music," he said. "It's trying to play clean and looking for the pretty notes."

Pushed further, he said that a distinctive feature of bop is its strong feeling for beat.

"The beat-in a bop band is with the music, against it, behind it," Charlie said. "It pushes it. It helps it. Help is the big thing. It has no continuity of beat, no steady chug-chug. Jazz has, and that's why bop is more flexible."

He admits the music eventually may be atonal. Parker himself is a devout admirer of Paul Hindemith, the German neo-classicist, raves about his *Kammermusik* and *Sonata for Viola and Cello*. He insists, however, that bop is not moving in the same direction as modern classical. He feels that it will be more flexible, more emotional, more colorful.

He reiterates constantly that bop is only just beginning to form as a school, that it can barely label its present trends, much less make prognostications about the future.

The closest Parker will come to an exact, technical description of what may happen is to say that he would like to emulate the precise...

Chicago, September 9, 1949

NEWS—FEATURES

12   DOWN BEAT

Bird: Lester Didn't Influence Me

(Jumped from Page 1)

in a state of surprise. But, actually, he himself has no roots in traditional jazz. During the years he worked with traditional jazzmen he wandered like a lost soul. In his formative years he never heard any of the music which is traditionally supposed to inspire young jazzists—no Louis, no Bix, no Hawk, no Rudy Vallee.

Tossed into the jazz world of the mid-30's with this kind of background, he had no familiar ground on which to stand. For three years he fumbled unhappy until he suddenly stumbled into the music which appealed to him. For Charlie insists, ing to him. For Charlie insists,

"I kept thinking about it," he recalls. "I could hear it sometimes but I couldn't play it."

Charlie's horn first came alive in a chili house on Seventh avenue between 139th street and none between 139th street. He was jamming there with a guitarist named Buddy Fleet. At the time, Charlie says, he was bored with the stereotyped changes being used then.

[Photo by Jerome Lacy]

Charlie Parker
"You've got to love it"

"(Photo by Jerome Lacy)

musician," said recently. "That's Charlie Parker. All the others say they're playing bop are just him trying to imitate him.

Despite his unwillingness to put anybody down, a slight note of irritation creeps into Charlie's voice when he contrasts the things which have been sidetracking those young jazzmen...

Lester Young
"But he didn't influence me"

"The main idea of the job," Charlie recalls, "was to be there and hold a note.

Soon after this, he tried jamming for the first time at the High Hat, at 22nd and Vine. He knew a little of *Lazy River* and *Honeysuckle Rose* and played the C-Melody sax...

Rock-A-Bye

Chicago—Earle Spencer and his pretty Marlene recently motored from Los Angeles to Chicago. At one stage Earle became sleepy, turned the wheel over to his wife, and curled up in the back seat for a snooze. Marlene drove until he fell asleep, then parked at the roadside for a two-hour nap herself. When Earle awakened, she was sweetly in motion again. But the speedometer showed only a five-mile gain.

New... RUNYON METAL MOUTHPIECE FOR TENOR SAX

• Sensational brass tenor mouthpiece, plated in chrome or gold

HERBIE FIELDS says "Volume, flexibility and tone quality never before experienced. It's the finest I've ever played"

Facings No. 2 to No. 8, inclusive

Distributed by
SANTY RUNYON PRODUCTS, H. & A. SELMER, INC
192 North Clark Street   Elkhart,
Chicago 1, Illinois   Indiana

SAT	1
SUN	2
MON	3
TUES	4
WED	5
THUR	6
FRI	7
SAT	8
SUN	9
MON	10
TUES	11
WED	12
THUR	13
FRI	14
SAT	15
SUN	16
MON	17
TUES	18
WED	19
THUR	20
FRI	21
SAT	22
SUN	23
MON	24
TUES	25
WED	26
THUR	27
FRI	28
SAT	29
SUN	30
MON	31

SATURDAY 1 OCTOBER 1949

Charlie appears with JATP at the Masonic Auditorium in Detroit. After the concert he appears as guest soloist with the Phil Hill Quintet at the Bluebird Inn in Detroit.

CHARLIE PARKER (alto sax), TATE HOUSTON (baritone sax), PHIL HILL (piano), JAMES 'BEANS' RICHARDSON (bass), ART MARDIGAN (drums), JACK TIANT (bongoes)
Now's The Time

Soon after the Detroit appearance, Charlie leaves the JATP tour to fulfil his contract to appear at the Three Deuces on 52nd Street.

THURSDAY 6 OCTOBER 1949

Charlie Parker Quintet open at the Three Deuces in New York for six weeks opposite Slam Stewart. The quintet is Bird, Red Rodney, Al Haig, Tommy Potter and Max Roach

The quintet play from 10pm to 4am for $1000 per week

Down Beat reviews the show:

SLAM STEWART / CHARLIE PARKER
Three Deuces

New York—New show at the Three Deuces features Charlie Parker's quintet and the Slam Stewart trio. Neither group is liable to make Deuces patrons forget Erroll Garner, who left after a three-month run there.

Stewart's trio is made up of Beryl Booker, piano; Johnny Collins, guitar, and Stewart on bass. Slam, of course, is still featuring his humming and bowing duets which are amusing on first hearing, but become duller and duller on successive repetitions. Possibly through association, Collins also is humming along with his guitar, although he fortunately lets his expert fingers do most of his work for him.

Miss Booker does most of the work in the trio, taking a pair of solos to each of the other's one and tossing in a vocal here and there. Her voice is nothing to vocalize about but her piano work is light, tasteful, and frequently quite interesting.

She evidently has been listening a lot to Garner, for quite a few typical Garner mannerisms are evident in her playing, along with stuff that is evidently her own.

The Bird's group is made up of Red Rodney, trumpet; Al Haig, piano; Tommy Potter, bass, and Max Roach drums. Charlie and Red currently are intrigued with the idea of using an English-round type of coda.

Dizzy Gillespie responds to Charlie's *Down Beat* interview:

Bird Wrong; Bop Must Get A Beat: Diz

New York—The Bird is wrong about the relationship of bop and jazz, says Dizzy Gillespie. "Bop is an interpretation of jazz," Diz told the *Beat*. "It's all part of the same thing." Last month Charlie Parker said that bop had no roots in jazz, was something entirely separate and apart from the older tradition (see *Down Beat*, Sept. 9) Parker identified the beat as the distinguishing factor of bop.

"It (bop) has no continuity of beat, no steady chug-chug," Parker said.

This lack of a steady beat, according to Dizzy, is what is wrong with bop today.

"Bop is part of jazz," Dizzy said, "and jazz music is to dance to. The trouble with bop as it's played now is that people can't dance to it. They don't hear those four beats. We'll never get bop across to a wide audience until they can dance to it. They're not particular about whether you're playing a flatted fifth or a ruptured 129th as

people can understand where the beat is. We'll use a lot of things which are in the book now, but we'll cut them and splice them together again like you would a movie so as to leave out the variations in beat.

"I'm not turning my back on bop. My band has a distinctive sound and I want to keep that. But I want to make bop bigger, get it a wider audience. I think George Shearing is the greatest thing that's happened to bop in the past year. He's the only one who has helped it along. He plays bop so the average person can understand it.

"Anybody can dance to Shearing's music. By doing that, he has

made it easier for me and for everybody else who plays bop."

They Were Unhappy

Main pressure on Dizzy to make the switch has come from his wife, Lorraine, a former dancer, and his manager, Willard Alexander. For the last year, Lorraine has circulated in the audience on his one-niters, getting audience reaction and trying to impress him that a lot of his numbers were making the dancers unhappy.

From Alexander's point of view, the big hurdle with Dizzy's band, as it was, was scarcity of places where a big band which didn't draw dancers could be booked.

"We can't play small places that hold 100 or 200 persons," Dizzy pointed out. "We're playing big auditoriums that hold a couple of thousand, and you can't rely on the extremists to support you there."

Alexander says he isn't asking
(Modulate to Page 13)

Wingy Paroled; Europe Trip Off

Hollywood—Wingy Manone, convicted recently on a morals charge filed against him by two L.A. vice squadsmen who peeked in on a party he was enjoying with a couple of girl friends, was granted probation.

But the European tour planned for him by Joe Glaser is out for the present, as he will have to report regularly to probation authorities here for an indefinite period.

Strand Won't Use Just Orks In Shows

New York — Return

TUES	**1**
WED	**2**
THUR	**3**
FRI	**4**
SAT	**5**
SUN	**6**
MON	**7**
TUES	**8**
WED	**9**
THUR	**10**
FRI	**11**
SAT	**12**
SUN	**13**
MON	**14**
TUES	**15**
WED	**16**
THUR	**17**
FRI	**18**
SAT	**19**
SUN	**20**
MON	**21**
TUES	**22**
WED	**23**
THUR	**24**
FRI	**25**
SAT	**26**
SUN	**27**
MON	**28**
TUES	**29**
WED	**30**

WEDNESDAY 16 NOVEMBER 1949
Charlie Parker Quintet close at the Three Deuces.

THURSDAY 17 NOVEMBER 1949
Charlie Parker Quintet open at Bop City opposite Billy Eckstine and Herbie Fields.

WEDNESDAY 23 NOVEMBER 1949
Charlie Parker Quintet close at Bop City.

Below: The first recording session with strings. L to r: Buddy Rich, Ray Brown, Bird, Max Hollander, Mitch Miller, Milton Lomask.

LATE NOVEMBER 1949
Charlie Parker Quintet at Pershing Ballroom, Chicago. CHARLIE PARKER (alto sax), RED RODNEY (trumpet), AL HAIG (piano), TOMMY POTTER (bass), ROY HAYNES (drums) Private recording at the Pershing:
Perdido / Allen's Alley / Hot House / Cheryl / I Can't Get Started / Groovin' High / I Cover The Waterfront / Confirmation / Now's The Time / Smoke Gets In Your Eyes / Ruby, My Dear / Big Foot / How High The Moon / Cool Blues / Unknown vocal / All The Things You Are / Stardust
Private recording at the Savoy Ballroom, Chicago:
Billie's Bounce

WEDNESDAY 30 NOVEMBER 1949
Charlie Parker makes his first recording with strings for Norman Granz and Mercury in New York City. CHARLIE PARKER (alto sax), STAN FREEMAN (piano), RAY BROWN (bass), BUDDY RICH (drums), MITCH MILLER (oboe), BRONISLAW GIMPEL, MAX HOLLANDER, MILTON LOMASK (violins), FRANK BRIEFF (viola), FRANK MILLER (cello), MEYER ROSEN (harp), JIMMY CARROLL (arranger/conductor)
Just Friends / Everything Happens To Me / April In Paris / Summertime / I Didn't Know What Time it Was / If I Should Lose You

THUR	1
FRI	2
SAT	3
SUN	4
MON	5
TUES	6
WED	7
THUR	8
FRI	9
SAT	10
SUN	11
MON	12
TUES	13
WED	14
THUR	15
FRI	16
SAT	17
SUN	18
MON	19
TUES	20
WED	21
THUR	22
FRI	23
SAT	24
SUN	25
MON	26
TUES	27
WED	28
THUR	29
FRI	30
SAT	31

MONDAY 5 DECEMBER 1949

Charlie's son, Leon Parker (born 10 January 1938) writes to his father:

Dear Charles
I have been blowing my saxophone I am trying to learn the scales. I hope you are having a nice time. Mother bought me a coat with the money you gave her. I saw your picture downtown. Mother and Ross said Hello. I would like to have a train set for Christmas
So long for now, your son, Leon Parker

THURSDAY 15 DECEMBER 1949

Birdland opens at 1678 Broadway between 52nd and 53rd Streets.

Charlie Parker Quintet is booked for 3 weeks as part of an All-Star package including bands led by Lester Young, Stan Getz, Hot Lips Page and Max Kaminsky plus singing star Harry Belafonte. Pee Wee Marquette is the MC and Symphony Sid broadcasts nightly from the club over station WJZ.

Below: Opening night at Birdland. L to r: Max Kaminsky, Lester Young, Hot Lips Page, Charlie Parker and Lennie Tristano.

SATURDAY 24 DECEMBER 1949

Charlie Parker Quintet appear at a Carnegie Hall Concert. The concert is broacast over Voice of America and is compered by Symphony Sid.

CHARLIE PARKER (alto sax), RED RODNEY (trumpet), AL HAIG (piano), TOMMY POTTER (bass), ROY HAYNES (drums)
Ornithology / Cheryl / Koko / Bird Of Paradise / Now's The Time

Birdland Again Sets Opening

New York—Birdland, Broadway bophouse which failed to open in September because of license difficulties, was scheduled to make its bow Dec. 15 under a different management. Music policy includes Dixie, swing, and bop.

Opening show, pencilled in for three weeks, includes three combos, three instrumental soloists, and two singers. Groups are Charlie Parker's, Lennie Tristano's, and Max Kaminsky's. Soloists are Lester Young, Stan Getz, Hot Lips Page, Harry Belafonte, and Florence Wright.

Parker is using Red Rodney, trumpet; Al Haig, piano; Tommy Potter, bass, and Roy Haynes, drums. With Tristano are Lee Ko-

SUN	1	WED	1
MON	2	THUR	2
TUES	3	FRI	3
WED	4	SAT	4
THUR	5	SUN	5
FRI	6	MON	6
SAT	7	TUES	7
SUN	8	WED	8
MON	9	THUR	9
TUES	10	FRI	10
WED	11	SAT	11
THUR	12	SUN	12
FRI	13	MON	13
SAT	14	TUES	14
SUN	15	WED	15
MON	16	THUR	16
TUES	17	FRI	17
WED	18	SAT	18
THUR	19	SUN	19
FRI	20	MON	20
SAT	21	TUES	21
SUN	22	WED	22
MON	23	THUR	23
TUES	24	FRI	24
WED	25	SAT	25
THUR	26	SUN	26
FRI	27	MON	27
SAT	28	TUES	28
SUN	29		
MON	30		
TUES	31		

Above: Doris and Bird at Birdland. Although they look happy, their relationship is close to ending.

WEDNESDAY 4 JANUARY 1950
Charlie Parker Quintet close at Birdland.

MONDAY 9 JANUARY 1950
Charlie Parker appears at the 421 Club in Philadelphia.

WEDNESDAY 1 FEBRUARY 1950
Buddy Stewart, the young bop vocalist, is killed in a car accident.

THURSDAY 2 FEBRUARY 1950
Charlie Parker Sextet (J.J.Johnson, Red Rodney, Al Haig, Tommy Potter & Roy Haynes) open at Birdland opposite Wynonie Harris and the Bobby Hackett Quartet.

TUESDAY 14 FEBRUARY 1950
Charlie Parker Sextet broadcast from Birdland
CHARLIE PARKER (alto sax), RED RODNEY (trumpet), J. J. JOHNSON (trombone), AL HAIG (piano), TOMMY POTTER (bass), ROY HAYNES (drums)
Hot House / Out Of Nowhere / Visa / 52nd Street Theme / Anthropology / Allen's Alley /What's New? / Little Willie Leaps / Yesterdays / 52nd Street Theme / 52nd Street Theme / DizzyAtmosphere / Wahoo / I Can't Get Started / Allen's Alley / 52nd Street Theme / Slow Boat To China / Night In Tunisia / 52nd Street Theme

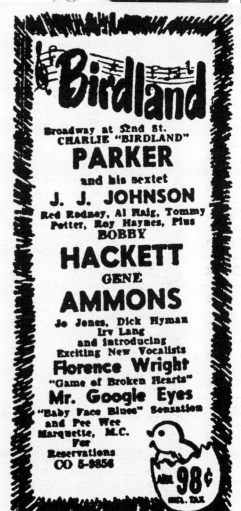

WED	**1**
THUR	**2**
FRI	**3**
SAT	**4**
SUN	**5**
MON	**6**
TUES	**7**
WED	**8**
THUR	**9**
FRI	**10**
SAT	**11**
SUN	**12**
MON	**13**
TUES	**14**
WED	**15**
THUR	**16**
FRI	**17**
SAT	**18**
SUN	**19**
MON	**20**
TUES	**21**
WED	**22**
THUR	**23**
FRI	**24**
SAT	**25**
SUN	**26**
MON	**27**
TUES	**28**

THURSDAY 16 FEBRUARY 1950
Charlie Parker Sextet close at Birdland.

SATURDAY 18 FEBRUARY 1950
Charlie Parker Quintet play a one-nighter at St Nicholas Ballroom, New York City. Bird and Chan are seen together in public for the first time. The session is privately recorded by Joe Maini and Don Lanphere.
CHARLIE PARKER (alto sax), RED RODNEY (trumpet), AL HAIG (piano), TOMMY POTTER (bass), ROY HAYNES (drums)
52nd Street Theme / Ornithology / I Didn't Know What Time It Was / Embraceable You / Scrapple From The Apple / Hot House / Now's The Time / Visa / Star Eyes / Confirmation / Out Of Nowhere / What's New? / Smoke Gets In Your Eyes / I Cover The Waterfront / 52nd Street Theme 52nd Street Theme / Perdido / I Can't Get Started / 52nd Street Theme / Anthropology / 52nd Street Theme / Groovin' High / 52nd Street Theme / Cheryl / 52nd Street Theme

Right: Charlie receives his Down Beat award for top alto man of 1949 from Charles Delaunay during the Birdland gig.
Below: Bird and Diz meet up at a Monday night Birdland benefit for Buddy Stewart, the young bop singer killed on the first of the month. Tommy Potter and 23 year old John Coltrane are also on hand.

WED	**1**
THUR	**2**
FRI	**3**
SAT	**4**
SUN	**5**
MON	**6**
TUES	**7**
WED	**8**
THUR	**9**
FRI	**10**
SAT	**11**
SUN	**12**
MON	**13**
TUES	**14**
WED	**15**
THUR	**16**
FRI	**17**
SAT	**18**
SUN	**19**
MON	**20**
TUES	**21**
WED	**22**
THUR	**23**
FRI	**24**
SAT	**25**
SUN	**26**
MON	**27**
TUES	**28**
WED	**29**
THUR	**30**
FRI	**31**

SATURDAY 11 MARCH 1950

Charlie Parker Quintet appear in Waukegan, North Chicago.

Through much of March the Charlie Parker Quintet tour with JATP. Tour starts in Buffalo and ends in Minneapolis. During the course of the tour, Norman Granz takes the opportunity to record Bird with a JATP rhythm section for Mercury/Verve in New York: CHARLIE PARKER (alto sax), HANK JONES (piano), RAY BROWN (bass), BUDDY RICH (drums)
Star Eyes / Blues (Fast) / I'm In The mood For Love

THURSDAY 30 MARCH 1950

Bird is present at rehearsals with The Gene Roland Orchestra – 'The Band That Never Was' – at the Nola Studios on Broadway. Trombonist Eddie Bert brings his camera to the rehearsal.

SAT	1
SUN	2
MON	3
TUES	4
WED	5
THUR	6
FRI	7
SAT	8
SUN	9
MON	10
TUES	11
WED	12
THUR	13
FRI	14
SAT	15
SUN	16
MON	17
TUES	18
WED	19
THUR	20
FRI	21
SAT	22
SUN	23
MON	24
TUES	25
WED	26
THUR	27
FRI	28
SAT	29
SUN	30

MONDAY 3 APRIL 1950

Bird is present at rehearsals with The Gene Roland Orchestra – 'The Band That Never Was' – at the Nola Studios on Broadway.

MARTY BELL, DON FERRARA, DON JOSEPH, JON NIELSOM, AL PORCINO, SONNY RICH, RED RODNEY, NEIL FRIEZ (trumpet), FRANK ORCHARD (valve trombone), EDDIE BERT, PORKY COHEN, JIMMY KNEPPER, PAUL SELDEN (trombone), JOE MAINI, CHARLIE PARKER (alto sax), AL COHN, DON LANPHERE, TOMMY MACKAGON, ZOOT SIMS (tenor sax), BOB NEWMAN, MARTY FLAX (baritone sax), HARRY BISS (piano), SAM HERMAN (guitar), BUDDY JONES (bass), FREDDIE GRUBER (drums), GENE ROLAND (arranger/conductor)

It's A Wonderful World (5 takes) / *Just You, Just Me* / *Unknown Title* / *Stardust* (4 takes) / *Limehouse Blues* / *Down Home Blues* / *East Side West Side*

Charlie spends much of April and May playing with the Bud Powell Trio at Birdland.

THURSDAY 20 APRIL 1950

Mrs Addie Parker, Bird's mother, graduates from the National Schools Institute of Practical Nursing in Kansas City.

FRIDAY 21 APRIL 1950

Down Beat carries this letter to the Editors:

> **Parker's 'Mood'**
>
> Charlie Parker played March 11 in North Chicago, three miles south of Waukegan. His showmanship was hell, and so was his music. I'm crazy about bop, and am one of the many Parker fans, or was, until his appearance here.
>
> *Parker's Mood* was the only decent piece of music he played. The dance was scheduled for 8 p.m. Parker sauntered in at 10:30. He announced his band would be in later. The admission was $1.75 in advance and $2.10 at the door. He had a great buildup.
>
> Parker could take lessons from Lionel Hampton, who played here in December. Hamp's band was set up at 8 p.m., played until midnight with three five-minute intermissions. Parker? Some 25 minutes for his two intermissions.
>
> Maybe I look at it wrong. Maybe that's what they do for us small town folks.

GENE ROLAND HAD THIS IDEA OF HAVING 8 SAXOPHONES, 5 TROMBONES, 8 TRUMPETS, 2 DRUMS I THINK, BASS, GUITAR AND PIANO. HE HAD THESE ARRANGEMENTS FOR THAT GROUP, SO WE GOT TOGETHER AND HAD ABOUT 4 OR 5 REHEARSALS ... I MADE 4, AND ON THE FIRST ONE I PHOTOGRAPHED... I HAD A SORT OF A BOX CAMERA AND I TOOK 8 BLACK AND WHITE PICTURES.

GENE SAID 'I'M GONNA WRITE A THING FOR A DOUBLE SECTION!' OH BOY, THAT BAND COULD HIT LIKE A HAMMER! A LOT OF REHEARSALS ENDED WITH JUST THE RHYTHM SECTION AND CHARLIE PARKER PLAYING... AND GUYS LISTENING.

YOU KNOW, PEOPLE THINK OF CHARLIE PARKER AS A DRUG ADDICT AND ALL THAT KIND OF STUFF, BUT HE WAS A GREAT GUY... HE WOULD TALK TO ANYBODY, HE WAS FRIENDLY, AND VERY KNOWLEDGEABLE, AND HE COULD TALK ON ANY SUBJECT.

Trombonist Eddie Bert (left) and drummer Freddie Gruber (right) remember the sessions:

MON	1
TUES	2
WED	3
THUR	4
FRI	5
SAT	6
SUN	7
MON	8
TUES	9
WED	10
THUR	11
FRI	12
SAT	13
SUN	14
MON	15
TUES	16
WED	17
THUR	18
FRI	19
SAT	20
SUN	21
MON	22
TUES	23
WED	24
THUR	25
FRI	26
SAT	27
SUN	28
MON	29
TUES	30
WED	31

MONDAY 1 MAY 1950

Bird is interviewed by Marshall Stearns and John Maher in New York City

STEARNS: *Now at 17 years old you were on an automobile trip…*

PARKER: Yeah.

STEARNS: *And you got in an accident…*

PARKER: Yeah.

STEARNS: *And was that in Kansas City?*

PARKER: That was going… that was between Kansas City and Jefferson City, Missouri.

STEARNS: *Oh… playing a gig or something?*

PARKER: Yeah. I was going on a Thanksgiving gig.

STEARNS: *Oh, I see.*

PARKER: And there was an accident.

STEARNS: *And what happened? You broke how many ribs?*

PARKER: I broke three ribs and had a spinal fracture.

STEARNS: *That was an awful thing to happen to you at that age, you know.*

PARKER: Oh yeah, it was. I mean everybody was so afraid that I wouldn't walk right no more… but everything was all right and… uh…

STEARNS: *Well, look! What happened? You say then you got a job…*

PARKER: Yeah.

STEARNS: *And you studied…*

PARKER: In Jefferson City… yeah…

STEARNS: *In Jefferson…*

PARKER: I got a job in this place, working, y'know, but prior to that, this was when they were laughing at me. I knew how to play…um… I figured… I had learned the scale. I'd learned how to play two tunes in a certain key, in the key of D for your saxophone, F concert. I learned to play the first eight bars of *Lazy River* and I knew the complete tune of *Honeysuckle Rose*. I didn't never stop to think about different keys or nothing like that. [laughter] So I took my horn out to this joint where a bunch of fellows I had seen around were… and the first thing they started playing was *Body And Soul*… Longbeat, y'know? Shit! So I got to playing my *Honeysuckle Rose*… I mean… an awful conglomeration. They laughed me off the bandstand. They laughed at me so hard.

STEARNS: *How old… how old were you then?*

PARKER: Oh, this was about along at the same time… 16… 17…

STEARNS: *Before the accident?*

PARKER: Yeah.

MAHER: *Ah, yeah.*

PARKER: 'bout a year before the accident.

STEARNS: *Where did you get your sax then?*

PARKER: Well, my mother brought me a horn for… oh, it was years before that, but I wasn't interested. I wasn't ready for it then. I didn't get interested in a horn until I got interested in the baritone horn when I was at High School. But I'd had that saxophone for a few years.

MAHER: *Where did you go to High School, Charlie?*

PARKER: Kansas City, Missouri. I went to Lincoln.

MAHER: *In Kansas City?*

PARKER: Yeah.

MAHER: *Did you play in the High School marching band?*

PARKER: Uh huh.

MAHER: *Oh, did you play in that? Did they have a symphony band in High School?*

PARKER: They had a… what they called a symphony band.

MAHER: *Did you play in that? Baritone horn?*

PARKER: Baritone horn, that's right.

STEARNS: *And you'd learned 'Honeysuckle Rose' and you'd learned the first eight bars of… which tune was it?*

PARKER: 'Up The Lazy River'.

STEARNS: *Lazy River… [laughter] And you were just innocent enough so that when you walked in …*

PARKER: I never thought about that… keys.

STEARNS: *And you played it all in… what key was it?*

PARKER: D for saxophone.

STEARNS: *In D for saxophone. Oh, what a story! [Chan laughs]*

MAHER: *What a slaughter of the innocents! [laughter]*

PARKER: They murdered that tune… oh, boy!

STEARNS: *Who did you play with? I mean, what band did you walk in on?*

PARKER: Oh, it was a band working in a joint. There was a bunch of young fellows that had a band around Kansas City. Uh, it was Jimmy Keith's Band then so it was Keith and a piano player… and Robert Wilson and James Ross and Shipley Gavan. That's the fellows names that were working at this club in Kansas City.

STEARNS: *Well… so after that you decided 'I'm going home and work it out'?*

PARKER: Yeah, that's it! [laughter] Yeah, then I knew it must be figured out some kind of way. [laughter] That was it.

STEARNS: *And then you went back and it was only… what? two or three months that you…?*

PARKER: Yeah, I was away for about two or three months.

STEARNS: *And then where did you go when you say you were away? Were you outside of Kansas City?*

PARKER: Yeah, actually I was on this job. The name of the town was Eldon, Missouri. It's about…

STEARNS: *Eldon. E-L-D-O-N?*

PARKER: Yeah, it's about 35 miles from Jefferson City.

STEARNS: *Oh, I see. And did you play a job there? Or was it…*

PARKER: Yeah, it was a job. It's a resort, a summer resort… about during all the summer months… June resort, something like that.

MAHER: *And that was where you had the chance to study while you were playing?*

PARKER: Yeah.

CHAN: *Bird bought his son a horn.*

PARKER: Yeah, he got an alto.

MAHER: *How old is he now?*

PARKER: Fourteen.

MAHER: *Fourteen? Does he play with it now?*

PARKER: … made him bring it to the dance… stay around. It sure is a lot of fun having a son that old, y'know?

STEARNS: *… only 12 years old. It's a lot of fun… she played a C-melody once and I'm not looking. [laughter] They never had any C-melody saxes, did they, when you were a kid?*

PARKER: Yeah! They were more popular then than alto.

STEARNS: *Were they?*

PARKER: Sure! '32… '33… there was Guy Lombardo was just getting popular then… that's when he was using it.

MON	**1**
TUES	**2**
WED	**3**
THUR	**4**
FRI	**5**
SAT	**6**
SUN	**7**
MON	**8**
TUES	**9**
WED	**10**
THUR	**11**
FRI	**12**
SAT	**13**
SUN	**14**
MON	**15**
TUES	**16**
WED	**17**
THUR	**18**
FRI	**19**
SAT	**20**
SUN	**21**
MON	**22**
TUES	**23**
WED	**24**
THUR	**25**
FRI	**26**
SAT	**27**
SUN	**28**
MON	**29**
TUES	**30**
WED	**31**

STEARNS: *Frankie Trumbauer was playing C-melody.*

…

STEARNS: *Charlie, what do you remember of your father? Was he around when you were growing up?*

PARKER: Some of the time. He died when I was…uh… oh, about when I was married and the baby was born.

STEARNS: *And what sort of work was he in?*

PARKER: He was like a… in his active years he was a waiter on this train… Santa Fe. Runs from Kansas City to Chicago… Los Angeles and back… Florida and back… Texas and back.

STEARNS: *I see.*

PARKER: He sure was a well-tutored guy. He spoke two, three languages.

STEARNS: *Yeah? Did he play any instruments?*

PARKER: Nah! He was a dancer in his real young years.

STEARNS: *Really?*

PARKER: … was in this circus on the TOB line. Ringling Brothers.

MAHER: *What was he on? Was he on TOBA?*

PARKER: Yeah, that was the circus, yeah.

MAHER: [sings] *He was with an old circus, yeah!*

STEARNS: *TOBA*

PARKER: Yeah, sure. Ha,ha!

MAHER: *Some years ago I heard about that, during the old Keith, Orpheum circuit days… it was dying out then… late twenties.*

STEARNS: *And he met your mother in Kansas City?*

PARKER: Yeah, they met in Kansas City.

STEARNS: *How is your mother now? She's still alive isn't she?*

PARKER: Yeah! She's very much alive! [laughter]

STEARNS: *Is she?*

PARKER: Fine, yeah!

STEARNS: *She got a lot of energy?*

PARKER: Activity, yeah! She just graduated from nurses' school a couple of months ago.

STEARNS: *No!*

CHAN: *No kidding!*

PARKER: Yeah… invitation… I sent her a watch.

CHAN: *How old is she?*

PARKER: Boy! … 62.

CHAN: *62.* [Parker laughs]

STEARNS: *How old did you say?*

PARKER: 62.

STEARNS: *62 years old.*

PARKER: [firmly] 62.

STEARNS: *Wonderful!*

PARKER: She's graduated from nurses' school. [laughter]

MAHER: *Hey, that's wonderful!*

PARKER: She's active as can be, man. She don't look and act it y'know. I mean, she's spryer than me, you know. She's very seldom ill.

STEARNS: *Yeah.*

PARKER: … she lives in that good climate in the country. She takes good care of herself, she owns her own home. She's got… she's very well… she's very well situated.

STEARNS: *Do you have any brothers and sisters, Charlie?*

PARKER: I got a brother.

STEARNS: *Older or younger?*

PARKER: Older.

STEARNS: *You got an older brother?*

PARKER: Yeah.

STEARNS: *Did he ever play any instruments?*

PARKER: No. He's a mail inspector at the Post Office at Kansas.

STEARNS: *And no sisters…Hi, darling!…* [Stearns is interrupted by Chan's 3 year old daughter, Kim] *So your mother is a very, very energetic, lively person, huh? Y'think, in a way, that's where you got your spirit?* [laughter]

PARKER: I guess so.

STEARNS: *Your dad was a dancer… that has the rhythm so, that could explain part of that, y'know?*

PARKER: Yeah, that's right.

MAHER: *When I first read that you ever played on a baritone horn with a marching band with a…*

PARKER: When I first went to High School, I was interested in music, y'know. So they gave me one of these…um… alto horns, y'know? 'Coop, coop! Coop, coop! Coop, coop! Coop, coop!' [laughter] so then I liked the baritone horn. When my successor graduated I got right in y'know? When what's-her-name graduated… the baritone player… the euphonium player….

MAHER: *Is that a big brass horn? Not like a tuba?*

PARKER: No, it isn't as big as a tuba. It's got three valves. It's between a tuba and an alto horn… pretty big. You hold it like this, y'know… like this… [Chan laughs]

STEARNS: *I can't figure you playing that! When did you get on reeds? When your mother gave you the saxophone, huh?*

PARKER: Yeah, well… I mean… she… I had the saxophone then but it was loaned out. A friend of mine was playing saxophone at the time. He had a band so he borrowed the horn from me. He kept it over two years, too. He kept it maybe a year after I got out of High School. I got out of High School in '35.

MAHER: *The year after I did.*

PARKER: Oh, a gang of things happened that year! I got the horn, I gotten married…

STEARNS: *Listen! You… when you were born… what was your… born in what? Nineteen…*

PARKER: Twenty.

STEARNS: *Twenty! Boy, you're awful recent!* [laughter]

MAHER: *I was born in 1918.*

PARKER: Oh boy!

STEARNS: *What happened in '36? You graduated from High School? You were playing saxophone by then weren't you?*

PARKER: Uh huh. Gotten married.

STEARNS: *Married…*

PARKER: Did a gang o' things that year.

STEARNS: *And this was all in Kansas City, huh?*

PARKER: Yeah.

STEARNS: *I was out through Kansas City in about '40 and I caught Harlan Leonard and Jay McShann out there and I don't know, maybe you were with McShann then. I've been kicking myself ever since, you know, I didn't.*

PARKER: Yeah, I was with McShann's band then…

STEARNS: *I came out with George Avakian.*

PARKER: McShann didn't have a big band then, did he?

STEARNS: *No, it was a little seven or eight piece.*

PARKER: I was in that band.

MON	**1**
TUES	**2**
WED	**3**
THUR	**4**
FRI	**5**
SAT	**6**
SUN	**7**
MON	**8**
TUES	**9**
WED	**10**
THUR	**11**
FRI	**12**
SAT	**13**
SUN	**14**
MON	**15**
TUES	**16**
WED	**17**
THUR	**18**
FRI	**19**
SAT	**20**
SUN	**21**
MON	**22**
TUES	**23**
WED	**24**
THUR	**25**
FRI	**26**
SAT	**27**
SUN	**28**
MON	**29**
TUES	**30**
WED	**31**

STEARNS: *You were?*

PARKER: It was at the Plaza, way out of Kansas City.

STEARNS: *Yes, we had to go outside of town to catch that band. And I heard that and I didn't know it!*

...

STEARNS: *I want to ask you about some of those recording dates, what happened on them, you know. What a story about that Rubberlegs Williams!* [laughter]

PARKER: He sure did that. The coffees got confused some kind of way and I was looking for the coffee that I had because I'd marked the container, y'know...

STEARNS: *You had the coffee in a...*

PARKER: It was all in containers. They sent out for coffee and sandwiches in a container. It was all in containers, y'know. Everybody was eating the sandwiches so I set my cup down beside the chair and dropped a benzedrine in it, y'know, and I was waiting for it to dissolve. Somehow or 'nother, Rubberlegs gets hungry and he goes to collect his coffee and he got it mixed up with mine. And about 20 minutes later he was <u>all</u> over the place. [laughter] You really ought to have seen him. He couldn't do nothing. He really got busy, you know what I mean? [laughter] It was a funny thing! [laughter]

STEARNS: *Well, he was really singing seriously, was he? He wasn't trying to kid you, was he?*

PARKER: No he wasn't... not a bit... and, ordinarily, if it hadn't been for that... I mean, he would... he'd have sung in a different style altogether.

STEARNS: *He would've?*

PARKER: Yeah. You never heard any of those records when he was, y'know... normal, y'know? He's got records out when, y'know, he was normal,

MAHER: *Much smoother.*

PARKER: <u>Much</u> smoother.

...

STEARNS: *These records you made with... uh... Trummy Young was on some of them.*

PARKER: Yeah.

STEARNS: *Remember? And All Stars? And some came out on Manor, some came out on...*

PARKER: Continental.

STEARNS: *Isn't that the one that...*

PARKER: Some came out on the Continental label.

CHAN: *Isn't that the one where you play 'I Can't Get Started'? That was made that day, wasn't it?*

PARKER: No.

CHAN: *It wasn't?*

PARKER: Um... 'Dream Of You'... 'Seventh Avenue'...

STEARNS: *Yeah.*

PARKER: Two other sides were made that day.

STEARNS: *Were they all made for the same company that day? Then they just got 'em out on different...*

PARKER: Oh, that date was made for Continental, yeah, but I have seen some of those records out on the Manor label, I tell you.

...

STEARNS: *Was it more fun playing with the Hines Band or the Eckstine Band on big bands?*

PARKER: I think it was more fun playing with the Eckstine Band.

STEARNS: *The Eckstine Band.*

PARKER: But the Hines Band was much smoother.

STEARNS: *Billy makes a very easy-going leader and everybody's having a ball.*

CHAN: *Swinging!*

STEARNS: *This Tiny Grimes date... you made 'Red Cross' and 'Tiny's Tempo' and so on... they since put it out with your name on it.*

PARKER: They did?

STEARNS: *Yeah. They figured it would sell more records, you see. Came out under Tiny's name.*

CHAN: *They're not allowed to do that, are they?*

STEARNS: *I don't know.*

PARKER: Yeah.

STEARNS: *Reissued under Parker's name.*

PARKER: They're not supposed to do that but, I mean... Herman Lubinsky does a gang of things he ain't supposed to do.

MAHER: *All guys do. It's the old, old story. You can't... you can copyright a label but you can't copyright a performance and... once you sell your time that day you're...*

CHAN: *I heard he has eleven sets of books... whoever wants to see the books...* [laughter]

STEARNS: *Well, Charlie, is it true that 'Mop, Mop' was your idea originally? Leonard [Feather] says here that 'Mop, Mop' was one of the things that you threw off and then, finally, I don't know who... somebody else...*

PARKER: It could've been, man, 'cause we used to do that a long time ago in Kansas City.

STEARNS: *You did 'Mop, Mop' in Kansas City?*

PARKER: Years ago. That was just... put in drum beats in there just for the four... we'd just play, when we got to the channel we used to play sometimes...[sings to demonstrate] y'know, just put it in.

CHAN: *Would you like to see these?* [shows photographs of the Gene Roland Band] *Did you hear about Gene Roland's Band?*

STEARNS: *No.*

CHAN: *Tell him about it Bird. It had eight reeds.*

PARKER: Yeah. Twenty seven piece band rehearsing.

STEARNS: *How long ago was this?*

PARKER: A month, three weeks ago... a month ago.

CHAN: *Do you know all those people?*

STEARNS: *No.*

PARKER: Eight reeds, six trombones and eight brass.

CHAN: *If you like...*

STEARNS: *But who... what label did they record for?*

CHAN: *They're not. They just rehearsed.*

PARKER: Didn't record, just rehearsed.

CHAN: [referring to photograph] *This is Sonny Rich, Eddie Bert, Zoot Sims and John Simmons... Al Cohn, Buddy Jones... this is Gene and the Band... and the trumpet section , of course, every day at rehearsal they had different people... Jon Nielson, Sonny Rich, Marty Bell, Red, Al Porcino... and here's Gene... Don and Zoot and Al Cohn, Bird, Joe Maini...*

STEARNS: *Wow! Look at that reed section! What a...*

PARKER: Eight saxophones.

STEARNS: *How'd it sound?*

CHAN: *Wonderful!*

PARKER: It was solid... Wild!

MON	**1**
TUES	**2**
WED	**3**
THUR	**4**
FRI	**5**
SAT	**6**
SUN	**7**
MON	**8**
TUES	**9**
WED	**10**
THUR	**11**
FRI	**12**
SAT	**13**
SUN	**14**
MON	**15**
TUES	**16**
WED	**17**
THUR	**18**
FRI	**19**
SAT	**20**
SUN	**21**
MON	**22**
TUES	**23**
WED	**24**
THUR	**25**
FRI	**26**
SAT	**27**
SUN	**28**
MON	**29**
TUES	**30**
WED	**31**

CHAN: *They had three drummers.*

STEARNS: *Who was doing the arrangements?*

PARKER: Gene Roland.

STEARNS: *Well, you did record 'em, didn't you?*

PARKER: On this tape recorder.

STEARNS: *Who has the tape? Do you have it?*

PARKER: Made one recording…no, I don't have it. Made one… made one record.

CHAN: *Gene has it.*

PARKER: But the balance was bad.

STEARNS: *Oh,where were they made?*

PARKER: It was made at Nola's.

STEARNS: *Nola's?*

PARKER: Gene has all those covered. He was recording all summer….

STEARNS: *It's awful hard to record a big sound in New York, because there are so few rooms that are…*

PARKER: Sure! You know, at first the theory was that they must have a very toned down room, something with a lot of soft things in it… to really get these acoustics… that's all wrong, man!

STEARNS: *Yeah!*

PARKER: Because in Europe they have much better balance on records than we do here… and they record in old temples and old cathedrals and old churches, backyards and everything… with no acoustics whatsoever… just nothing but a chamber… an echo chamber, and the records come out with a great big sound.

MAHER: *You know, in these small rooms, I guess, particularly in the higher register, everything compresses, it gets squeezed.*

Red Rodney goes into hospital around this time for an appendicitis operation.

Charlie spends much of May playing at Birdland with the Bud Powell Trio and Fats Navarro.

TUESDAY 2 MAY 1950

Charlie Parker, George Shearing and the Slam Stewart Trio appear in concert at the Metropolitan in Philadelphia.

WEDNESDAY 17 MAY 1950

Charlie Parker, Fats Navarro and the Bud Powell Trio broadcast from Birdland.
CHARLIE PARKER (alto sax), FATS NAVARRO (trumpet), BUD POWELL (piano), CURLEY RUSSELL (bass), ART BLAKEY (drums)
52nd Street Theme / Wahoo / Round Midnight / This Time The Dream's On Me / Dizzy Atmosphere / Move / 52nd Street Theme
CHARLIE PARKER (alto sax), FATS NAVARRO, MILES DAVIS (trumpet), WALTER BISHOP (piano), CURLEY RUSSELL (bass), ART BLAKEY (drums)
Conception

THURSDAY 18 MAY 1950

Charlie Parker, Fats Navarro and the Bud Powell Trio broadcast from Birdland.
CHARLIE PARKER (alto sax), FATS NAVARRO (trumpet), BUD POWELL (piano), CURLEY RUSSELL (bass), ART BLAKEY (drums)
52nd Street Theme / A Night in Tunisia /The Street Beat / Out Of Nowhere
WALTER BISHOP (piano) replaces BUD POWELL:
Cool Blues / 52nd Street Theme

FRIDAY 19 MAY 1950

Charlie Parker appears with Machito's large Afro-Cuban band at the Renaissance Ballroom in Harlem. Probable personnel: CHARLIE PARKER (alto sax), HOWARD MCGHEE, MARIO BAUZA, FRANK DAVILLA, BOB WOODLEN (trumpet), GENE JOHNSON, FRED SKERRIT (alto sax), JOSE MADERA, FRANK SOCOLOW (tenor sax), LESLIE JOHNAKINS (baritone sax), RENE HERNANDES (piano), ROBERT RODRIGUEZ (bass), JOSE MANGUEL (bongo), LUIS MIRANDA (conga), UBALDO NIETO (timbales), MACHITO (maraccas)
Reminiscing At Twilight / Mambo / Lament For The Congo

SATURDAY 20 MAY 1950

Charlie Parker, Fats Navarro and the Bud Powell Trio broadcast from Birdland.
CHARLIE PARKER (alto sax), FATS NAVARRO (trumpet), BUD POWELL (piano), CURLEY RUSSELL (bass), ART BLAKEY (drums)
Little Willie Leaps / 52nd Street Theme

SUNDAY 21 MAY 1950

Charlie Parker, Fats Navarro and the Bud Powell Trio broadcast from Birdland.
CHARLIE PARKER (alto sax), FATS NAVARRO (trumpet), BUD POWELL (piano), CURLEY RUSSELL (bass), ART BLAKEY (drums)
Ornithology / I'll Remember April / 52nd Street Theme
WALTER BISHOP (piano) replaces BUD POWELL, 'LITTLE JIMMY' SCOTT (vocal):
Embraceable You (vocal)

TUESDAY 23 MAY 1950

Monday night is jam session night at Birdland and the Charlie Parker All Stars broadcast in the early hours of Tuesday:
CHARLIE PARKER (alto sax), BUDDY DE FRANCO (clarinet), CHARLIE ROUSE (tenor sax) ERROLL GARNER (piano), TOMMY POTTER (bass), MAX ROACH (drums)
Lover Come Back To Me

THUR	**1**
FRI	**2**
SAT	**3**
SUN	**4**
MON	**5**
TUES	**6**
WED	**7**
THUR	**8**
FRI	**9**
SAT	**10**
SUN	**11**
MON	**12**
TUES	**13**
WED	**14**
THUR	**15**
FRI	**16**
SAT	**17**
SUN	**18**
MON	**19**
TUES	**20**
WED	**21**
THUR	**22**
FRI	**23**
SAT	**24**
SUN	**25**
MON	**26**
TUES	**27**
WED	**28**
THUR	**29**
FRI	**30**

Bird and Chan begin living together at 422 East 11th Street in New York City

SUNDAY 4 JUNE 1950

Bird is involved in some private recordings at the home of Joe Maini and Don Lanphere in the William Henry Apartments in New York City. Others probably involved include Jon Eardley, Jimmy Knepper, Joe Maini, Don Lanphere, John Williams, Buddy Jones, Frank Isola and Buddy Bridgeford.

TUESDAY 6 JUNE 1950

Charlie Parker Quintet recording session for Mercury/ Verve in New York City.
CHARLIE PARKER (alto sax), DIZZY GILLESPIE (trumpet), THELONIOUS MONK (piano), CURLEY RUSSELL (bass), BUDDY RICH (drums)
Bloomdido / An Oscar For Treadwell (2 takes) / *Mohawk* (2 takes) / *My Melancholy Baby* (3 takes) / *Leap Frog* (11 takes) / *Relaxing With Lee* (6 takes)

THURSDAY 8 JUNE 1950

Charlie Parker Quintet (Kenny Dorham, Al Haig, Tommy Potter and Roy Haynes) open at Café Society Downtown for a 4-week engagement. Also on the bill are Art Tatum, a plump comic named Jack Prince and the intermission pianist is Cliff Jackson.

During the 4-week engagement the Quintet often broadcast from Café Society Downtown, sometimes with added guests TONY SCOTT (clarinet) or BREW MOORE (tenor sax).
CHARLIE PARKER (alto sax), KENNY DORHAM (trumpet), AL HAIG (piano), TOMMY POTTER (bass), ROY HAYNES (drums)
52nd Street Theme (Scott) / *Just Friends* (Scott) / *April in Paris* (Scott) / *Night in Tunisia* into *52nd Street Theme* / *52nd Street Theme* / *Just Friends* (Moore) / *April in Paris* (Moore) / *Bewitched* / *Summertime* / *I Cover The Waterfront* / *Easy To Love*

SUNDAY 11 JUNE 1950

Bird is involved in some private recordings at the home of Joe Maini and Don Lanphere in the William Henry Apartments in New York City. Others probably involved include Jon Eardley, Jimmy Knepper, Joe Maini, Don Lanphere, John Williams, Buddy Jones, Frank Isola and Buddy Bridgeford.

SUNDAY 18 JUNE 1950

Bird is involved in some private recordings at the home of Joe Maini and Don Lanphere in the William Henry Apartments in New York City. Others probably involved include Jon Eardley, Jimmy Knepper, Joe Maini, Don Lanphere, John Williams, Buddy Jones, Frank Isola and Buddy Bridgeford.

WEDNESDAY 21 JUNE 1950

British impresario Harold Davison writes to Bird offering work in Europe.

SUNDAY 25 JUNE 1950

Bird is involved in some private recordings at the home of Joe Maini and Don Lanphere in the William Henry Apartments in New York City. Others probably involved include Jon Eardley, Jimmy Knepper, Joe Maini, Don Lanphere, John Williams, Buddy Jones, Frank Isola and Buddy Bridgeford.

FRIDAY 30 JUNE 1950

Down Beat carries a record review of *Charlie's Wig* (tepid) and *Klactoveedsedstene* (tasty):

Quintet formation with Miles Davis, JJ Johnson, Max Roach, Duke Jordan, and Tommy Potter. JJ operates well on *Wig* as does Miles. *Klacto*–is an esoteric title, graced with fair solos. Charlie himself is heard to better advantage here than on *Wig*. (Dial 1040)

SAT	1
SUN	2
MON	3
TUES	4
WED	5
THUR	6
FRI	7
SAT	8
SUN	9
MON	10
TUES	11
WED	12
THUR	13
FRI	14
SAT	15
SUN	16
MON	17
TUES	18
WED	19
THUR	20
FRI	21
SAT	22
SUN	23
MON	24
TUES	25
WED	26
THUR	27
FRI	28
SAT	29
SUN	30
MON	31

WEDNESDAY 5 JULY 1950

Charlie Parker with Strings recording session for Mercury / Verve in New York City

CHARLIE PARKER (alto sax), JOSEPH SINGER (french horn), EDWIN C BROWN (oboe), SAM CAPLAN, HOWARD KAY, HARRY MELNIKOFF, SAM RAND, ZELLY SMIRNOFF (violin), ISADORE ZIR (viola), MAURICE BROWN (cello), VERLEY MILLS (harp), BERNIE LEIGHTON (piano), RAY BROWN (bass), BUDDY RICH (drums), JOE LIPPMAN (arranger/conductor)

Dancing In The Dark / Out Of Nowhere / Laura (2 takes) / *East Of The Sun / They Can't Take That Away From Me / Easy To Love / I'm In The Mood For Love* (2 takes) / *I'll Remember April* (3 takes)

Around this time, possibly at a rehearsal for the Strings session, Bird and the rhythm section record.

CHARLIE PARKER (alto sax), BERNIE LEIGHTON (piano), RAY BROWN (bass), BUDDY RICH (drums)

I Can't Get Started

Charlie Parker Quintet close at Café Society.

FRIDAY 7 JULY 1950

Fats Navarro dies.

TUESDAY 11 JULY 1950

Charlie Parker and Strings open at Birdland opposite the Sonny Stitt-Gene Ammons Band and the Stan Getz Trio.

The band consists of Charlie Parker (alto sax), Al Haig (piano), Tommy Potter (bass), Roy Haynes (drums), Tommy Mace (oboe), Wallace McManus (harp), Sam Kaplan, Seymour Barab, Dave Uchitel, Jerry Molfese and Al Feller (strings).

THURSDAY 13 JULY 1950

Charlie attends the funeral service for Fats Navarro in Harlem.

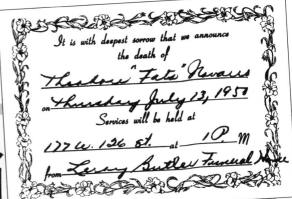

Bird, Backed By Strings, Disappoints At Birdland

Reviewed at Birdland, NYC

Violins: Sam Caplan, Jerry Molfese, and Al Feller.
Viola: Dave Uchitel.
Cello: Seymour Barab.
Oboe: Tommy Macy.
Harp: Wallace McManus.
Rhythm: Al Haig, piano; Charles T. Potter, bass, and Roy Haynes, drums.
Charlie Parker—leader and alto.

New York—After several false starts, Charlie Parker has finally managed to get in front of a string section in a night club. Shortly after his *Charlie Parker with Strings* album was released, plans were afoot to put the Bird and strings into Birdland but it fell through. Later the group was supposed to make its in-the-flesh bow at Cafe Society but, again, it didn't pan out. Finally, in July, the deed was accomplished at Birdland.

To date the string backing has done a lot for the Bird so far as general public acceptance is concerned. The album has made several appearances on the best-selling albums list, an unusual experience for a musician as determinedly esoteric as Parker.

Even Sylvester

And his work with the strings at Birdland caused the *Daily News'* mouldly figging Robert Sylvester to completely revise his previous low opinion of the Bird.

In view of such successes, this report will have to be considered a dissenting opinion. For, to this listener, what artistry the Bird has shown in his work with small

to be replaced by heavy-handed stodginess. His tone becomes a flat, monotonous, squawking thing, and his work in general appears to have little relationship to what is going on around him.

Contrast

The contrast between standard Parker and Parker with strings is brought out sharply when he ends a set by going into a brief display of thematic material with only the rhythm section behind him. Suddenly he seems relaxed and at home. His horn is in proper juxtaposition to his accompaniment, and the Parkerian phrases flow easily and pleasantly once more.

The string section, headed by Sam Caplan, does a fine job and provides a more lush, ear-caressing sound than has ever been heard in Birdland before. Tommy Macy, on oboe, gets frequent but very brief moments on his own which show

Buck Clayton, trumpet; Dickie Wells, trombone, and Buddy Tate, tenor. Crew broke in at the Savoy ballroom in July.

stood all kinds of treatment. In this case, however, the undue lack of unity of approach between the soloist and his accompaniment is more than these stalwart tunes can take.

Whether the Bird is bored by his material or baffled by his accompaniment, he has allowed his playing to degenerate into a tasteless and raucous hullabaloo.

Granz To Film 'JATP' Short

New York—Norman Granz has completed plans to make a *Jazz at the Philharmonic* film short in September before his *JATP* troupe starts out on its regular concert tour. Film will be shot at Gjon Mili's studio here. In addition to regular movie outlets, Granz hopes to show the film on TV, provided he can get an okay from the AFM.

Granz' 1950 tour opens on Sept. 16 at Carnegie hall here. Roster of *JATP* for this tour will be the usual Granz assortment, including Ella Fitzgerald, Oscar Peterson, Buddy Rich, and Flip Phillips.

SAT	**1**
SUN	**2**
MON	**3**
TUES	**4**
WED	**5**
THUR	**6**
FRI	**7**
SAT	**8**
SUN	**9**
MON	**10**
TUES	**11**
WED	**12**
THUR	**13**
FRI	**14**
SAT	**15**
SUN	**16**
MON	**17**
TUES	**18**
WED	**19**
THUR	**20**
FRI	**21**
SAT	**22**
SUN	**23**
MON	**24**
TUES	**25**
WED	**26**
THUR	**27**
FRI	**28**
SAT	**29**
SUN	**30**
MON	**31**

MONDAY 24 JULY 1950
Bird signs a contract to appear with strings at the Blue Note in Chicago in September. He also signs a rider in case of failure to appear. The contract calls for 11 musicians working 38 hours per week for $2800 per week payable at the end of each week.

THURSDAY 27 JULY 1950
Dizzy Gillespie's Band and Coleman Hawkins replace the Stitt-Ammons and Stan Getz Bands alongside Charlie at Birdland.

RIDER ATTACHED TO AND MADE A PART OF AGREEMENT DATED July 24, 1950, between CHARLIE PARKER AND TRIPLE ELL CORPORATION:
If for any reason whatsoever Charlie Parker shall fail to appear for any scheduled show (Schedule of shows to be given to Charlie Parker before beginning of engagement) then it is understood and agreed that the employer shall have the right to deduct $50.00 per show for each show missed by said Charlie Parker.

Below: Charlie and Dizzy on stage at Birdland. Opposite page: On the same night, Charlie fronts his string section.

SAT   **1**
SUN   **2**
MON   **3**
TUES   **4**
WED   **5**
THUR   **6**
FRI   **7**
SAT   **8**
SUN   **9**
MON   **10**
TUES   **11**
WED   **12**
THUR   **13**
FRI   **14**
SAT   **15**
SUN   **16**
MON   **17**
TUES   **18**
WED   **19**
THUR   **20**
FRI   **21**
SAT   **22**
SUN   **23**
MON   **24**
TUES   **25**
WED   **26**
THUR   **27**
FRI   **28**
SAT   **29**
SUN   **30**
MON   **31**

TUES **1**
WED **2**
THUR **3**
FRI **4**
SAT **5**
SUN **6**
MON **7**
TUES **8**
WED **9**
THUR **10**
FRI **11**
SAT **12**
SUN **13**
MON **14**
TUES **15**
WED **16**
THUR **17**
FRI **18**
SAT **19**
SUN **20**
MON **21**
TUES **22**
WED **23**
THUR **24**
FRI **25**
SAT **26**
SUN **27**
MON **28**
TUES **29**
WED **30**
THUR **31**

FRIDAY 4 AUGUST 1950

Billy Shaw writes to Charlie agreeing to release him from his contract on receipt of money owing to him.

SUNDAY 6 AUGUST 1950

Tommy Potter gives two weeks notice

WEDNESDAY 16 AUGUST 1950

Charlie Parker & Strings close at Birdland.

THURSDAY 17 AUGUST 1950

Charlie Parker and the string unit open for a one-week engagement at the Apollo Theatre opposite Stan Getz' Four Brothers Band.

Charlie and Gerry Mulligan buy food from a street vendor during a break in rehearsals at the Apollo Theatre.

FRIDAY 18 AUGUST 1950

Bird signs a contract for Charlie Parker & Strings (11 musicians) to appear at Club Harlem, 5530 Haverford Ave., Philadelphia 9 October thru 17 October 1951, 6 day week, 6 hours daily, matinee Saturday afternoon. $2000 per week plus $571.42 for two extra days, total $2571.42. $2000 to be paid at end of first week, balance at end of engagement.

TUES	1
WED	2
THUR	3
FRI	4
SAT	5
SUN	6
MON	7
TUES	8
WED	9
THUR	10
FRI	11
SAT	12
SUN	13
MON	14
TUES	15
WED	16
THUR	17
FRI	18
SAT	19
SUN	20
MON	21
TUES	22
WED	23
THUR	24
FRI	25
SAT	26
SUN	27
MON	28
TUES	29
WED	30
THUR	31

WEDNESDAY 23 AUGUST 1950

A private recording is made of 4 sets by Charlie Parker and the String Unit at the Apollo Theatre.
CHARLIE PARKER (alto sax), TOMMY MACE (oboe), TEDDY BLUME, SAM KAPLAN, STAN KARPENIA (violin), DAVE UCHITEL (viola), BILL BUNDY (cello), WALLACE MCMANUS (harp), BILLY TAYLOR (piano), TOMMY POTTER (bass), ROY HAYNES (drums) SARAH VAUGHAN (vocal), SYMPHONY SID TORIN (mc)
Repetition / April In Paris / Easy To Love / What Is This Thing Called Love / I Cried For You (vocal) / Repetition / April In Paris / Easy To Love / What Is This Thing Called Love / Repetition / April In Paris / Easy To Love / What Is This Thing Called Love / Repetition / April In Paris / Easy To Love / What Is This Thing Called Love

THURSDAY 24 AUGUST 1950

Charlie Parker & Strings close at the Apollo Theatre.

SATURDAY 26 AUGUST 1950

Kenny Clarke hears about the the Swedish/French tour and writes to Bird from Paris:
Hey Bird-shit
We shall all be waiting for your arrival, and I know you'll be a tremendous success. Here's waiting for you. Your boy always.
Klook

MONDAY 28 AUGUST 1950

Charlie Parker Quintet appear at New Brunswick, New Jersey.
CHARLIE PARKER (alto sax), AL HAIG (piano), TOMMY POTTER (bass), ROY HAYNES (drums) plus unknown trombonist (possibly JIMMY KNEPPER)
Hot House / I May Be Wrong / Indiana / S'Wonderful / Parker's Mood

TUESDAY 29 AUGUST 1950

Bird celebrates his 29th birthday at Birdland with a party organised by Oscar Goodstein.

THURSDAY 31 AUGUST 1950

Charlie Parker & Strings open a 2-week engagement at Birdland opposite the Oscar Pettiford Trio and Stan Getz.

Bird To Cut 2 More Albums With Strings

New York — Following the success of the *Charlie Parker with Strings* album, Mercury records plans to cut two more albums with the Bird in front of a string ensemble. Slicings will be made next winter. Parker and his strings are currently playing at Birdland.

Symphony Sid To Spin From Birdland

New York — Symphony Sid, WJZ's all night, all frantic disc jockey, will start doing his platter spinning from Birdland on Aug. 1. He'll do his complete broadcast, midnight to 5:45 a.m., from the jazz joint six nights a week. Sid has severed his connections with other music spots and will concentrate his plugs on Birdland.

Operators of Birdland have also gotten the mortgage on the fixtures of the old Royal Roost. Purpose of this is to tie up the spot to prevent a competitive room from being opened there.

Bird Celebrates His Birthday

New York—Charlie Parker celebrated his 30th birthday on Aug. 29, and what better place to fete the event than at the spot named after Parker, Birdland? Lots of folks showed up to wish Bird well, including Billy Eckstine, who's breaking up in this shot. Parker recently closed at Chicago's Blue Note with his string section, went into Philly's Club Harlem on Oct. 9.

FRI	**1**
SAT	**2**
SUN	**3**
MON	**4**
TUES	**5**
WED	**6**
THUR	**7**
FRI	**8**
SAT	**9**
SUN	**10**
MON	**11**
TUES	**12**
WED	**13**
THUR	**14**
FRI	**15**
SAT	**16**
SUN	**17**
MON	**18**
TUES	**19**
WED	**20**
THUR	**21**
FRI	**22**
SAT	**23**
SUN	**24**
MON	**25**
TUES	**26**
WED	**27**
THUR	**28**
FRI	**29**
SAT	**30**

In early September Charlie appears in a Gjon Mili film made for Norman Granz's Jazz at the Philharmonic troupe. Also featured in the film are Coleman Hawkins, Ella Fitzgerald, Hank Jones, Flip Phillips and Harry Edison.

It may also be the occasion on which Charlie and Coleman Hawkins recorded together for Norman Granz.

CHARLIE PARKER (alto sax), COLEMAN HAWKINS (tenor sax), HANK JONES (piano), RAY BROWN (bass), BUDDY RICH (drums)

Celebrity / Ballade

The film is never released, but some footage remains of Bird.

SUNDAY 3 SEPTEMBER 1950

Charles Delaunay writes to Bird from Paris

Dear Charlie

I found your letter as I came back to Paris from my summer vacation. I also had a letter from Billy Shaw who asked me which conditions I was ready to pay for having you over here. I answer him that having previous experience (Ellington, Goodman, Hawkins...) there was not two ways I could work out for you or any artist. This is the way I have been working lately with Sidney Bechet & Roy Eldridge. It's as personal manager. There is not much money to expect from Europe, apart a few places such as Scandinavia, and the way we operate, we try to get as much money as possible from each deal. For instance we will be able to line up some series of concerts in Western Europe (Italy, Switzerland, Germany, Belgium...) some in France, and get from there the most we can, and in the mean time, we can find a club in Paris which will be able to secure you a permanent job when you won't be playing elsewhere. So you know you always can count on a real decent living in this town and manage to study…

The way we operate, you sign the contract and collect all the monies, and we only manage to deal all the bookings and just get our 10% commission as agents. This is how we have been working with Sidney and Roy.

If I am right, I understood that Billy Shaw had some offers for you in Scandinavia, so let's started there and get the trip expenses payed by these people.

When we know about which time you are to come over we will settle some concerts to advertise your coming over and then it will be rather easy to settle some club engagement. Roy has been playing

Mili Makes 'JATP' Film

New York—Norman Granz completed a two-reel film built around his *Jazz at the Philharmonic* troupe here in September. Film was directed by Gjon Mili and was made at his studio.

Mili made the famous *Jammin' the Blues* short, produced by Warner Bros. in 1944. Talent used in the current film included Ella Fitzgerald, Flip Phillips, Charlie Parker, Coleman Hawkins, Buddy Rich, Harry Edison, Hank Jones, and Ray Brown.

FRI	1
SAT	2
SUN	3
MON	4
TUES	5
WED	6
THUR	7
FRI	8
SAT	9
SUN	10
MON	11
TUES	12
WED	13
THUR	14
FRI	15
SAT	16
SUN	17
MON	18
TUES	19
WED	20
THUR	21
FRI	22
SAT	23
SUN	24
MON	25
TUES	26
WED	27
THUR	28
FRI	29
SAT	30

for three months at the same club, while Sidney who started early June played the same club (both in Paris and South Coast) since, and will soon open again the same club in Paris and do some concerts.

For concerts you could obtain an average 50.000 francs, (70.000 in some places, 40.000 in other places) and with such prices you will be given much more concerts and make more money you could make in asking more (which would limit a tour to a few towns only).

After Ellington & Goodman tours which were financially disastrous, and with the idea that jazz doesn't pay, there is now but few people who is ready to go in such a venture.

In clubs, you should get between 5 & 10.000 francs (a day) which definitely is the maximum a club can give presently for a jazz musician, as know this can be, and which is twice as much as you can spend you and your wife. You will appear only twice a night (half an hour) and be free to work and study. Not to mention broadcasts and one-nighters we may settle.

Here is an almost complete picture of the situation, which in a whole is very depressing right now with all the war talks.

As soon as you have made up your mind let me know so I can get at work immediately.

With kindest regards, Charles

WEDNESDAY 13 SEPTEMBER 1950
Charlie Parker & Strings close at Birdland.

SATURDAY 16 SEPTEMBER 1950
Charlie Parker & Strings appear at a Jazz at the Philharmonic concert at Carnegie Hall, New York City. Also appearing are Ella Fitzgerald, Coleman Hawkins, Flip Phillips, Buddy Rich, Lester Young, Oscar Peterson, Ray Brown and Hank Jones.
CHARLIE PARKER (alto sax), TOMMY MACE (oboe), TEDDY BLUME, SAM KAPLAN, STAN KARPENIA (violin), DAVE UCHITEL (viola), BILL BUNDY (cello), WALLACE MCMANUS (harp), AL HAIG (piano), TOMMY POTTER (bass), ROY HAYNES (drums)
What Is This Thing Called Love? / April In Paris / Repetition / Easy To Love / Rocker

Teddy Blume becomes Bird's manager.

SUNDAY 17 SEPTEMBER 1950
Charlie Parker & Strings appear at a Jazz at the Philharmonic concert at the National Guard Armory in Washington.

TUESDAY 19 SEPTEMBER 1950
Charlie Parker is summoned to be in court for Special Sessions Part 1 for a traffic violation.

FRIDAY 22 SEPTEMBER 1950
Charlie Parker & Strings open at the Blue Note in Chicago for a two-week engagement.

Armory Gets Jazz Concert

The rafters of the National Guard Armory will rock once more tonight when impresario Norman Granz presents his tenth annual "Jazz at the Philharmonic" concert.

Sponsored by Down Beat magazine, this year's concert once again stars "The First Lady of Swing," Ella Fitzgerald.

As a special feature, Granz will present the increasingly popular subdued "bop" of Charlie Parker and his unusual string ensemble which has been breaking attendance records at a New York nightspot.

Also featured is Granz' crew of outstanding jazz musicians.

SUN	1
MON	2
TUES	3
WED	4
THUR	5
FRI	6
SAT	7
SUN	8
MON	9
TUES	10
WED	11
THUR	12
FRI	13
SAT	14
SUN	15
MON	16
TUES	17
WED	18
THUR	19
FRI	20
SAT	21
SUN	22
MON	23
TUES	24
WED	25
THUR	26
FRI	27
SAT	28
SUN	29
MON	30
TUES	31

6   DOWN BEAT

CHICAGO N

CHICAGO BAND BRIEFS
Konitz Joins Russo Five: Bird With Strings In Town

By JACK TRACY

Chicago—The two great alto men in jazz are playing in Chicago right now. Charlie Parker and his string section are at the Blue Note and Lee Konitz, in a surprising, but heartily-welcome move, has joined the Bill Russo quintet at the Airliner. Bird will be around until Oct. 5, Lee will remain until at least Oct. 26, option time for the group at the club.

In coming in, Konitz replaced Don Carone, now busily occupied teaching school. Other personnel change found drummer George Rott leaving and Frank Duffy coming in.

No Concessions

The Russo group has made a remarkably long stay out of what had started out to be off-night-only sessions back in July. And they've done it without making any concessions, musically or otherwise.

booking following Fields. Diz changed his mind about joining *JATP* when some bookings came through for his own group. So now it's Harry Edison who'll be playing trumpet when Granz and stars come house on Oc

Jacl

Jackie Ca the Hi-Note time manage up a replace ing somethii stays on as vocalist

New Philly Spot Features Parker

Philadelphia—The Club Harlem, town's newest room which was set up by vet cafe man Si Kaliner, has Charlie Parker and strings moving into the spot Oct. 9 for two weeks. Also on the bill will be Slim Gaillard and singer Ann Cornell.

Sarah Vaughan comes into the club Oct. 30.

Steve Gibson and the Red Caps are carrying on this month at

these parts a few y back in town with a playing nightly at the

Mr. B

Billy Eckstine com Regal theater on Oc nothing definite set at houses at presstime.

David LeWinter, wh tight little band at Room for just about tv now, got a five-year (v year) extension. W keep him satisfied ur thereabouts.

And no longer wil sounds of Dave Garro as a disc jockey. He's afternoon platter spot sorting with live taler radio shows and TV

Perkins at S

Chubby's, across the lingswood, N. J. And son, one of the town's players, has her own Cats and a Kitten, a lounge here.

Joe Frasetto took ov Casino bandstand this was held by Harry many years previous.

Jackie Davis, swi who created much in lantic City all summ here for the first Moravian bar.

THURSDAY 5 OCTOBER 1950
Charlie Parker & Strings close at the Blue Note, Chicago

MONDAY 9 OCTOBER 1950
Charlie Parker & Strings open at Club Harlem in Philadelphia for a nine-day engagement.

TUESDAY 10 OCTOBER 1950
Billy Shaw writes to Bird about the opening.

Dear Charlie:

It was nice to see you the other night at your opening in Philadelphia, and I enjoyed talking with you. I have been thinking over your conversation, and you know how I feel about you Charlie. I would never at any time want to hold you back if I thought you could better yourself elsewhere.

However, on August 4th, I wrote you a letter stating that upon receipt of the balance of monies due us, which at that time amounted to $815.76, we would be happy to give you a release from our management contract. As you well know Charlie since that time we have advanced you additional

money, such as transportation to Chicago, and then more transportation money to get you back home, so naturally, if you should desire a release at any time we would have to sit down and discuss the financial settlement necessary for me to give you said release. In other words it has been over two months since I wrote you, and since that time you came in the office and told me to go ahead and accept bookings, which I have certainly done. This letter will serve to revoke all statements made in my previous letter of August 4th.

Charlie, I will be happy to sit down with you at any time and work out a new financial agreement whereby you can obtain your release if you so desire. However, I want you to know that I personally do not want it this way, as you know that I am the only one that has confidence in you, and now that you are starting to make progress, after all the heartaches we have had together, I think we should go on together.

Looking forward to seeing you when you get back to New York.

Kindest regards.
Sincerely, BILLY SHAW

SUN	**1**
MON	**2**
TUES	**3**
WED	**4**
THUR	**5**
FRI	**6**
SAT	**7**
SUN	**8**
MON	**9**
TUES	**10**
WED	**11**
THUR	**12**
FRI	**13**
SAT	**14**
SUN	**15**
MON	**16**
TUES	**17**
WED	**18**
THUR	**19**
FRI	**20**
SAT	**21**
SUN	**22**
MON	**23**
TUES	**24**
WED	**25**
THUR	**26**
FRI	**27**
SAT	**28**
SUN	**29**
MON	**30**
TUES	**31**

WEDNESDAY 11 OCTOBER 1950

Charlie is due in court for trial in Special Sessions Part 2, but the case is put off until Monday 6 November.

TUESDAY 17 OCTOBER 1950

Charlie Parker & Strings close at Club Harlem, Philadelphia.

MONDAY 23 OCTOBER 1950

Charlie Parker plays a one-night gig at the Pershing Ballroom in Chicago.
A young fan named Donald Coy records the session on his portable tape recorder:
'I arrived early at the Pershing, but later than I intended and there was already a crowd in the front of the bandstand waiting for Bird to appear. There was no room left to set up to record and there were already a couple of other tape machines set up on the front edge of the low stage. In desperation, I went around to the rear of the bandstand backstage, and found an unused dressing room with a single wall speaker, controlled by a single off-on switch, that was used to monitor the central on-stage microphone; the one that Bird would be using. I set up my machine, and although I would not be able to see Bird (a great disappointment), at least I would have his music on my own tape.

Things went fairly well for the first set, however, my solitude was interrupted by the appearance of some unknown individual, somewhere between Hot House and Embraceable You, who insisted on staying and rapping —sometimes about Bird, but mostly about nothing.

Fortunately, he left during the beginning of All The Things You Are, so during those tracks, you will hear muffled voices in the background.'

CHARLIE PARKER (alto sax), EARL LAVON FREEMAN (tenor sax), CHRIS ANDERSON (piano), GEORGE FREEMAN (guitar), LEROY JACKSON (bass), BRUZ FREEMAN (drums)
Early set: *Indiana / I Can't Get Started / Anthropology / Out Of Nowhere / Get Happy*
Late set: *Hot House / Embraceable You* (unknown vocalist) / *Body And Soul* (unknown vocalist) / *Cool Blues / Stardust* (unknown vocalist) / *All The Things You Are / Billie's Bounce / Pennies From Heaven*
Late set: *There's A Small Hotel / These Foolish Things / Keen And Peachy / Hot House / Bird, Bass And Out / Goodbye*

THURSDAY 9 OCTOBER 1950

Charlie Parker & Strings open at Soldier Meyers in Brooklyn for a one-week engagement.

WEDNESDAY 23 OCTOBER 1950

Charlie Parker & Strings close at Soldier Meyers.

THURSDAY 26 OCTOBER 1950

Charlie Parker Quintet opens at Birdland for a one-week engagement.

TUESDAY 31 OCTOBER 1950

Charlie appears on comedian Jerry Lester's TV show 'Broadway Open House' on channel 5, New York City.

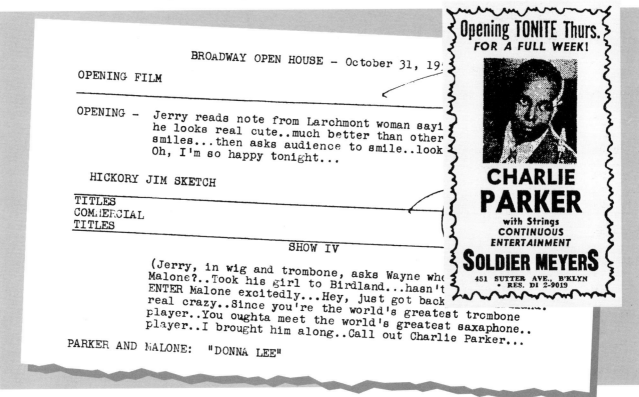

WED	**1**
THUR	**2**
FRI	**3**
SAT	**4**
SUN	**5**
MON	**6**
TUES	**7**
WED	**8**
THUR	**9**
FRI	**10**
SAT	**11**
SUN	**12**
MON	**13**
TUES	**14**
WED	**15**
THUR	**16**
FRI	**17**
SAT	**18**
SUN	**19**
MON	**20**
TUES	**21**
WED	**22**
THUR	**23**
FRI	**24**
SAT	**25**
SUN	**26**
MON	**27**
TUES	**28**
WED	**29**
THUR	**30**

THURSDAY 2 NOVEMBER 1950
Charlie Parker Quintet close at Birdland.

FRIDAY 3 NOVEMBER 1950
The contracts are signed for the Swedish tour by Nils Helstrom, the Swedish promoter.

TUESDAY 14 NOVEMBER 1950
Charlie Parker is fined for a traffic offence in Manhattan.

SATURDAY 18 NOVEMBER 1950
Bird leaves New York by air for Stockholm.

SUNDAY 19 NOVEMBER 1950
Bird arrives at Bromma Airport, Stockholm with Roy Eldridge for a one week tour of Sweden.

Below: Roy Eldridge and Bird join Swedish trumpeter Rolf Ericson for a taxi ride from Bromma airport to central Stockholm. Bird is clutching a bunch of flowers presented to him by his Swedish admirers.

MONDAY 20 NOVEMBER 1950
Bird sends a cablegram to Chan, who sends two in return to the Hotel Plaza in Stockholm where Charlie is staying:
I'M ASHAMED OF MY LACK OF UNDERSTANDING LAST WEEK. THE NEW YOU THRILLS ME. REAL THANKSGIVING THIS YEAR. MY LOVE FOREVER. CHAN

CONFIRMATION OF **RADIOGRAM**
2 **TELEPHONED**
TO
RCA COMMUNICATIONS, Inc.
1950 nov 20 pm 12 15 6
"Via RCA"
CHARLES PARKER HOTEL PLAZA STOCKHOLM
PUDDIN YOUR CABLEGRAM THRILLED ME KIM AND I MISS YOU
TERRIBLY IM ONLY HALF ALIVE TEDDY IS HAPPY ABOUT YOUR
HEALTH HE SAID KEEP UP THE GOOD WORK HURRY BACK TO ME
I ADORE YOU
CHAN

WED	**1**
THUR	**2**
FRI	**3**
SAT	**4**
SUN	**5**
MON	**6**
TUES	**7**
WED	**8**
THUR	**9**
FRI	**10**
SAT	**11**
SUN	**12**
MON	**13**
TUES	**14**
WED	**15**
THUR	**16**
FRI	**17**
SAT	**18**
SUN	**19**
MON	**20**
TUES	**21**
WED	**22**
THUR	**23**
FRI	**24**
SAT	**25**
SUN	**26**
MON	**27**
TUES	**28**
WED	**29**
THUR	**30**

MONDAY 20 NOVEMBER 1950

The opening concert is at the Konserthuset in Stockholm. Roy Eldridge opens with a group of Swedish musicians. Charlie follows with ROLF ERICSON (trumpet), YNGVE ÅKERBERG (piano), GUNNAR SVENNSON (bass), JACK NOREN (drums) *Anthropology / Cool Blues / Cheers / Lover Man / Stupendous*

Afterwards Charlie is whisked off to the Headquarters of Swedish Jazz Clubs for a jam session.

Above right: Bird surrounded by Swedish musicians. L to r: Thore Jederby (b), Arne Domnerus (as), Gösta Theselius (p/ts), Rolf Ericson (t), Jack Noren (d). Right: The jam session in the cellar of the Stockholm Jazz Association with Lars Gullin (bs), Simon Brehm (b), Rolf Larsson (p). Sven Bollhem (d) is out of shot. Below: In concert at Stockholm's Konserthuset. L to r: Gunnar Svensson (p), Bird, Rolf Ericson (t), Jack Noren (d), Yngve Åkerberg (b).

WED	**1**
THUR	**2**
FRI	**3**
SAT	**4**
SUN	**5**
MON	**6**
TUES	**7**
WED	**8**
THUR	**9**
FRI	**10**
SAT	**11**
SUN	**12**
MON	**13**
TUES	**14**
WED	**15**
THUR	**16**
FRI	**17**
SAT	**18**
SUN	**19**
MON	**20**
TUES	**21**
WED	**22**
THUR	**23**
FRI	**24**
SAT	**25**
SUN	**26**
MON	**27**
TUES	**28**
WED	**29**
THUR	**30**

TUESDAY 21 NOVEMBER 1950
The tour begins with a double concert in Gothenburg. Charlie and Roy Eldridge are photographed walking about in the snow.

WEDNESDAY 22 NOVEMBER 1950
Matinee concert at the Amiralen Dance Hall in Malmö.
CHARLIE PARKER (alto sax), ROLF ERICSON (trumpet), GÖSTA THESELIUS (piano), THORE JEDERBY (bass), JACK NOREN (drums)
Anthropology / Cheers / Lover Man / Cool Blues

After the matinee, they drive a few miles north to the University of Lund where a jam session is held at the Akademiska Foreningen.

Danspalatset
|||||| **Amiralen** ||||||
I morgon onsdag kl. 20—24
Direkt från Broadway,
den moderna jazzens främste
ALTSAXOFONISTEN
Charlie Parker
med sensationell, svensk elit-orkester:
**Arne Domnerus - Rolf Ericsson
Thore Jederby - Gösta Theselius
Jack Norén**
Konsert — Dans
Biljetter: Arbetets kundtjänst,
SDS och Svenska Dagbladet,
G. Ad. torg samt i Amiralens biljettkontor onsdag kl. 19.

Charlie Parker och de andra 5

Malmö har nu sett den moderna jazzens båda okrönta kungar — först Dizzie Gillespie för något år sedan och nu Charlie Parker, altsax-matadoren från många bop-plattor. Han turnerar i Sverige biträdd av några av landets bästa jazzmusiker, och i går var turen kommen till Amiralen vars arena ingalunda var späckad med folk men dock ganska välbesatt. Fem fina svenska musiker inledde programmet med tre—fyra nummer av jämförelsevis traditionellt slag — den förträffligo tenor-saxofonisten Gösta Theselius vann speciellt publikens bevågenhet med ett balanserat men ändå djärvt spel, medan Rolf Ericsons trumpetspel egentligen var bara djärvt. Sedan kom den svarte Charlie och satte luften i dallring med några hastiga melodier — utpräglat avancerade saker som man många känner igen från gång till gång, antas det, och

CHARLIE PARKER skivor STOLTENS

WED	**1**
THUR	**2**
FRI	**3**
SAT	**4**
SUN	**5**
MON	**6**
TUES	**7**
WED	**8**
THUR	**9**
FRI	**10**
SAT	**11**
SUN	**12**
MON	**13**
TUES	**14**
WED	**15**
THUR	**16**
FRI	**17**
SAT	**18**
SUN	**19**
MON	**20**
TUES	**21**
WED	**22**
THUR	**23**
FRI	**24**
SAT	**25**
SUN	**26**
MON	**27**
TUES	**28**
WED	**29**
THUR	**30**

A fan writes from Lund:

Dear Charlie,

We want to thank you for your wonderful playing both in Malmö and Lund. We all think that it is a lovely dream that you spent last night with us, a few students and music lovers. We just can't understand you were so human just like one of us cause you are a star a genius and we just nothing. We will always remember you as one of the greatest human beings we ever met and a wonderful guy.

The first thing I said to you was 'there's only one Bird' and I sure hope to meet that Bird very soon again. You said that I talk English like a man from Florida and I hope I'll be able to talk real English with you next time but we don't need to talk just play cause music is an international language.

That was awful nice of you coming to Lund just to play for a few music lovers and I have no words to explain how grateful we are. One day when you are tired of U.S.A. come back to Sweden and be one of us. Your playing, your talk, your wonderful smile, your cry of happiness, you in person gave me (and a bunch of other guys too) the happiest moments of my life.

Once again thank you and may you live long and see a better world growing up with more fun, understanding, humanity and lots of good music.

Regards, Slim

THURSDAY 23 NOVEMBER 1950

Charlie and Roy appear at a big concert at K.B.Hallen in Copenhagen, Denmark, where they are joined by the Norwegian Quintet of Rowland Greenberg whom Charlie had met in 1949 at the Paris Jazz Festival. Benny Goodman is in Copenhagen and joins in the jamming.

WED	**1**
THUR	**2**
FRI	**3**
SAT	**4**
SUN	**5**
MON	**6**
TUES	**7**
WED	**8**
THUR	**9**
FRI	**10**
SAT	**11**
SUN	**12**
MON	**13**
TUES	**14**
WED	**15**
THUR	**16**
FRI	**17**
SAT	**18**
SUN	**19**
MON	**20**
TUES	**21**
WED	**22**
THUR	**23**
FRI	**24**
SAT	**25**
SUN	**26**
MON	**27**
TUES	**28**
WED	**29**
THUR	**30**

FRIDAY 24 NOVEMBER 1950

The party returns to Sweden for a matinee performance at Folkets Park, a beer garden and dance pavilion in Helsingborg.

CHARLIE PARKER (alto sax), ROLF ERICSON (trumpet), GÖSTA THESELIUS (piano), THORE JEDERBY (bass), JACK NOREN (drums)

Anthropology / Scrapple From The Apple / Embraceable You / Cool Blues / Star Eyes / All The Things You Are / Strike Up The Band

After the concert, they jam until the small hours. The jam session is recorded and later released on the Swedish label, Sonet.

CHARLIE PARKER (alto sax), ROLF ERICSON, ROWLAND GREENBERG (trumpet), GÖSTA THESELIUS (tenor sax), LENNART NILSSON (piano), FOLKE HOLST (bass), JACK NOREN (drums)

How High The Moon into *Ornithology / Body And Soul / Fine And Dandy*

WED	1
THUR	2
FRI	3
SAT	4
SUN	5
MON	6
TUES	7
WED	8
THUR	9
FRI	10
SAT	11
SUN	12
MON	13
TUES	14
WED	15
THUR	16
FRI	17
SAT	18
SUN	19
MON	20
TUES	21
WED	22
THUR	23
FRI	24
SAT	25
SUN	26
MON	27
TUES	28
WED	29
THUR	30

SATURDAY 25 NOVEMBER 1950
Concert in a large sports building in Jönköping.

SUNDAY 26 NOVEMBER 1950
Concert in Gävle. Due to a missed train connection, Charlie arrives late and the concert is delayed.

MONDAY 27 NOVEMBER 1950
Charlie returns to Stockholm where he rests during his last day in Sweden.

TUESDAY 28 NOVEMBER 1950
In Paris, Charlie is met at Le Bourget Airport by a heavily pregnant Annie Ross and Charles Delaunay who asks Charlie to appear at a concert the following weekend. Delaunay has arranged hotel accommodation for Parker, but when Annie gives Bird a note from Kenny Clarke, he decides to stay with Klook and Annie at their shared flat.

> Hey Bird;
>
> At this, sorry I had to leave town, but I sincerely hope I'll make it back before you leave. I had planned to stay and have a long talk with you concerning conditions back home. At any rate, I'll be back Friday morning and I hope you're still in Paris when I return. By the By, the bearer of this little note is my future wife, and anything you think you might want to tell me just tell it to her. C'est la même chose dig?????
>
> I hope your picture of the States is a much brighter one, but that I doubt. (a little) My fiancées name is _Annabella_. Here's hoping to see you anyway.
>
> All the best Bird and return soon.
>
> Klook

Charlie records at the Studio Washington with the Maurice Moufflard Orchestra.
CHARLIE PARKER (alto sax), ROGER GUERIN, GEORGES JOUVIN, PIERRE FASSIN, YVES ALOUTTE (trumpet), ANDRE PAQUINET, MAURICE GLADIEU, CHARLES HUSS (trombone), ROBERT MERCHEZ, ROGER SIMON (alto sax), JACQUES TESS, MARCEL POMES (tenor sax), HONORE TRUC (baritone sax), ROBERT CAMBIER (piano), HENRI KAREN (bass), PIERRE LOTEGUY (drums), MAURICE MOUFFLARD (arranger/conductor)
Lady Bird

Charlie spends the week visiting the Montmartre jazz bistros including 'Le Boeuf sur le Toit'.

THURSDAY 30 NOVEMBER 1950
Eddy Bernard writes to Bird from Paris:

Dear Charlie,

I don't know if you remember me: I'm Eddy Bernard, the little man with a beard, playing the piano in Fats Waller's styling; I was backing up Sidney Bechet at the 1949 Jazz Festival in Salle Pleyel and talked a little with you about Omar Khayyam (your favourite poet) and about Edgar Poe (my favourite poet). I'd love to see you and have a chance to talk a little more with you while you're in Paris; my mother too (she's a fan of Greek mythology, remember?). I've been trying to get you on the phone but, I couldn't get in touch with you. Would it be too much asking you to call me, at meals hours, at KLEber 28-01? I'd be so happy to have you, someday, for tea or supper, and talk and dream about music and Omar Khayyam and Edgar Poe.

In that hope, I'll cut here, hoping to see you soon.

Please find here my friendly regards combined with my deep admiration for your music.

Eddy Bernard

Toots Thielemans writes from Stockholm:

Dear Charlie,

In case you forgot my name – I am the harmonica player from Belgium.

Just wanted to tell you how profoundly you impressed me as a person besides as the musician I 'stole' most from and will always with or without your approval.

I felt really glad to be able to dedicate to you my modest tribute with 'Lover Man'.

Maybe you'll think that's corny but I don't think people are corny when they say what they really feel. I guess I said what I had to say.

Hope you come back in good shape from that 'Gay Paree', Oui Oui, Say See boon...

How is my harmonica doing? Isn't your alto yet jealous.

I plan to make some records real soon with Reinhold Svensson which is, besides a great personality, one of the musicians who listened the most to what others are playing around them.

As soon as possible I'll send them up to you. I understand Norman Granz is coming soon to Sweden. I wrote to him. If you think it might be of any help for me may I ask you to speak to him about me.

So, Charlie, thanks once more for everything, excuse my 'schoolboy' English – I'm sorry I'm not hep.

All the best, very sincerely yours,

Toots Thielemans

FRI	**1**
SAT	**2**
SUN	**3**
MON	**4**
TUES	**5**
WED	**6**
THUR	**7**
FRI	**8**
SAT	**9**
SUN	**10**
MON	**11**
TUES	**12**
WED	**13**
THUR	**14**
FRI	**15**
SAT	**16**
SUN	**17**
MON	**18**
TUES	**19**
WED	**20**
THUR	**21**
FRI	**22**
SAT	**23**
SUN	**24**
MON	**25**
TUES	**26**
WED	**27**
THUR	**28**
FRI	**29**
SAT	**30**
SUN	**31**

SATURDAY 2 DECEMBER 1950

On the day of the planned Paris concert, Charlie feels stomach pains and flies back to New York via London.

In the evening, in New York, Charlie is persuaded to appear on Leonard Feather's radio show, which is broadcast overseas. Through a special hook up, Charlie is able to explain his absence to the French concert audience.

After days of misery Charlie goes to Medical Arts Hospital in Manhattan where X-rays confirmed an acute peptic ulcer. He was admitted and put on a special diet with 24-hour nursing.

After a week Charlie begins to improve. After the doctor prescribes another week of intensive care, Charlie flees the hospital and takes a cab to Birdland where he drowns many whiskies. Oscar Goodstein, the manager, persuades him to return to the hospital.

Chan discovers she is pregnant, and writes to tell Annie Ross and Kenny Clarke.

Ulcer Attack Beds Parker

New York—Charlie Parker was just released from Medical Arts hospital here after being suddenly stricken with a recurrence of an ulcer condition less than 24 hours after his return from Europe.

Charlie reported his week in Sweden as a great success, and reports from Swedish impresario Nils Hellstrom indicate that both his promoter and the Scandinavian public agreed.

A surprise element was the appearance of Roy Eldridge on four of the seven concerts. Roy has since returned to Paris. Featured in the small group with Bird on the tour was Rolf Ericson, bop trumpet ace who returned home a few months ago after working in this country with Herman, Ventura, and other name bands.

Charlie says his accompaniment, notably the drumming of Jack Norris and the bass of Thore Jederby, was excellent, and that the Swedish people are "the coolest and the nicest."

DECEMBER 1950

Charlie Parker Quintet play at Birdland. They broadcast over station WJZ.

CHARLIE PARKER (alto sax), RED RODNEY (trumpet), KENNY DREW (piano), CURLEY RUSSELL (bass), ART BLAKEY (drums), SYMPHONY SID (mc), BOB GARRITY (announcer)

Jumpin' With Symphony Sid / Anthropology / Embraceable You / Cheryl / Salt Peanuts / Jumpin' With Symphony Sid

WEDNESDAY 13 DECEMBER 1950

Annie Ross writes to Chan and Bird:

Dear Chan and Bird,

Was so very happy to get your letter. Klook and I were asleep and the moment Jany saw it was a letter from you she woke us up. Believe me, it was just the tonic we needed. We translated the letter to Jany and Henri and they were gassed also.

Oh, I'm so happy, Chan that you are pregnant!! When Bird was here, he said he wished you were and I can imagine how he felt when he found out! What a fine strong little baby that will be! Chan, tell me if you want things knitted in pink or in blue, and I shall start right away to knit some little sweaters and booties and things for your layette. Also, take Kim's hand and draw the outline on a piece of paper and yours too so that I can make you both a pair of mittens.

Melody Maker

INCORPORATING 'RHYTHM'

VOL. 26. No. 898   DECEMBER 2, 1950 [Registered at the G.P.O. as a Newspaper]   EVERY FRIDAY - 4d.

CHARLIE PARKER TO PLAY AT PARIS SALON DU JAZZ

Death of famous MD, Percival Mackey

THE MELODY MAKER announces with the deepest regret the death of famous conductor-composer Percival Mackey, who passed away very suddenly at his Edgware home on Thursday, November 23. He was 56.

The cremation took place at Golders Green last Tuesday. By special request, the ceremony was private, only Mrs. Mackey and one or two special friends being present.

(See full story on page 7)

Graham replaces Dankworth in international jazz hook-up

PARIS, WEDNESDAY.

LAST-MINUTE addition to the galaxy of stars lined up to appear in Paris on December 1, is the world-renowned altoist Charlie Parker.

Arriving in Stockholm last week from the U.S., he was at once contacted by trumpeter Roy Eldridge and invited to appear at the Fair. He agreed at once, and on Tuesday afternoon this week arrived in Paris. He will be playing at the Fair tomorrow.

"MM" Paris Correspondent Henry Kahn, interviewing him on arrival, asked how he had enjoyed his stay in Sweden.

SWEDEN? IT WAS TERRIFIC!—PARKER

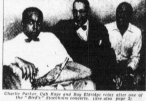

Charlie Parker, Cab Kaye and Roy Eldridge relax after one of the "Bird's" Stockholm concerts. (see also page 3)

DANCE MUSIC IS RICH INSTONE

Melody Maker
★ CHRISTMAS ★ ISSUE ★ 1950 ★

VOL. 26. No. 899   DECEMBER 9, 1950 [Registered at the G.P.O. as a Newspaper]   EVERY FRIDAY - 4d.

Xmas Greetings to all our readers

THE INCREDIBLE STORY OF PARKER IN PARIS

Fans besiege the Salon du Jazz— then find Bird has flown

MOST widely discussed personality of all the stars associated with the sensational Paris Jazz Fair—which ended its five-day run at the Centre Marcellin Berthelot on Tuesday last—was the man who did not appear at all.

Excitement prior to the opening of this feast of jazz reached its zenith with the announcement, on Tuesday last week, that ace altoist Charlie Parker had promised to play.

His assent excited thousands—not only in Paris, where the French Press splashed the announcement, but also in London, where ardent fans made hasty preparations to cross the Channel in order to hear him, or

Anne Shelton to have own

FRI	1
SAT	2
SUN	3
MON	4
TUES	5
WED	6
THUR	7
FRI	8
SAT	9
SUN	10
MON	11
TUES	12
WED	13
THUR	14
FRI	15
SAT	16
SUN	17
MON	18
TUES	19
WED	20
THUR	21
FRI	22
SAT	23
SUN	24
MON	25
TUES	26
WED	27
THUR	28
FRI	29
SAT	30
SUN	31

How did you and Leon like your scarves? And little Kim, I bet she looks like a little flower in her bonnet!

We have a little bed for our son. Part of a laundry basket in wicker. Nothing fancy as financial situations don't permit it, but I don't suppose little Klook will care whether its fancy or not. It's so weird to awaken in the morning and see that little bed and think that someday soon, our little son will be in it! Every morning when I wake Klook up, he asks me if I have any pains yet. He is so anxious to see the finished product.

Still the same stuff going down here. The other day Klook went over to the Hot Club to see if he had any mail. Delaunay handed him a letter which he had already opened and told Klook he thought it was for him! Of course he said he hadn't read it, but then you know how Delaunay is. He was furious when you and Klook didn't play at the Jazz Concerts. They are really out of their minds here! Some cat went to the Club where Henri works and told Henri that you and Klook were both fags and were making it together here in Paris. Henri just laughed in his face. You dig the mentality? Oh, well, thank God we won't be here forever.

We were all terribly sorry to hear you were in the hospital, Bird. But in a way it will rest you up a bit so that when you do come out, you'll feel much better.

Laba is fine and says hello and keep well. Perk is as tall, thin, vague and always in a stupor, as usual.

I guess this just about makes it for now. Remember that you both are in our thoughts always. Bird, take care of Chan and the little ones and Chan, I know you'll take care of your "homme".

And I know the little little little one will take care of all of you!! (smiles!)

With fondest love from
X Annie X

THURSDAY 14 DECEMBER 1950
Annie Ross sends a postcard to Bird:

Dear Chan and Bird –

This is the square at the top of the road where we live. The little 'X' marks Rue de Clichy. The other 'X' marks Sacré Coeur, the famous church. Everyone is fine and sends their love. Jany, Klook and I are all in the kitchen drinking coffee as it's cold, cold, cold outside – Jany says to say "Everything's cool!!"

Annie XX

WEDNESDAY 20 DECEMBER 1950
Kenny Clarke writes to Bird:

Dear Bird;

All day you've been running through my mind, and all of a sudden, impulsively, I grabbed a pen and paper and started a letter to you, hoping all the time that you'd be able to read it immediately after the closing phrase (Your sincere friend).

Not withstanding the fact that I hope it reaches you with all the expedience possible. I trust and pray that this letter upon reaching you, finds you in an approved and improved state of health. How do you feel Bird? May God give all attending you the power to administer all that is necessary to bring about your speedy recovery, and renewed strength in your material form to which we all owe so much to.

By the Bye, your Godson will be coming into the world any minute now, so, the moments near at hand find Annie and me hoping and praying that God will be kind and give us a child healthy and strong in mind and body and spirit. And too, we hope that Chan and the family are all well. I've just received news that Beezy [?] is gravely ill. Is this true? God forfend. A few gigs are coming my way which I must take to help foot the bills the baby'll eventually pile up. Nevertheless, all is well. Courage Bird and the best for the New Year and always. The rumors of War are still circulating and causing unrest among the populace, and the death knell is sounding, and getting louder every day for Europeans and their culture, fini!! All happens for the best, and may the best and good prevail. Sincere best wishes again to Chan and the kids from the both of us on this end, and please get well Bird, our hearts are with you always.

Affectionately
Klook & Annie

THURSDAY 21 DECEMBER 1950
Charlie Parker and Flip Phillips record as guest soloists with Machito and his Orchestra for Mercury/Verve in New York City.
CHARLIE PARKER (alto sax), FLIP PHILLIPS (tenor sax), MARIO BAUZA, FRANK 'PAQUITO' DAVILLA, HARRY EDISON, AL STEWART, BOB WOODLEN (trumpet), UNKNOWN (clarinet), GENE JOHNSON, FRED SKERRITT (alto sax), JOSE MADERA, SOL RABINOWITZ (tenor sax), LESLIE JOHNAKINS (baritone sax), RENE HERNANDEZ (piano), ROBERTO RODRIGUEZ (bass), BUDDY RICH (drums), JOSE MANGUEL (bongos), RAFAEL MIRANDA, CHINO POZO (conga), UMBALDO NIETO (timbales), MACHITO (maraccas), CHICO O'FARRILL (arranger/conductor)
The Afro Cuban Jazz Suite: *Cancion / Mambo Part 1 / Mambo Part 2 / Rhumba Abierta / 6/8 / Jazz*

SUNDAY 24 DECEMBER 1950
Annie Ross gives birth to a son, Kenny Clarke Jr.

THURSDAY 28 DECEMBER 1950
Kenny Clarke and Annie Ross cable Bird from Paris with news of the birth of their son:
LITTLE KLOOK ARRIVED DEC 24TH AT 5.05 BEST OF HEALTH SENDS ALL THE BEST TO HIS GOD FATHER
KLOOK ET ANNIE

MON	**1**	THUR	**1**
TUES	**2**	FRI	**2**
WED	**3**	SAT	**3**
THUR	**4**	SUN	**4**
FRI	**5**	MON	**5**
SAT	**6**	TUES	**6**
SUN	**7**	WED	**7**
MON	**8**	THUR	**8**
TUES	**9**	FRI	**9**
WED	**10**	SAT	**10**
THUR	**11**	SUN	**11**
FRI	**12**	MON	**12**
SAT	**13**	TUES	**13**
SUN	**14**	WED	**14**
MON	**15**	THUR	**15**
TUES	**16**	FRI	**16**
WED	**17**	SAT	**17**
THUR	**18**	SUN	**18**
FRI	**19**	MON	**19**
SAT	**20**	TUES	**20**
SUN	**21**	WED	**21**
MON	**22**	THUR	**22**
TUES	**23**	FRI	**23**
WED	**24**	SAT	**24**
THUR	**25**	SUN	**25**
FRI	**26**	MON	**26**
SAT	**27**	TUES	**27**
SUN	**28**	WED	**28**
MON	**29**		
TUES	**30**		
WED	**31**		

WEDNESDAY 3 JANUARY 1951
Red Rodney, Kenny Drew, Curley Russell and Phil Brown file claims against Charlie with Local 802.

TUESDAY 9 JANUARY 1951
Charlie Parker Quintet open at the 421 Club in Philadelphia for one-week engagement.

THURSDAY 11 JANUARY 1951
Charlie Parker is summoned by Local 802 of the AF of M to attend a meeting of the Trial Board, to be held at 1267 Sixth Avenue, NYC at 11 a.m. to answer charges against him by Dillon 'Curley' Russell, Kenny Drew, Phil Brown and Robert 'Red Rodney' Chudnick.

SUNDAY 14 JANUARY 1951
Charlie Parker Quintet close at the 421 Club in Philadelphia

WEDNESDAY 17 JANUARY 1951
Recording session as Charlie Parker Quintet for Mercury/Verve in New York City
CHARLIE PARKER (alto sax), MILES DAVIS (trumpet), WALTER BISHOP (piano), TEDDY KOTICK (bass), MAX ROACH (drums)
Au Privave (2 takes) / *She Rote* (2 takes) / *K.C. Blues* / *Star Eyes*

MONDAY 22 JANUARY 1951
Contracts are signed for Charlie Parker & Strings (10 musicians) to appear at the Paradise Theatre, Detroit for 1 week in March. $2750 flat guarantee – pro rata extra shows.

TUESDAY 23 JANUARY 1951
Contracts are signed for Charlie Parker & Strings (10 musicians) to appear at the Towne Casino, Main Street, Buffalo for 1 week in February. $2250 guarantee in cash at conclusion of engagement.

WEDNESDAY 25 JANUARY 1951
Contracts are signed for Charlie Parker & Strings (10 musicians) to appear at the Johnny Brown's, Frankstown Ave., Pittsburgh for 8 days in February. $3000 for eight days to be paid at end of engagement

FRIDAY 9 FEBRUARY 1951
Charlie Parker & Strings open at Johnny Brown's in Pittsburgh for an 8-day engagement, playing 4 shows daily. Weekdays: 8.30, 10.15, 11.30, 1.00 Saturdays: 3.00, 8.00, 10.00, 12.00

SUNDAY 11 FEBRUARY 1951
On the off night at Johnny Brown's Charlie Parker flies into Chicago for a special dance engagement at the Pershing Ballroom.

MONDAY 12 FEBRUARY 1951
Charlie Parker back at Johnny Brown's in Pittsburgh .

SATURDAY 17 FEBRUARY 1951
Charlie Parker & Strings close at Johnny Brown's in Pittsburgh.

MONDAY 19 FEBRUARY 1951
Charlie Parker & Strings open at Towne Casino, Buffalo for 7 days. Rehearsal at 2pm.

SUNDAY 25 FEBRUARY 1951
Charlie Parker & Strings close at Towne Casino, Buffalo

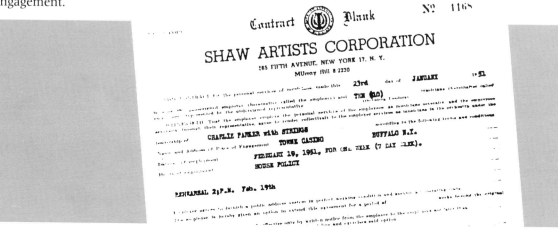

THUR	1
FRI	2
SAT	3
SUN	4
MON	5
TUES	6
WED	7
THUR	8
FRI	9
SAT	10
SUN	11
MON	12
TUES	13
WED	14
THUR	15
FRI	16
SAT	17
SUN	18
MON	19
TUES	20
WED	21
THUR	22
FRI	23
SAT	24
SUN	25
MON	26
TUES	27
WED	28
THUR	29
FRI	30
SAT	31

While in Detroit Bird visits with his son, Leon, and his first wife, Rebecca.
L to r: Rebecca and her second husband, Teddy Blume, Bird and Leon.

FRIDAY 2 MARCH 1951
Charlie Parker & Strings open at Paradise Theatre, Detroit for one week.

THURSDAY 8 MARCH 1951
Charlie Parker & Strings close at Paradise Theatre, Detroit.

MONDAY 12 MARCH 1951
Charlie Parker recording session in New York for Mercury/Verve.
CHARLIE PARKER (alto sax), WALTER BISHOP (piano), TEDDY KOTICK (bass), ROY HAYNES (drums), JOSE MANGUEL (bongos), LUIS MIRANDA (conga)
My Little Suede Shoes / Un Poquito De Tu Amor / Tico Tico / Fiesta / Why Do I Love You? (3 takes)

FRIDAY 16 MARCH 1951
Contracts are signed for Charlie Parker and a 17-piece Orchestra to appear at the Apollo Theatre in Harlem for one week in April. 30 shows for $3,131 to be paid at the conclusion of the engagement.

THURSDAY 22 MARCH 1951
Charlie Parker & Strings open at Birdland for a 3-week engagement. Also on the bill are Slim Gaillard and the Erroll Garner Trio.
Charlie Parker and Strings broadcast from Birdland over station WJZ.
CHARLIE PARKER (alto sax), WALTER BISHOP (piano), TEDDY KOTICK (bass), ROY HAYNES (drums) unknown string section, SYMPHONY SID TORIN (mc)
Easy To Love / Rocker / Jumpin' With Symphony Sid (theme)

SATURDAY 24 MARCH 1951
Charlie Parker and Strings broadcast from Birdland over station WJZ.
CHARLIE PARKER (alto sax), WALTER BISHOP (piano), TEDDY KOTICK (bass), ROY HAYNES (drums) unknown string section, SYMPHONY SID TORIN (mc)
Jumpin' With Symphony Sid (theme) */ Just Friends / Everything Happens To Me / East Of The Sun / Laura / Dancing In The Dark / Jumpin' With Symphony Sid* (theme)

THUR	**1**
FRI	**2**
SAT	**3**
SUN	**4**
MON	**5**
TUES	**6**
WED	**7**
THUR	**8**
FRI	**9**
SAT	**10**
SUN	**11**
MON	**12**
TUES	**13**
WED	**14**
THUR	**15**
FRI	**16**
SAT	**17**
SUN	**18**
MON	**19**
TUES	**20**
WED	**21**
THUR	**22**
FRI	**23**
SAT	**24**
SUN	**25**
MON	**26**
TUES	**27**
WED	**28**
THUR	**29**
FRI	**30**
SAT	**31**

During the Birdland engagement, Bird is interviewed by Leonard Feather for a Voice of America radio broadcast:

FEATHER: *Do you have any plans at the moment about any future engagement?*

PARKER: Well… about future engagements… no, not any exact plans… I guess you heard I'm breaking with my manager.

FEATHER: *Yes, as a matter of fact, I sent an item to Down Beat about that just last week.*

PARKER: Yes, well, I mean after that maybe plans can be made but no… nothing special right now.

FEATHER: *Well, lets talk about your recent trip to Europe, because I have a couple of records coming up by people you probably met over there, and I know you had a very interesting experience. It was quite a short trip, but a very eventful one. How long were you over there?*

PARKER: Well… I was in Scandinavia eleven days and I was in Paris for four days… in Europe.

FEATHER: *The Paris part was not for… actually for playing, was it? Just… it was a visit.*

PARKER: Oh, just a visit… I went there strictly for a visit.

FEATHER: *What did you do in Scandinavia? Who was with you there?*

PARKER: Well, in Scandinavia I had the pleasure of working with Roy Eldridge, along with a Swedish band which consisted of Rolf Ericson… I guess you remember him? He was here with Woody Herman.

FEATHER: *Oh, I certainly do.*

PARKER: And I… er, some of the names I can't pronounce… anyway, there were five musicians with me all the while, and then Roy had his own band and he did his… thing with them… I did the thing…

FEATHER: *Yeah, and where is Roy Eldridge now? Is he back?*

PARKER: Well… he's in Paris.

FEATHER: *Aha, does he intend to come back here? Or is he going to stay over indefinitely?*

PARKER: Well… I don't know. I think he intends to come back. Anyway, he has his ticket back.

FEATHER: *Oh, well, that's good news because we sure miss him. I got some records that he made in Paris and I want to play them on the show some day. I have one thing where he sings the blues in French. It's really strange.*

PARKER: Yes, I think I've heard that.

FEATHER: *Yeah, that's great. Well… while we're talking about that, how about cutting in for a moment for some music that comes from over there. James Moody is the chief musician on this next side. Did you meet him over there?*

PARKER: Yes, I saw him over there. I met him here first though.

FEATHER: *Did you work with him ever?*

PARKER: No, I haven't, he's a very fine… only on the concert in 1949… in Paris that was.

FEATHER: *Oh, I see. This is one of the sides he made I believe in Scandinavia and the title is 'Blue and Moody'.*

[plays record]

FEATHER: *Do you know who Reinhold Svenson is?*

PARKER: Reinhold Svenson? Sure, I know Reinhold Svenson.

FEATHER: *Tell me about him.*

PARKER: Well… he's a blind pianist, he's blond, he weighs about two hundred 35, 40 pounds…

FEATHER: *No kidding?*

PARKER: …very clever, very good musician, very jovial.

FEATHER: *He certainly is very talented, too. He made a whole series of sides with a quintet over there… I think patterned after George Shearing, wasn't it?*

PARKER: Yes, yes, that could be.

FEATHER: *Sounds very much like it. Anyway, we have one of those sides here. They just brought out an LP consisting of eight Reinhold Svenson numbers and I think you'll like this one… 'Dearly Beloved'.*

[plays record]

FEATHER: *Say one thing for that record… it has a fine surface… a lot of surface, anyway. Well… the music is good. Well… Charlie, I would like to get your opinion on something. I read a very interesting article just a few days ago in Ebony Magazine under the byline of Cab Calloway. Did you read it?*

PARKER: Yes, Leonard… I saw such an article, and I've never read or heard of such a violent and contentious thing against musicians of today.

FEATHER: *Well, that's a pretty strong statement. I think we'd better tell our listeners what the article is about.*

PARKER: Well, OK… let's tell our listeners. Let's tell them this way… if they should like to read the article, it's published in Ebony Magazine under the name of Cab Calloway, the rest will speak for itself.

FEATHER: *Well… ah… can I go into a few details anyway? Cab Calloway says in the article, or implies in the article, that narcotics are ruining the music business, and, oh… he makes it very clear that he thinks a large number of musicians are using narcotics, and that he goes into a great number of details about this thing… which we won't go into on the air… but, anyway, it's a very provocative article. Would you say that it represents the true picture of the situation?*

PARKER: I'd rather say that it was poorly written, poorly expressed… and poorly meant. It was just poor.

FEATHER: *Well… that makes it pretty definite. As a matter of fact, I'm inclined to agree with you, Charlie. I think the article was perhaps badly timed, and perhaps didn't go into a careful enough examination of the real facts. As a matter of fact, it quoted something that I wrote several years ago about the same subject in Esquire, and it misquoted… or rather made an incomplete quote that gave a wrong picture of my feeling about the thing. I certainly don't think that a musician necessarily plays better under the influence of any stimulus of any kind, and I am pretty sure you agree with me, don't you?*

THUR **1**
FRI **2**
SAT **3**
SUN **4**
MON **5**
TUES **6**
WED **7**
THUR **8**
FRI **9**
SAT **10**
SUN **11**
MON **12**
TUES **13**
WED **14**
THUR **15**
FRI **16**
SAT **17**
SUN **18**
MON **19**
TUES **20**
WED **21**
THUR **22**
FRI **23**
SAT **24**
SUN **25**
MON **26**
TUES **27**
WED **28**
THUR **29**
FRI **30**
SAT **31**

Above: Bird with strings at Birdland. Walter Bishop can be seen on piano, with Teddy Kotick on bass.

PARKER: Well, um… yes… I'd rather agree with you to an extent. I think you are quoting something that I once said to you about this.

FEATHER: *That's right, exactly. You said that to me quite a while ago.*

PARKER: That's exactly right. Well… nobody's fooling themselves… never, anymore… anyway, we'll put it that way… and in case an investigation should be conducted, it should be done in the right way instead of trying to destroy musicians and their names. I don't think it's quite a good idea.

FEATHER: *Yeah, well… I think that maybe Cab is going to think twice about whether it was a good idea to have that article appear in…*

PARKER: He has already expressed his thoughts.

FEATHER: *He has? You mean in the magazine? Well, that's true.*

PARKER: That's exactly right.

FEATHER: *Well, that's true, but I haven't talked to him since the article came out, and I'd be very interested to hear what he has to say about the musicians' reaction to that article, because there's going to be a pretty violent reaction, just as yours is.*

PARKER: Well, would you expect anything less?

FEATHER: *No, as a matter of fact, you're right. I think it's bound to cause a lot of talk, and a lot of unfavourable talk, certainly. Well, Charlie… it's been very, very good talking about all these subjects with you, and before you go, I'd like* to say that as soon as you have your plans set, please come up here and tell us all about it, tell us who your new manager is, and where your new bookings will be and, of course, as far as what your new records are, we'll be keeping in touch with that and reviewing them as they come along, and I know they'll be all A's and B's.

PARKER: All right, Leonard… thanks a lot.

WEDNESDAY 28 MARCH 1951

Contracts are signed for Charlie Parker & Strings (10 musicians) to appear at Uline's Arena, Washington D.C. on Saturday 21 April from 8.30 to midnight for $1200. $600 deposit to be paid upon signing of contract; balance of $600 to be paid to leader in cash during intermission.

Charlie Parker & Strings close at Birdland.

THURSDAY 29 MARCH 1951

Charlie, without the strings, joins Dizzy Gillespie's Band at Birdland.

SATURDAY 31 MARCH 1951

Charlie Parker and the All Stars broadcast from Birdland over station WJZ.
CHARLIE PARKER (alto sax), DIZZY GILLESPIE (trumpet), BUD POWELL (piano), TOMMY POTTER (bass), ROY HAYNES (drums), SYMPHONY SID TORIN (mc)
Introduction / Blue'n'Boogie / Anthropology / Round About Midnight / Night In Tunisia / Jumpin' With Symphony Sid (theme)

SUN	**1**
MON	**2**
TUES	**3**
WED	**4**
THUR	**5**
FRI	**6**
SAT	**7**
SUN	**8**
MON	**9**
TUES	**10**
WED	**11**
THUR	**12**
FRI	**13**
SAT	**14**
SUN	**15**
MON	**16**
TUES	**17**
WED	**18**
THUR	**19**
FRI	**20**
SAT	**21**
SUN	**22**
MON	**23**
TUES	**24**
WED	**25**
THUR	**26**
FRI	**27**
SAT	**28**
SUN	**29**
MON	**30**

SATURDAY 7 APRIL 1951

Charlie Parker and Strings broadcast from Birdland over station WJZ.

CHARLIE PARKER (alto sax), WALTER BISHOP (piano), TEDDY KOTICK (bass), ROY HAYNES (drums) unknown string section, SYMPHONY SID TORIN (mc)
What Is This Thing Called Love? / Laura / Repetition / They Can't Take That Away From Me / Easy To Love

WEDNESDAY 11 APRIL 1951

Charlie Parker and Strings close at Birdland.

THURSDAY 12 APRIL 1951

Charlie Parker and a 17-piece Orchestra rehearse for the Friday's opening at the Apollo.

In the evening he takes part in a jam session at Christy's Restaurant, Framingham, Massachusetts.
CHARLIE PARKER (alto sax), DICK WELLINGTON (alto sax), WARDELL GRAY (tenor sax), NAT PIERCE, WALTER BISHOP, DICK TWARDZIK (piano), TOMMY POTTER (bass), ROY HAYNES (drums)
Scrapple From The Apple / Lullaby In Rhythm / I Remember April / Happy Bird Blues

FRIDAY 13 APRIL 1951

Charlie Parker and a 17-piece Orchestra open at the Apollo Theatre, Harlem for a one-week engagement. 30 shows for $3131 per week.

THURSDAY 19 APRIL 1951

Charlie Parker and a 17-piece Orchestra close at the Apollo.

SATURDAY 21 APRIL 1951

Charlie Parker & Strings play a one-nighter opposite Johnny Hodges and his All Stars (Billy Strayhorn, Al Sears, Emmett Berry, Lawrence Brown and Sonny Greer) at Uline's Arena in Washington D.C. Charlie supplies a 10-piece orchestra for $1200.

MONDAY 30 APRIL 1951

Charlie Parker & Strings open in St Paul, Minnesota for a one-week engagement.

Bird Meets The Rabbit

New York — The Rabbit ran head-on into the Bird April 21 at Uline's arena in Washington, when both Johnny Hodges and Charlie Parker were featured, along with June Christy, in a Symphony Sid jazz concert presentation.

Charlie and Johnny are also both booked for Cleveland, but not together — Charlie and strings will be there the week of May 7, Hodges following two weeks later. Spot is Lindsay's Sky bar.

TUES	**1**
WED	**2**
THUR	**3**
FRI	**4**
SAT	**5**
SUN	**6**
MON	**7**
TUES	**8**
WED	**9**
THUR	**10**
FRI	**11**
SAT	**12**
SUN	**13**
MON	**14**
TUES	**15**
WED	**16**
THUR	**17**
FRI	**18**
SAT	**19**
SUN	**20**
MON	**21**
TUES	**22**
WED	**23**
THUR	**24**
FRI	**25**
SAT	**26**
SUN	**27**
MON	**28**
TUES	**29**
WED	**30**
THUR	**31**

TUESDAY 1 MAY 1951

Teddy Blume, manager of the Strings unit, writes to Allen Miller, accountant, from the Hotel Lowry, St Paul, Minnesota:

Allen Miller, Miller & Miller,
Room 518, 565 Fifth Avenue, New York

Dear Allen
I must apologize for not being able to get this out sooner, but conditions beyond my control necessitated the delay. However, in separate parcel, I have sent you Parker's folio and in it you will find the reports for the last quarter of 1950 plus the two copies of the witholding report with Parker's signatures affixed. At the moment I'm not able to make out the other reports regarding costs of band operations as I haven't the necessary contracts of the past engagements. However, you can obtain that information from Billie Miller. I spoke to Parker and he said it was O.K. for me to send you fifty dollars towards your fee. I will do so at the end of this engagement (May 6, 1951). Keep well and if you want to contact me, write me at the spots wherever we might be at the time.
Best regards,
Teddy Blume

SUNDAY 6 MAY 1951

Charlie Parker & Strings close in St Paul, Minnesota.

MONDAY 7 MAY 1951

Charlie Parker & Strings open at Lindsay's in Cleveland for one week.

SUNDAY 13 MAY 1951

Charlie Parker & Strings close at Lindsay's in Cleveland.

From Cleveland the Charlie Parker Quintet move on to Philadelphia to play a one-week engagement. Clifford Brown deps with the quintet when Benny Harris leaves.

> BENNY HARRIS LEFT PARKER SHORTLY AFTER THE ENGAGEMENT BEGAN, SO I WORKED IN HIS PLACE FOR A WEEK. BIRD HELPED MY MORALE A GREAT DEAL. ONE NIGHT HE TOOK ME INTO A CORNER AND SAID "I DON'T BELIEVE IT. I HEAR WHAT YOU'RE SAYING, BUT I DON'T BELIEVE IT".

CLIFFORD BROWN (interviewed by Nat Hentoff):

Charlie Parker fronting his quintet, probably at Lindsay's in Cleveland, during the Strings tour. Roy Haynes (drums) and Teddy Kotick (bass) can just be glimpsed. Missing from the picture are Walter Bishop (piano) and Benny Harris (trumpet).

SUNDAY 27 MAY 1949

Charlie Parker Quintet with Benny Harris, Walter Bishop, Teddy Kotick and Roy Haynes play a concert at Kleinham's Music Hall in Buffalo, N.Y.

FRI	1
SAT	2
SUN	3
MON	4
TUES	5
WED	6
THUR	7
FRI	8
SAT	9
SUN	10
MON	11
TUES	12
WED	13
THUR	14
FRI	15
SAT	16
SUN	17
MON	18
TUES	19
WED	20
THUR	21
FRI	22
SAT	23
SUN	24
MON	25
TUES	26
WED	27
THUR	28
FRI	29
SAT	30

THURSDAY 14 JUNE 1951

Charlie Parker opens as a guest with Machito's Band at Birdland. Also on the bill are the Stan Getz Quartet and Slim Gaillard. This is Bird's last NYC club appearance for 15 months because of a State Liquor Authority ban.

WEDNESDAY 20 JUNE 1951

Charlie Parker and Machito's Band close at Birdland.

SATURDAY 23 JUNE 1951

Charlie Parker Quintet appear at the Eastern Parkway Ballroom in Brooklyn.
A private recording is made.
CHARLIE PARKER (alto sax), UNKNOWN (trumpet), AL HAIG (piano), TEDDY KOTICK (bass), ROY HAYNES (drums)

52nd Street Theme / Ornithology / Embraceable You / Steeplechase / 52nd Street Theme / Now's The Time / Be My Love / April In Paris / Dance Of The Infidels / 52nd Street Theme / Wee / This Time The Dream's On Me / Don't Blame Me / A Night In Tunisia / All The Things You Are / Cool Blues / 52nd Street Theme

Based on the evidence of these two receipts for advances, it seems likely that Bird played a one-week engagement at Club 421 in Philadelphia, probably from Monday 25 June.

FRIDAY 29 JUNE 1951

The new issue of *Down Beat* features Charlie in the 'My Best on Wax' series:

My Best On Wax
By Charlie Parker

I'm sorry, but my best on wax has yet to be made. When I listen to my records I always find that improvements could be made on each one. There's never been one that completely satisfied me.

If you want to know my worst on wax, though, that's easy. I'd take *Lover Man*, a horrible thing that should never have been released—it was made the day before I had a nervous breakdown. No, I think I'd choose *Be-Bop*, made at the same session, or *The Gypsy*. They were all awful.

Getz, Parker Play Birdland

New York—Pairing a team that has made several records for Mercury, Birdland brought in Machito's Afro-Cubans with Charlie Parker as soloist on June 14. And also on the big bill is the Stan Getz quartet and Slim Gaillard doing a single.

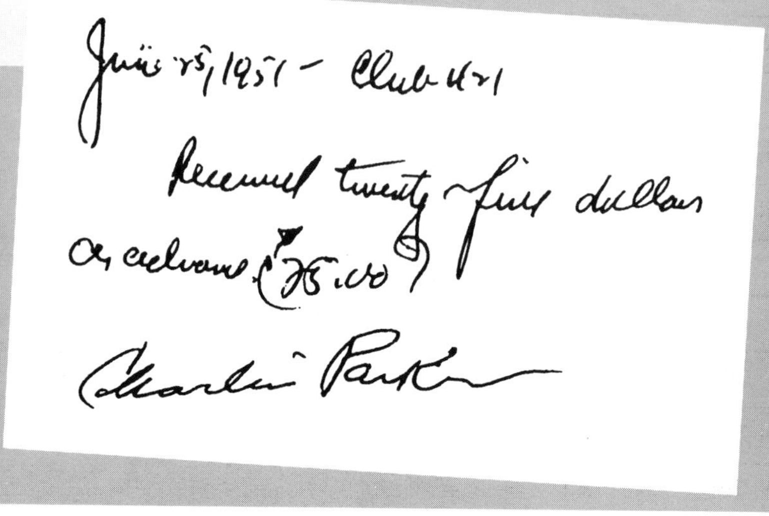

Duke Ellington returns on June 21 for 10 days, with vocalist Lurlean Hunter also bowing on that date. From July 1 to 18 it'll be the George Shearing quintet.

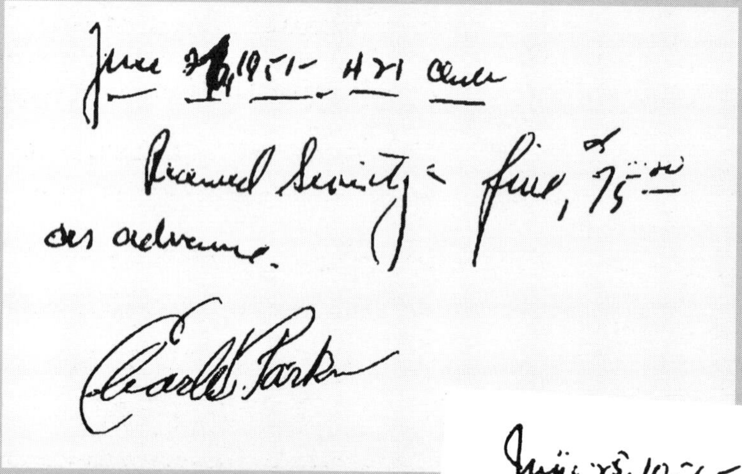

SUN	**1**	WED	**1**
MON	**2**	THUR	**2**
TUES	**3**	FRI	**3**
WED	**4**	SAT	**4**
THUR	**5**	SUN	**5**
FRI	**6**	MON	**6**
SAT	**7**	TUES	**7**
SUN	**8**	WED	**8**
MON	**9**	THUR	**9**
TUES	**10**	FRI	**10**
WED	**11**	SAT	**11**
THUR	**12**	SUN	**12**
FRI	**13**	MON	**13**
SAT	**14**	TUES	**14**
SUN	**15**	WED	**15**
MON	**16**	THUR	**16**
TUES	**17**	FRI	**17**
WED	**18**	SAT	**18**
THUR	**19**	SUN	**19**
FRI	**20**	MON	**20**
SAT	**21**	TUES	**21**
SUN	**22**	WED	**22**
MON	**23**	THUR	**23**
TUES	**24**	FRI	**24**
WED	**25**	SAT	**25**
THUR	**26**	SUN	**26**
FRI	**27**	MON	**27**
SAT	**28**	TUES	**28**
SUN	**29**	WED	**29**
MON	**30**	THUR	**30**
TUES	**31**	FRI	**31**

TUESDAY 17 JULY 1951

Chan gives birth to a little girl, Pree.

THURSDAY 19 JULY 1951

Charlie signs a contract with Spencer Presentations in Kansas City to appear as guest soloist with Woody Herman at the Municipal Auditorium on the following Sunday. A flat fee of $200 to be paid at the end of the engagement.

SUNDAY 22 JULY 1951

Charlie Parker does 4 spots as guest soloist with the Woody Herman Orchestra at the Municipal Auditorium in Kansas City while holidaying at his mother's home.

CHARLIE PARKER (alto sax), ROY CATON, DON FAGERQUIST, JOHNNY MACOMBE, DOUG METTOME (trumpet), JERRY DORN, URBIE GREEN, FRED LEWIS (trombone), WOODY HERMAN (alto sax/clarinet), DICK HAFER, BILL PERKINS, KENNY PINSON (tenor sax), SAM STAFF (baritone sax), DAVE McKENNA (piano), RED WOOTTEN (bass), SONNY IGOE (drums)
You Go To My Head / Leo The Lion / Cuban Holiday / The Nearness Of You / Lemon Drop / The Goof And I / Laura / Four Brothers / Leo The Lion / More Moon

AUGUST 1951

During August , Bird makes some private recordings in Lennie Tristano's apartment in New York City.

CHARLIE PARKER (alto sax), LENNIE TRISTANO (piano), KENNY CLARKE (brushes on phone book)
All Of Me / I Can't Believe That You're In Love With Me

FRIDAY 3 AUGUST 1951

Contracts are signed with Associated Booking Corporation and Cleo Elders for Charlie to appear at Union Park Temple, Chicago on 3 September – Labor Day, 9.00pm to 2.00am. $600 guarantee with a privilege of 60%. $350 deposit, balance on night of the engagement. $175 is paid by Elders as part payment on the deposit.

WEDNESDAY 8 AUGUST 1951

Charlie Parker Quintet record at RCA Victor studios in New York for Mercury/Verve.

CHARLIE PARKER (alto sax), RED RODNEY (trumpet), JOHN LEWIS (piano), RAY BROWN (bass), KENNY CLARKE (drums)
Blues For Alice / Si Si / Swedish Schnapps (2 takes) / *Back Home Blues* (2 takes) / *Lover Man*

MONDAY 27 AUGUST 1951

Charlie Parker & Strings open at Lindsay's in Cleveland for a one-week engagement.

WEDNESDAY 29 AUGUST 1951

Charlie Parker's 31st birthday.

Petrillo sends a telegram to Bird at 2.38 PM:

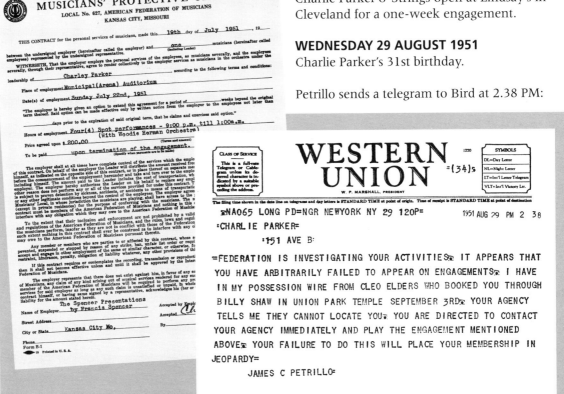

SAT	1	MON	1	THUR	1
SUN	2	TUES	2	FRI	2
MON	3	WED	3	SAT	3
TUES	4	THUR	4	SUN	4
WED	5	FRI	5	MON	5
THUR	6	SAT	6	TUES	6
FRI	7	SUN	7	WED	7
SAT	8	MON	8	THUR	8
SUN	9	TUES	9	FRI	9
MON	10	WED	10	SAT	10
TUES	11	THUR	11	SUN	11
WED	12	FRI	12	MON	12
THUR	13	SAT	13	TUES	13
FRI	14	SUN	14	WED	14
SAT	15	MON	15	THUR	15
SUN	16	TUES	16	FRI	16
MON	17	WED	17	SAT	17
TUES	18	THUR	18	SUN	18
WED	19	FRI	19	MON	19
THUR	20	SAT	20	TUES	20
FRI	21	SUN	21	WED	21
SAT	22	MON	22	THUR	22
SUN	23	TUES	23	FRI	23
MON	24	WED	24	SAT	24
TUES	25	THUR	25	SUN	25
WED	26	FRI	26	MON	26
THUR	27	SAT	27	TUES	27
FRI	28	SUN	28	WED	28
SAT	29	MON	29	THUR	29
SUN	30	TUES	30	FRI	30
		WED	31		

SUNDAY 2 SEPTEMBER 1951
Charlie Parker & Strings close at Lindsay's in Cleveland.

MONDAY 3 SEPTEMBER 1951
Charlie Parker appears as a solo performer at Union Park Temple in Chicago from 9 to 2am for $600.

FRIDAY 7 SEPTEMBER 1951
Charlie Parker Quintet opens at the Apollo Bar on 125th Street for a two-week engagement.

THURSDAY 20 SEPTEMBER 1951
Charlie Parker Quintet closes after a successful two weeks at the Apollo Bar.

SATURDAY 22 SEPTEMBER 1951
Charlie Parker & Strings open at the Blue Note in Chicago for a two-week engagement.

FRIDAY 5 OCTOBER 1951
Charlie Parker & Strings close at the Blue Note in Chicago.

TUESDAY 16 OCTOBER 1951
Charlie Parker & Strings open a 2-night engagement at Johnny Brown's in Pittsburgh.

WEDNESDAY 17 OCTOBER 1951
Charlie Parker & Strings close at Johnny Brown's in Pittsburgh.

SUNDAY 4 NOVEMBER 1951
Charlie Parker & his All Stars – Red Rodney (trumpet), Roy Haynes (drums), Rudy Williams (tenor sax), Teddy Brandon (piano), Bonnie Wetzel (bass) – play a one-nighter at Reynolds Hall in Philadelphia.

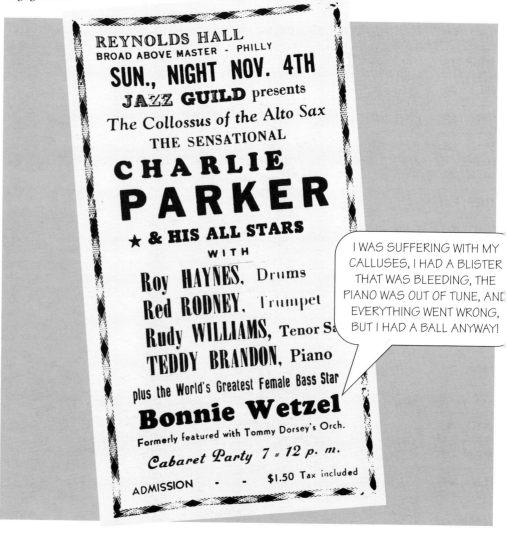

THUR	**1**
FRI	**2**
SAT	**3**
SUN	**4**
MON	**5**
TUES	**6**
WED	**7**
THUR	**8**
FRI	**9**
SAT	**10**
SUN	**11**
MON	**12**
TUES	**13**
WED	**14**
THUR	**15**
FRI	**16**
SAT	**17**
SUN	**18**
MON	**19**
TUES	**20**
WED	**21**
THUR	**22**
FRI	**23**
SAT	**24**
SUN	**25**
MON	**26**
TUES	**27**
WED	**28**
THUR	**29**
FRI	**30**

WEDNESDAY 7 NOVEMBER 1951

Charlie Parker makes an agreement with Shaw Artists Corporation that he is indebted to the sum of $650.17 and will pay in equal payments at the finish of the weeks commencing 19 November, 26 November and 3 December 1951.

He also accepts 3 weeks engagements as follows:
At the SHOWBOAT, Philadelphia, Pennsylvania at a salary of $1300.00 per week;
Two weeks at the LINDSAY SKYBAR, Cleveland, Ohio, at a salary of $1375.00 per week
for a total of $2750.00 for the engagement.
Of the above mentioned sum, there is to be paid to SHAW ARTISTS CORP., the sum of $100.00 per week commission and the sum of $216.66 per week towards paying off the aforementioned indebtedness in full. Upon the making of the above payments, CHARLIE PARKER shall be released from his contract with SHAW ARTISTS CORP., and shall be free to make any arrangements he may desire in connection with his musical career.

MONDAY 19 NOVEMBER 1951

Charlie Parker opens at the Showboat in Philadelphia for a one-week engagement.

SUNDAY 25 NOVEMBER 1951

Charlie Parker closes at the Showboat in Philadelphia.

MONDAY 26 NOVEMBER 1951

Charlie Parker opens at Lindsay's Skybar in Cleveland, Ohio for a two-week engagement.

Below: Jimmy Knepper (trombone) deputises for Red Rodney at the Showboat in Philadelphia. Roy Haynes is on drums.

SAT	1	TUES	1
SUN	2	WED	2
MON	3	THUR	3
TUES	4	FRI	4
WED	5	SAT	5
THUR	6	SUN	6
FRI	7	MON	7
SAT	8	TUES	8
SUN	9	WED	9
MON	10	THUR	10
TUES	11	FRI	11
WED	12	SAT	12
THUR	13	SUN	13
FRI	14	MON	14
SAT	15	TUES	15
SUN	16	WED	16
MON	17	THUR	17
TUES	18	FRI	18
WED	19	SAT	19
THUR	20	SUN	20
FRI	21	MON	21
SAT	22	TUES	22
SUN	23	WED	23
MON	24	THUR	24
TUES	25	FRI	25
WED	26	SAT	26
THUR	27	SUN	27
FRI	28	MON	28
SAT	29	TUES	29
SUN	30	WED	30
MON	31	THUR	31

SUNDAY 9 DECEMBER 1951
Charlie Parker closes at Lindsay's Skybar in Cleveland, Ohio.

Charlie then goes back to Kansas City to visit his mother and to rest. Charlie's mother recalls a redheaded girl who 'pushed dope, and he had met her through one of those numbers on a match cover people were always slipping him'. According to Tootie Clarkin: 'We got word somehow that she was trying to frame him on a narcotics charge for the government. He only had time to play eight bars of 'How High The Moon' when we motioned him off the bandstand and helped him to skip town.'

FRIDAY 4 JANUARY 1952
Charlie Parker Quintet play a one-nighter at the Chateau Gardens on Houston Street in NYC.

WEDNESDAY 23 JANUARY 1952
Charlie Parker & Strings recording session in New York City for Mercury/Verve.
CHARLIE PARKER (alto sax), CHRIS GRIFFIN, AL PORCINO, BERNIE PRIVIN (trumpet), BILL BRADLEY, BILL HARRIS (trombone), TOOTS MONDELLO, MURRAY WILLIAMS (alto sax), HANK ROSS, ART DRELINGER (tenor sax), STANLEY WEBB (baritone sax), VERLEY MILLS (harp), LOU STEIN (piano), ART RYERSON (guitar), BOB HAGGART (bass), DON LAMOND (drums), unknown string section, JOE LIPPMAN (arranger/conductor)
Temptation / Lover / Autumn In New York / Stella By Starlight

Above: Bird in Kansas City with Red Rodney (3rd right).

FRIDAY 25 JANUARY 1952
Down Beat's Jack Tracy reviews a 2-volume LP of Charlie on Savoy:

CHARLIE PARKER
Now's The Time / Donna Lee / Chasing The Bird / Red Cross / Ko-Ko / Warming Up A Riff / Half Nelson / Sipping At Bell's
Billie's Bounce / Cheryl / Milestones / Another Hair-Do / Thriving On A Riff / Buzzy / Little Willie Leaps / Klaunstance
Two volumes of Charlie Parker reissues on Savoy that offer an immense amount of Birdlore. Some of Parker's greatest sides, most of which have become well-nigh unavailable on 78 rpm, are now here on LP. Though we're getting late to them, they're well worth mentioning.

There are incalculable riches here. And the great session with Dizzy, Curly Russell, and Max Roach that resulted in *Warming Up A Riff* and *Ko-Ko*, the two wonderful flights on Cherokee's changes, rates right at the top.

Though most of these don't have the polish and ensemble ease of later Bird records, many contain the fire and inventiveness of Parker at his best, which is more than enough reason to see that you own them. (Savoy LPs MG 9000 and 9001.)

MONDAY 28 JANUARY 1952
Charlie Parker Septet recording session in New York City for Mercury/Verve.
CHARLIE PARKER (alto sax), BENNY HARRIS (trumpet), WALTER BISHOP (piano), TEDDY KOTICK (bass), MAX ROACH (drums), LUIS MIRANDA (conga), JOSE MANGUEL (bongos)
Mama Inez / La Cucaracha (4 takes) / *Estrellita* (4 takes) / *Begin The Beguine / La Paloma*

FRI **1**

SAT **2**

SUN **3**

MON **4**

TUES **5**

WED **6**

THUR **7**

FRI **8**

SAT **9**

SUN **10**

MON **11**

TUES **12**

WED **13**

THUR **14**

FRI **15**

SAT **16**

SUN **17**

MON **18**

TUES **19**

WED **20**

THUR **21**

FRI **22**

SAT **23**

SUN **24**

MON **25**

TUES **26**

WED **27**

THUR **28**

FRI **29**

SUNDAY 24 FEBRUARY 1952

Charlie Parker and Dizzy Gillespie appear on a TV programme on Channel 5, New York. They are presented with *Down Beat* plaques by Earl Wilson and Leonard Feather before playing a number with the resident pianist Dick Hyman. This is the only known surviving film of Parker actually playing.

EARL WILSON: *Here they are, this is Charlie Parker and the famous Dizzy Gillespie. Now, fellas, Leonard says I'm supposed to be the toastmaster... the sort of Georgie Jessel of jazz. So Charlie, I want to award you now the Down Beat award for the best alto sax man of 1951. Congratulations to you. And Diz, this is to you from Down Beat for being one of the top trumpet men of all time. Congratulations Diz, I mean Dizzy, I got a little informal there. Er... you boys got anything more to say?*

CHARLIE PARKER: Well, Earl, they say music speaks louder than words, so we'd rather voice our opinion that way... if you don't mind.

EARL WILSON: *I think that'd be all right with everybody if you really wanna do it. OK, now while you fellas are getting up there, I'd better tell the public... we're gonna hear some really torrid tempo with Charlie Parker (alto sax), Diz at the trumpet and Dick Hyman at the piano... they're gonna play... what is it?*

LEONARD FEATHER: *I think it's 'Hot House'.*

EARL WILSON: *Hot House? OK fellas, let's go.*

CHARLIE PARKER (alto sax), DIZZY GILLESPIE (trumpet), DICK HYMAN (piano), SANDY BLOCK (bass), CHARLIE SMITH (drums)
Hot House

Below: Bird receives his Down Beat award from Earl Wilson (l). Looking on are Leonard Feather and Dizzy Gillespie.
Right: Bird solos on 'Hot House'. The drummer is Charlie Smith.

SAT	**1**	TUES	**1**
SUN	**2**	WED	**2**
MON	**3**	THUR	**3**
TUES	**4**	FRI	**4**
WED	**5**	SAT	**5**
THUR	**6**	SUN	**6**
FRI	**7**	MON	**7**
SAT	**8**	TUES	**8**
SUN	**9**	WED	**9**
MON	**10**	THUR	**10**
TUES	**11**	FRI	**11**
WED	**12**	SAT	**12**
THUR	**13**	SUN	**13**
FRI	**14**	MON	**14**
SAT	**15**	TUES	**15**
SUN	**16**	WED	**16**
MON	**17**	THUR	**17**
TUES	**18**	FRI	**18**
WED	**19**	SAT	**19**
THUR	**20**	SUN	**20**
FRI	**21**	MON	**21**
SAT	**22**	TUES	**22**
SUN	**23**	WED	**23**
MON	**24**	THUR	**24**
TUES	**25**	FRI	**25**
WED	**26**	SAT	**26**
THUR	**27**	SUN	**27**
FRI	**28**	MON	**28**
SAT	**29**	TUES	**29**
SUN	**30**	WED	**30**
MON	**31**		

Above: Bird and Chan at Birdland. Chan is pregnant with Baird.

TUESDAY 25 MARCH 1952

Charlie Parker Big Band recording session in New York City for Mercury/Verve

CHARLIE PARKER (alto sax), JIMMY MAXWELL, CARL POOLE, AL PORCINO, BERNIE PRIVEN (trumpet), BILL HARRIS, LOU McGARITY, BART VARSALONA (trombone), HARRY TERRILL, MURRAY WILLIAMS (alto sax), FLIP PHILLIPS, HANK ROSS (tenor sax), DANNY BANKS (baritone sax), OSCAR PETERSON (piano), FREDDIE GREENE (guitar), RAY BROWN (bass), DON LAMOND (drums), JOE LIPPMAN (arranger/conductor)

Night And Day / Almost Like Being In Love / I Can't Get Started / What Is This Thing Called Love?

In the evening Charlie appears in a Jerry Jerome Concert at Loew's Valencia Theatre in Jamaica, New York.

CHARLIE PARKER (alto sax), BUDDY DE FRANCO (clarinet), BILL HARRIS (trombone), DICK CARY (piano), EDDIE SAFRANSKI (bass), DON LAMOND (drums)

Ornithology

CHARLIE PARKER (alto sax), TEDDY WILSON (piano), EDDIE SAFRANSKI (bass), DON LAMOND (drums)

Cool Blues

FRIDAY 4 APRIL 1952

Contracts are signed for the Charlie Parker Quintet to appear at the Howard Theatre, Washington D.C. for 1 week from 18 April for $1275. Rehearsal promptly at 8.30am on opening day of the engagement.

FRIDAY 18 APRIL 1952

Charlie Parker Quintet – Kenny Dorham, Walter Bishop, Teddy Kotick, Stan Levey – open at the Howard Theatre, Washington D.C. for a one-week engagement.

WEDNESDAY 23 APRIL 1952

Charlie Parker sends a Western Union Money Order message to Chan from Washington D.C.

TAKE CARE OF YOURSELF FOR ME LOVE

THURSDAY 24 APRIL 1952

Charlie Parker Quintet close at the Howard Theatre, Washington D.C.

THUR	1
FRI	2
SAT	3
SUN	4
MON	5
TUES	6
WED	7
THUR	8
FRI	9
SAT	10
SUN	11
MON	12
TUES	13
WED	14
THUR	15
FRI	16
SAT	17
SUN	18
MON	19
TUES	20
WED	21
THUR	22
FRI	23
SAT	24
SUN	25
MON	26
TUES	27
WED	28
THUR	29
FRI	30
SAT	31

WEDNESDAY 7 MAY 1952

Down Beat reviews Charlie's latest record release:

CHARLIE PARKER
** Star Eyes
*** Au Privave

Nothing much happens on *Star Eyes*, but turn it over and
catch some bop reminiscent of the halcyon days. Bird, Miles,
young Walter Bishop (the songsmith's pianist son) and Max
all blow their best on this fast blues. Teddy Kotick completes
the quintet. The title, we understand on unimpeachable
authority, means nothing. (**Mercury 11087**)

MAY 1952

Charlie Parker plays a week at the Times Square Hotel
in Rochester, NY with the house rhythm section. On
the Wednesday, Art Taylor and Walter Bishop are
imported to salvage the week.

THURSDAY 29 MAY 1952

Charlie Parker opens at the Tiffany Club in Los
Angeles.

*Below: Bird on stage at the Tiffany Club in LA with 22 year
old Chet Baker on trumpet and Harry Babasin on bass.*

Bird Flies To LA's Tiffany

Hollywood—Charlie Parker, who
hasn't made an appearance in Los
Angeles for several years, opened
at the Tiffany club starting May
29.

Chuck Landis, operator of the
Tiffany, has sold his other nitery,
the Surf. He said: "In trying to
run two jazz clubs here I was just
competing with myself."

Landis has Nat Cole set for the
Tiffany starting July 3, and Louis
Jordan, who hasn't played a local
spot for a long time, coming in
July 28.

SUN	1
MON	2
TUES	3
WED	4
THUR	5
FRI	6
SAT	7
SUN	8
MON	9
TUES	10
WED	11
THUR	12
FRI	13
SAT	14
SUN	15
MON	16
TUES	17
WED	18
THUR	19
FRI	20
SAT	21
SUN	22
MON	23
TUES	24
WED	25
THUR	26
FRI	27
SAT	28
SUN	29
MON	30

THURSDAY 5 JUNE 1952

Jazz at the Philharmonic recording session for Norman Granz in Los Angeles.

CHARLIE PARKER, BENNY CARTER, JOHNNY HODGES (alto sax), BEN WEBSTER, FLIP PHILLIPS (tenor sax), CHARLIE SHAVERS (trumpet), OSCAR PETERSON (piano), BARNEY KESSEL (guitar), RAY BROWN (bass), J.C.HEARD (drums)
Jam Blues / What Is This Thing Called Love? / Ballad Medley / Funky Blues

Esther Bubley takes photographs as a guest of David Stone Martin who designs the album cover.

Charlie Parker sends a Western Union Money Order message to Chan from Los Angeles.

LOVE MISS AND NEED YOU WILL WRITE SOON

3 Alto Kings In Granz Date

New York—Norman Granz cut a jazz session recently that stacks up as the most provocative of the past several months. Granz managed to get together within one unit the three sparkplugs of the jazz alto sax field—Charlie Parker, Johnny Hodges, and Benny Carter.

To round out the session, Granz used tenorists Flip Phillips, and Ben Webster, trumpeter Charlie Shavers, pianist Oscar Peterson, guitarist Barney Kessel, bassist Ray Brown, and drummer J. C. Heard.

The slicings made at the session were all cut for LP length, with four sides expected to come out of the bash. One of the unusual aspects of the session was Granz's handling of a ballad side. He got each of the men gathered to blow a chorus of their favorite ballad, rather than run down a single tune. The disks will be put on the market sometime in the early fall.

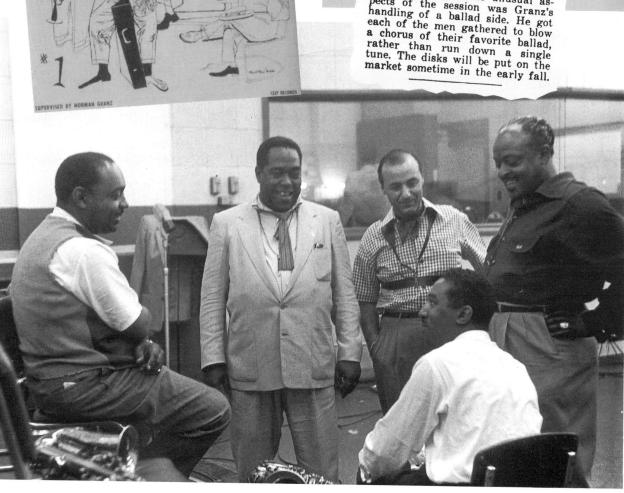

SUN	**1**
MON	**2**
TUES	**3**
WED	**4**
THUR	**5**
FRI	**6**
SAT	**7**
SUN	**8**
MON	**9**
TUES	**10**
WED	**11**
THUR	**12**
FRI	**13**
SAT	**14**
SUN	**15**
MON	**16**
TUES	**17**
WED	**18**
THUR	**19**
FRI	**20**
SAT	**21**
SUN	**22**
MON	**23**
TUES	**24**
WED	**25**
THUR	**26**
FRI	**27**
SAT	**28**
SUN	**29**
MON	**30**

WESTERN UNION
MONEY ORDER MESSAGE
QUICK SERVICE — LOW RATES
Money Sent by Telegraph and Cable to All the World
W. P. MARSHALL, PRESIDENT

Form 3308C

N₀ NA134   137 AVE A   DATE JUNE 5 19 52
OFFICE

To MRS CHAN PARKER   TRANSIT TIME OF THIS MONEY ORDER MINUTES

151 AVE B   ADDRESS   CHARLES PARKER
NAME

The Money Order paid you herewith is from

at WN LOSANGELES CALIF   and included the following message:

LOVE MISS AND NEED YOU WILL WRITE SOON.

THE WESTERN UNION TELEGRAPH COMPANY

SATURDAY 14 JUNE 1952
Charlie Parker closes at the Tiffany Club in Los Angeles

MONDAY 16 JUNE 1952
Charlie Parker is featured with the Harry Babasin All Stars at the Trade Winds Club in Inglewood, California. The session is privately recorded.
CHARLIE PARKER, SONNY CRISS (alto sax), CHET BAKER (trumpet), DONN TRENIER, RUSS FREEMAN (piano), HARRY BABASIN (bass), LAWRENCE MARABLE (drums)
The Squirrel / Irresistible You / Indiana (Donna Lee) / Liza

Billy Shaw writes to Charlie Parker:
c/o Say When Club, 952 Busch Street, San Francisco:

SAC

SHAW ARTISTS CORPORATION
BILLY SHAW, President

565 FIFTH AVENUE   •   NEW YORK 17, N. Y.
MUrray Hill 8-2230   Cable Address "Shawart"
NEW YORK   •   CHICAGO   •   HOLLYWOOD

June 16, 1952

Mr. Charlie Parker
c/o Say When Club
952 Busch Street
San Francisco Calif.

Dear Charlie:

I understand that you are back to your old tricks again, making various promises, and not living up to them.

When you were in my office, you signed deduction orders, and asked me to have your money sent here; now, I understand you threatened to walk out if there were any deductions, etc. Also understand you made some very ugly remarks about me.

In the first place, Charlie, rest assured I will not take your word again in the future; as a matter of fact, we do not have to worry about anything but our own monies. We advanced you transportation money to California, and you only allowed them to deduct our commissions.

We are instructing Cliff Aronson to deduct the transportation we advanced you, our commissions, plus the $15.00 per week on the old balance. I am sending a copy of this letter to Cliff Aronson.

Charlie, you are indebted to us in the sum of $734.98. You promised to give us $15.00 a week towards the balance; since you are getting $750.00 a week, I am sure you can spare a stinking $15. per week. In the event you give Cliff Aronson anymore trouble with regarding the deductions orders, we will be forced to take this up with the Federation. As far as I am concerned, your word doesn't mean a thing to me anymore; we have tried to help you in every way, but to no avail. I am tired of always getting a run around.

Sincerely

Billy Shaw

BILLY SHAW

BS:BM

SUN	1
MON	2
TUES	3
WED	4
THUR	5
FRI	6
SAT	7
SUN	8
MON	9
TUES	10
WED	11
THUR	12
FRI	13
SAT	14
SUN	15
MON	16
TUES	17
WED	18
THUR	19
FRI	20
SAT	21
SUN	22
MON	23
TUES	24
WED	25
THUR	26
FRI	27
SAT	28
SUN	29
MON	30

WEDNESDAY 18 JUNE 1952

Charlie's latest record release:

CHARLIE PARKER
** Autumn In New York
** Temptation

The resplendent sheen of novelty and excitement that coated Bird's string experiments, back in the days when they were experiments, seems to have worn off. Whether because the freshness has worn off or because the arrangements are logey and a little pretentious, there's no real excitement here.

Charlie's tone is loud and unsubtle and the only mild surprise is the insertion of a couple of solos by other horns, for the first time in this series — a trombone bit here, a trumpet there.

Charlie should have made that first fine album with strings and then moved on to something new. He is too great a musician to get into a rut. (**Mercury 11068.**)

THURSDAY 19 JUNE 1952

Charlie Parker opens at the Say When Club in San Francisco.

SUNDAY 29 JUNE 1952

San Francisco Chronicle reports:

> **Charlie Parker has been missing an occasional act at the Say When but he hasn't missed many at that after-hours spot he hits each morning...**

Down Beat reviews the show at the Say When:

The heralded Charlie Parker-Flip Phillips battle-of-the-saxes at the Say When disintegrated into one of the most miserable foul-ups in local history. Both instrumentalists were salty at having to work with the house band and Parker finally brought in a unit of his own. Flip and the club parted company after the first week, both being wholeheartedly dissatisfied. Parker remained for part of the next week, but that ended in a Class "A" hassle. After appearing twice on the Cerebral Palsy TV marathon, Parker took up a collection in the club, asked club op Dutch Neiman for a contribution, was refused (because Neiman said he had already contributed), took the mike, called the house "cheap" and then Neiman and the Bird engaged in a gentle shoving contest with Parker losing. Neiman refused to pay him off and Bird was stranded in town for almost a week. The mix-up was still being batted around at the union at presstime.

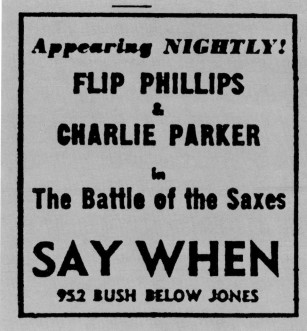

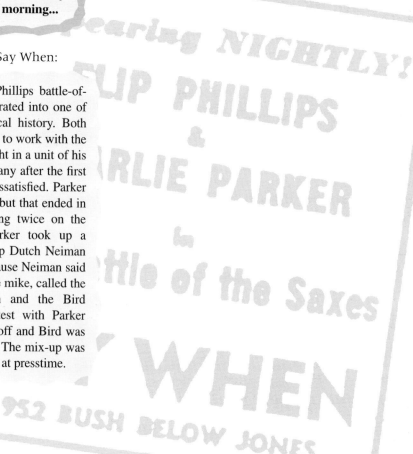

TUES	**1**	FRI	**1**
WED	**2**	SAT	**2**
THUR	**3**	SUN	**3**
FRI	**4**	MON	**4**
SAT	**5**	TUES	**5**
SUN	**6**	WED	**6**
MON	**7**	THUR	**7**
TUES	**8**	FRI	**8**
WED	**9**	SAT	**9**
THUR	**10**	SUN	**10**
FRI	**11**	MON	**11**
SAT	**12**	TUES	**12**
SUN	**13**	WED	**13**
MON	**14**	THUR	**14**
TUES	**15**	FRI	**15**
WED	**16**	SAT	**16**
THUR	**17**	SUN	**17**
FRI	**18**	MON	**18**
SAT	**19**	TUES	**19**
SUN	**20**	WED	**20**
MON	**21**	THUR	**21**
TUES	**22**	FRI	**22**
WED	**23**	SAT	**23**
THUR	**24**	SUN	**24**
FRI	**25**	MON	**25**
SAT	**26**	TUES	**26**
SUN	**27**	WED	**27**
MON	**28**	THUR	**28**
TUES	**29**	FRI	**29**
WED	**30**	SAT	**30**
THUR	**31**	SUN	**31**

THURSDAY 3 JULY 1952

Charlie Parker closes at the Say When Club in San Francisco.

TUESDAY 8 JULY 1952

Charlie is recorded during a session at Zorthian's Ranch in Altadena.

CHARLIE PARKER, FRANK MORGAN (alto sax), DON WILKERSON (tenor sax), AMOS TRICE (piano), DAVE BRYANT (bass), LAWRENCE MARABLE (drums)

Scrapple From The Apple / Au Privave / Dance Of The Infidels

WEDNESDAY 9 JULY 1952

Charlie Parker sends a Western Union Money Order message to Chan from Los Angeles.

`I LOVE YOU BELIEVE IN ME`

MONDAY 14 JULY 1952

Charlie is again recorded during a session at Zorthian's Ranch in Altadena.

CHARLIE PARKER, FRANK MORGAN (alto sax), DON WILKERSON (tenor sax), AMOS TRICE (piano), DAVE BRYANT (bass), LAWRENCE MARABLE (drums)

Hot House / Embraceable You / Night In Tunisia / How High The Moon (Ornithology)

MONDAY 28 JULY 1952

Charlie is again recorded during a session at Zorthian's Ranch in Altadena, joined for one number by Chet Baker on trumpet.

CHARLIE PARKER, FRANK MORGAN (alto sax), DON WILKERSON (tenor sax), AMOS TRICE (piano), DAVE BRYANT (bass), LAWRENCE MARABLE (drums)

Cool Blues / Dixie, Yankee Doodle / Scrapple From The Apple (CHET BAKER added)

SUNDAY 10 AUGUST 1952

Chan gives birth to a son, Charles Baird Parker (7lbs 6oz) in New York City.

THURSDAY 14 AUGUST 1952

Charlie writes to James Petrillo of the AF of M:

> Dear Sir and Brother,
>
> I hereby request a stay of judgement so that I may file an appeal against the decision of Local 767 in fining me $350.00, of this amount $250.00 is held in abeyance. However, I am a family man and have been out of work for a long time and find it impossible to pay this amount.
>
> Fraternally yours,
>
> *Charlie Parker*
>
> Charlie Parker

FRIDAY 29 AUGUST 1952

Charlie Parker's 32nd birthday.

MON	**1**
TUES	**2**
WED	**3**
THUR	**4**
FRI	**5**
SAT	**6**
SUN	**7**
MON	**8**
TUES	**9**
WED	**10**
THUR	**11**
FRI	**12**
SAT	**13**
SUN	**14**
MON	**15**
TUES	**16**
WED	**17**
THUR	**18**
FRI	**19**
SAT	**20**
SUN	**21**
MON	**22**
TUES	**23**
WED	**24**
THUR	**25**
FRI	**26**
SAT	**27**
SUN	**28**
MON	**29**
TUES	**30**

FRIDAY 12 SEPTEMBER 1952
Charlie plays on an excursion boat SS Peter Stuyvesant.

SATURDAY 20 SEPTEMBER 1952
Charlie Parker Quartet broadcast from Birdland.
CHARLIE PARKER (alto sax), DUKE JORDAN (piano), CHARLES MINGUS (bass), PHIL BROWN (drums)
Ornithology / 52nd Street Theme

WEDNESDAY 24 SEPTEMBER 1952
Leo Cluesmann of the A F of M writes to Dutch Neiman, manager of the Say When Club in San Francisco, advising him that Charlie Parker is filing charges against him.

Down Beat carries reviews of Charlie's latest record releases:

CHARLIE PARKER
*** Stella By Starlight
**** Lover
Joe Lipmann handles the strings and arrangements on two of Bird's better recent big-band sides. *Lover*, the first wild-tempo thing Charlie has done with strings, has him blowing brilliantly, swinging the band right off its plodding feet, and leaving room for good solos by Bill Harris and pianist Lou Stein. This could have been an even better side with just a straight swinging band sans strings. **(Mercury 11089.)**

Bird and Diz
Leap Frog / An Oscar For Treadwell / Mohawk / Visa / Bloomdido / Melancholy Baby / Relaxing With Lee / Passport
Album Rating: ****
A collation of numbers previously issued as singles, this presents the two bop pioneers along with Monk, Curly Russell and Buddy Rich, except *Passport* and *Visa*. Latter two have Kinny Dorham, Max Roach, Al Haig and Tommy Potter with Bird, though they get no album credit. Though there is no mention of the word bop in Norman Granz' notes, we owe him a salvo for reminding us through this LP that this music is still very much alive. **(Mercury LP C-512)**

FRIDAY 26 SEPTEMBER 1952
Charlie Parker Quintet plus Strings play a one-nighter at the Rockland Palace Ballroom in Harlem, New York City. The dance is a benefit for Benjamin Davis, an attorney and City Council Officer, the last Communist to hold elected office in the US. Davis had been sentenced to 5 years and had become a cause célèbre. Chan records the evening on the tape recorder Bird has given her as a birthday present.

CHARLIE PARKER (alto sax), WALTER BISHOP (piano), MUNDELL LOWE (guitar), TEDDY KOTICK (bass), MAX ROACH (drums), unknown oboe and string section
This Time The Dream's On Me / Cool Blues / Noodling / I'll Remember April / Laura / What Is This Thing Called Love? / Noodling / My Little Suede Shoes / Lester Leaps In / I Didn't Know What Time It Was / Repetition / Just Friends / Rocker / April In Paris / Out Of Nowhere / Rocker / East Of The Sun / Sly Mongoose / Moose The Mooche / Stardust / Easy To Love / Dancing In The Dark / Just Friends / Ornithology / Don't Blame Me / What Is This Thing Called Love? / Everything Happens To Me / Repetition / Gold Rush / Star Eyes / East Of The Sun / 52nd Street Theme / Scrapple From The Apple / Scrapple From The Apple / Easy To Love / Repetition / Sly Mongoose

SATURDAY 27 SEPTEMBER 1952
Dutch Neiman, manager of the Say When Club in San Francisco, writes to Leo Cluesmann:

```
Re: Case 623, 1952-53

Dear Sir, In reply to your letter of September 24th,
regarding charges filed against me by CHARLIE PARKER.

With respect to claims, checks No 1480-1489 were issued
to Mr. Parker on June 23rd, and 30th for $750.00 each,
leaving a balance due at that time for three (3) days
only. The food bills, and personal withdrawals plus
advances paid to his musicians more than offset any
salaries Mr. Parker had coming.

I would like to say at this opportunity that Mr. Parker
was not authorized at any time to collect any monies for
the Cerebral Palsy drive. In fact said collection was
taken one and a half hours after the drive had closed.
Mr. Parker was "loaded", and promised the audience I
would give $50.00. After I refused to give $50.00, he
went back to the bandstand, and told the people I was a
no good "son of a .....". This is when I pulled him off
of the stand. At no time during the length of the
engagement was he ever on time, and when he did come he
was always "loaded". As a matter of fact Mr.Forbes was
in the club twice, and told him the next time he came in
at 11.00 PM he would take him off of the job.

Regarding the extract from the San Francisco Chronicle,
the interview was given by Mr. Parker directly to the
headquarters of the paper. The statements are his, and
are not true. Also the night after he left the 'Say When
Club', he went to the 'Blackhawk' and played, sending
someone to the 'Say When Club' to tell the customers he
was appearing at the 'Blackhawk'. Naturally we lost
customers who had come to hear this particular artist.

Very truly yours,

DUTCH NEIMAN Manager
SAY WHEN CLUB.
```

WED	**1**
THUR	**2**
FRI	**3**
SAT	**4**
SUN	**5**
MON	**6**
TUES	**7**
WED	**8**
THUR	**9**
FRI	**10**
SAT	**11**
SUN	**12**
MON	**13**
TUES	**14**
WED	**15**
THUR	**16**
FRI	**17**
SAT	**18**
SUN	**19**
MON	**20**
TUES	**21**
WED	**22**
THUR	**23**
FRI	**24**
SAT	**25**
SUN	**26**
MON	**27**
TUES	**28**
WED	**29**
THUR	**30**
FRI	**31**

WEDNESDAY 1 OCTOBER 1952

A. V. Forbes, Secretary of Local 669 AF of M writes to Leo Cluesmann:

Re: Case No 406, 1952-53

Dear Sir and Brother:

In reply to your letter of September 23rd, Our rebuttal regarding the CHARLIE PARKER case in the matter of charges preferred by us against him for violations of the laws of the A F of M are:

Regarding Paragraph (1):

The 'Say When Club' had their own five (5) men, but when Parker arrived he brought two (2) men; a trumpet man from Local 47, and a drummer from Local 767, and said he worked with these men only. After the first night, he got two (2) local men; piano and bass. I called the Milton Deutsch Agency, and they informed me that this was unknown to them, they booked Parker alone. I called Parker, and he promised to come in with the contract on three (3) different occasions, but failed to do so. I then went on his job, and he agreed to come in the office, and make a contract.

Regarding Paragraph (2):

He did collect his salary, for the Business Agent of Local 6, and myself talked with him at the Club, at which time he promised he would be in the office the following day, and pay his 10% surcharges; at first he claimed he didn't know he was supposed to pay it. Again he failed to come in. When I called him he said he wasn't coming in to pay tax or anything else.

Regarding Paragraph (3):

He played the entire evening at the 'Blackhawk', for Vido Musso called the following evening pleading that he only wanted to help Charlie, and there was no intention on his part of breaking any local law, but Charlie needed money. I asked Musso how much was paid Parker, and he said he was going to give him some money to get home with, and wouldn't we assist since his (Parker's) home Local would not advance him any monies. I then informed Musso that if he allowed Parker to play again, charges would be brought against him.

Regarding Paragraph (4):

He not only intended to ignore the Local, but was most insulting to the officers, and created a scene which was unprovoked. As for his conduct both at the Club, and the Local, it was without precedent. The man appeared constantly under the influence of something.

Fraternally yours,
A. V. Forbes, Sec Local 669 AFM

FRIDAY 3 OCTOBER 1952

Charlie Parker writes to Leo Cluesmann:

Dear Sir and Brother:

In reply to the copy of the letter sent to me through your office from Dutch Neiman, manager of the Say When Club, September 27, 1952; point by point, Mr Neiman claims I received two checks for $750 each which was my salary per week. I only worked a week and four days, was paid for the first week, was not paid for the extra four days. The full contract read two weeks, three days. There were no food bills or personal withdrawals, and only one check was

issued me.

Point number two: Mr Neiman was informed of the collection of monies incident for the Cerebral Palsy Fund, and I asked Mr Neiman if it was all right to say he would contribute with the people. To which he agreed.

Not understanding thoroughly the meaning of the word loaded which he mentions in his reply... If he means intoxicated, I finished my engagement that particular night satisfactorily to the people in the club. Furthermore the only drinking that was done by me in the club that night was sponsored by one or two parties at most. Certainly not enough to get drunk.

As far as my making time is concerned, at the end of the first week Mr Neiman told me himself, Quote, "Good work Charlie. It was a good week. I made money. Keep it up."

His accusation concerning the write-up in the San Francisco Chronicle, that I went directly to the headquarters of the paper can be proven false merely by contacting the columnist who wrote same.

The night after I left the Say When Club I did not play in the Blackhawk or anywhere else. As far as his losing customers is concerned, Mr Neiman used my name for the fulfilment of the contract.

Monies owed me by Mr. Neiman amount to $1,125. That is the fulfilment of contract price. Mr Neiman first fired my band without my knowledge, and the next night when I came to report for work he said my services were no longer required.

These are the facts of the case in its entirety.

Thanking you for the chance to explain it as it really was, I remain your friend and brother.

CHARLIE PARKER

TUESDAY 7 OCTOBER 1952

Charlie replies to the letter from A. V. Forbes.

FRIDAY 17 OCTOBER 1952

Charlie Parker appears at a midnight show 'Jazz at Midnight' at the Howard Theatre in Washington.
A private recording is made.
CHARLIE PARKER (alto sax), EARL SWOPE (trombone), CHARLIE BYRD (guitar), BILL SHANAHAN (piano), MERTON OLIVER (bass), DON LAMOND (drums), UNKNOWN (bongos). CHARLIE WALP (trumpet), ZOOT SIMS (tenor sax) and ROB SWOPE (trombone) are added on *Now's The Time* and the first version of *Cool Blues*.
Scrapple From The Apple / Out Of Nowhere / Now's The Time / 52nd Street Theme / Cool Blues / Cool Blues

TUESDAY 21 OCTOBER 1952

Charlie Parker appears at the Metropolitan Hall, Philadelphia. Charlie is due to be paid $450 for the engagement, but promoter Herb Gordy only pays him $100 deposit and promises to pay the balance in a few days. The dispute is to rumble on for two years.

SAT	**1**
SUN	**2**
MON	**3**
TUES	**4**
WED	**5**
THUR	**6**
FRI	**7**
SAT	**8**
SUN	**9**
MON	**10**
TUES	**11**
WED	**12**
THUR	**13**
FRI	**14**
SAT	**15**
SUN	**16**
MON	**17**
TUES	**18**
WED	**19**
THUR	**20**
FRI	**21**
SAT	**22**
SUN	**23**
MON	**24**
TUES	**25**
WED	**26**
THUR	**27**
FRI	**28**
SAT	**29**
SUN	**30**

SATURDAY 1 NOVEMBER 1952

Charlie Parker and the Milt Jackson Quartet broadcast from Birdland, New York City.

CHARLIE PARKER (alto sax), MILT JACKSON (vibes), JOHN LEWIS (piano), PERCY HEATH (bass), KENNY CLARKE (drums), BOB GARRITY (announcer)

How High The Moon / Embraceable You / 52nd Street Theme

FRIDAY 14 NOVEMBER 1952

Charlie Parker appears in two concerts at Carnegie Hall, New York, on an All Star bill including Duke Ellington, Billie Holiday, Dizzy Gillespie, Stan Getz and Ahmad Jamal.

WNBC Radio broadcast both concerts, introduced by Bob Garrity.

First Concert: CHARLIE PARKER (alto sax), WALTER BISHOP (piano), WALTER YOST (bass), ROY HAYNES (drums), CANDIDO (conga), TEDDY BLUME (violin), Unknown string section

Just Friends / Easy To Love / Repetition / Strings Theme

Second Concert: CHARLIE PARKER (alto sax), WALTER BISHOP (piano), WALTER YOST (bass), ROY HAYNES (drums), CANDIDO (conga), TEDDY BLUME (violin), Unknown string section plus DIZZY GILLESPIE (trumpet) on *Night In Tunisia* and *52nd Street Theme*.

Just Friends / Easy To Love / Repetition / Strings Theme / Night In Tunisia / 52nd Street Theme

Bill Coss reviews the concert in *Metronome*:

> As the [Ahmad Jamal] trio left the stage, four violinists, one cellist, one harpist, an English hornist and a three-man rhythm section filed on, followed, naturally enough by Charlie Parker. This was a paucity of strings, considering Carnegie's size, but Charlie has never been in better form. *Just Friends* and *Easy To Love* were especially lovely; *Repetition*, with Candido on bongos and conga, was nearly the high spot in the evening for me. This was The Bird with the longest wing span.

WEDNESDAY 19 NOVEMBER 1952

Charlie Parker signs a contract to appear at Springfield Auditorium, Springfield, Massachusetts on 5 December.

Below: A shy young visitor to the Carnegie Hall dressing rooms is entertained by Tony Scott, Billie Holiday and Bird.

MON	**1**
TUES	**2**
WED	**3**
THUR	**4**
FRI	**5**
SAT	**6**
SUN	**7**
MON	**8**
TUES	**9**
WED	**10**
THUR	**11**
FRI	**12**
SAT	**13**
SUN	**14**
MON	**15**
TUES	**16**
WED	**17**
THUR	**18**
FRI	**19**
SAT	**20**
SUN	**21**
MON	**22**
TUES	**23**
WED	**24**
THUR	**25**
FRI	**26**
SAT	**27**
SUN	**28**
MON	**29**
TUES	**30**
WED	**31**

MONDAY 1 DECEMBER 1952

Herb Gordy, promoter of the Met Hall engagement in Philadelphia, sends a telegram to Charlie at 3.10 PM:

CHARLIE PARKER
151 AVE B

JUST GOT JOB EVERYONE HAS ATTACHED MY
SALARY WILL RUSH MONEY TO YOU AS SOON
AS I CAN GET IT GIVE ME MORE TIME

HERB GORDY

TUESDAY 2 DECEMBER 1952

The AF of M write to Charlie concerning the Say When affair, fining him $100.

FRIDAY 5 DECEMBER 1952

Charlie Parker appears at Springfield Auditorium, Springfield, Massachusetts. Charlie makes two appearances during the evening, backed by the Milt Buckner Trio (Milt Buckner, organ; Bernie McKay, guitar; Cornelius Thomas, drums), for a fee of $300.

SUNDAY 7 DECEMBER 1952

Charlie Parker and his band play a one-nighter at the Hunts Point Palace in the Bronx.

MONDAY 8 DECEMBER 1952

Charlie Parker opens at the Hi Hat Club in Boston.

TUESDAY 9 DECEMBER 1952

Charlie sends a Western Union Money Order message to Chan from Boston:

WILL CALL LATER TONITE LOVE FOREVER BIRD

THURSDAY 11 DECEMBER 1952

Charlie sends a Western Union Money Order message to Chan from Boston:

DARLING KEEP IN TOUCH WITH ME ALL MY LOVE

SATURDAY 13 DECEMBER 1952

Charlie sends a Western Union Money Order message to Chan from Boston:

FOREVER YOURS BIRD

SUNDAY 14 DECEMBER 1952

Charlie Parker closes at the Hi Hat Club in Boston.

TUESDAY 30 DECEMBER 1952

Charlie Parker Quartet recording session in New York City for Verve.
CHARLIE PARKER (alto sax), HANK JONES (piano), TEDDY KOTICK (bass), MAX ROACH (drums)
The Song Is You / Laird Baird / Kim (2 takes) / *Cosmic Rays* (2 takes)

THUR	**1**
FRI	**2**
SAT	**3**
SUN	**4**
MON	**5**
TUES	**6**
WED	**7**
THUR	**8**
FRI	**9**
SAT	**10**
SUN	**11**
MON	**12**
TUES	**13**
WED	**14**
THUR	**15**
FRI	**16**
SAT	**17**
SUN	**18**
MON	**19**
TUES	**20**
WED	**21**
THUR	**22**
FRI	**23**
SAT	**24**
SUN	**25**
MON	**26**
TUES	**27**
WED	**28**
THUR	**29**
FRI	**30**
SAT	**31**

FRIDAY 23 JANUARY 1953

Joe Maini writes from Los Angeles:

Dear Bird, Chan, Kim etc ?

It felt good to get your warm letter while I was in the "hospital". Nep [Jimmy Knepper] and I got out Nov 17th. I have become a solid citizen and good musician. No more raucous living for me. That 16 months changed me.

About you, I hope everything is fine. I sure miss you. I'm still buying your records (even though I got no box). I'm looking forward to seeing you although it'll be a little while before I can split to the "apple". Jerry Mulligan is making a lot of money out here. He's got a small group with no piano. I played with him the other night on his gig and it was a lot of fun. Sure is pretty weather we're having here – warm – Nep and I have a small library for alto, tenor, trom and 3 rhythm. Can't seem to find a tenor man who can read them. All my love and best wishes to you all.

Joe Maini

SUNDAY 25 JANUARY 1953

Charlie signs a contract with N. R. Wattam of the New Jazz Society of Toronto to appear at a Massey Hall concert on Friday 15 May, 8.30–11.00 pm. $200 guarantee plus 21.7% of the musicians share of the net profit. $200 to be paid before commencement of the engagement; percentage immediately after engagement.

TUESDAY 27 JANUARY 1953

Charlie Parker opens at the Times Square Night Club in Rochester, New York

Above: Art Granatstein and Bird at the Hartnett Studios in New York. Art and three other members of the New Jazz Society (Dick Wattam, Bill Hoare and Roger Feather) had driven down from Toronto to sign up musicians for a Massey Hall concert in May.

THUR	1
FRI	2
SAT	3
SUN	4
MON	5
TUES	6
WED	7
THUR	8
FRI	9
SAT	10
SUN	11
MON	12
TUES	13
WED	14
THUR	15
FRI	16
SAT	17
SUN	18
MON	19
TUES	20
WED	21
THUR	22
FRI	23
SAT	24
SUN	25
MON	26
TUES	27
WED	28
THUR	29
FRI	30
SAT	31

WEDNESDAY 28 JANUARY 1953

In the new issue of *Down Beat* Bird defends his 'commercial' string recordings in an interview with Nat Hentoff:

"When I recorded with strings," said Charlie Parker, "some of my friends said, 'Oh, Bird is getting commercial.' That wasn't it at all. I was looking for new ways of saying things musically. New sound combinations.

"Why, I asked for strings as far back as 1941, and then, years later, when I went with Norman [Granz], he okayed it. I liked Joe Lipman's fine arrangements on the second session, and I think they didn't turn out too badly.

"Now," said the always far-ranging Bird, "I'd like to do a session with five or six woodwinds, a harp, a choral group, and full rhythm section. Something on the line of Hindemith's *Kleine Kammermusik*. Not a copy or anything like that. I don't want ever to copy. But that sort of thing."

Charlie is really in love with the classics and unlike a number of people who say they are, Charlie knows them intimately. "I first began listening seven or eight years ago. First I heard Stravinsky's *Firebird Suite*. In the vernacular of the streets, I flipped. I guess Bartok has become my favourite. I dig all the moderns. And also the classical men, Bach, Beethoven, etc.

"It's a funny thing, listening to music, any kind," Bird went on. "What you hear depends on so many things in yourself. Like I heard Bartok's *Second Piano Concerto* over here and later, I heard it again in France. I was more acclimated to life, then, and I heard things in it I never heard before. You never know what's going to happen when you listen to music. All kinds of things can suddenly open up."

Charlie doesn't feel, as some musicians do, that modern jazz and classical music are becoming too closely interrelated. "They're different ways of saying things musically, and don't forget, classical music has that long tradition. But in 50 or 75 years, the contributions of present-day jazz will be taken as seriously as classical music. You wait and see."

The Bird went on to talk about some of the men in contemporary jazz he especially admires. "As long as I live, I'll appreciate the accomplishments of Thelonious Monk. And Bud Powell plays so much.

"As for Lennie Tristano, I'd like to go on record as saying I endorse his work in every particular. They say he's cold. They're wrong. He has a big heart and it's in his music. Obviously, he also has tremendous technical ability, and, you know, he can play anywhere with anybody. He's a tremendous musician. I call him the great acclimatizor.

"And I like Brubeck. He's a perfectionist, as I try to be. And I'm very moved by his altoist, Paul Desmond."

Talk of perfectionism led Charlie to ruminate about his records. "Every time I hear a record I've made, I hear all kind of things I could improve on, things I should have done. There's always so much more to be done in music. It's so vast. And that's why I'm always trying to develop, to find new and better ways of saying things musically."

And that is also why Charlie Parker has become so respected here and abroad as one of the focal figures in the evolutionary history of jazz.

FRIDAY 30 JANUARY 1953

Miles Davis Sextet recording session in New York City for Prestige features Charlie Parker on tenor sax.
MILES DAVIS (trumpet), CHARLIE PARKER (tenor sax), SONNY ROLLINS (tenor sax), WALTER BISHOP (piano), PERCY HEATH (bass) PHILLY JOE JONES (drums)
Compulsion / The Serpent's Tooth (2 takes) / *Round About Midnight*

Right: Bird on tenor sax at the Miles Davis Sextet recording session. Because of his exclusive contract with Mercury, he appears on the record under the pseudonym of Charlie Chan.

SUN	**1**
MON	**2**
TUES	**3**
WED	**4**
THUR	**5**
FRI	**6**
SAT	**7**
SUN	**8**
MON	**9**
TUES	**10**
WED	**11**
THUR	**12**
FRI	**13**
SAT	**14**
SUN	**15**
MON	**16**
TUES	**17**
WED	**18**
THUR	**19**
FRI	**20**
SAT	**21**
SUN	**22**
MON	**23**
TUES	**24**
WED	**25**
THUR	**26**
FRI	**27**
SAT	**28**

THURSDAY 5 FEBRUARY 1953

Bird flies into Montreal in the afternoon and is transported immediately to the CBC studios for a live TV performance on CBFT's 'Jazz Workshop'. Without rehearsal, and backed by Paul Bley (piano), Dick Garcia (guitar), Neil Michaud (bass) and Ted Paskert (drums), Bird is introduced by Don Cameron.

DON CAMERON: *... Our outstanding jazz artist this evening on the show, a man that we're very proud to be able to bring to you people here in Canada, possibly the gentleman who's considered tops on the alto saxophone, Mr Charlie Parker ... Charlie! ... It's all yours, boy ... Good to see you, Bird ...*

CHARLIE PARKER: Good to be here ...

CAMERON: *Fine. Could this be your first trip to Canada?*

PARKER: In many a year, yes ...

CAMERON: *Many a year. Well, how would you like to kick off with something in a nice bouncy tempo to get us all warmed up?*

PARKER: All right. I think first I'll take a tune that was recorded on the Dial label, 1948, Co-o-o-l Blues.

CAMERON: *Cool Blues. Here it is.*

After 'Cool Blues' comes a song by Laura Berkeley and 'Bernie's Tune' by Brew Moore.

DON CAMERON: *The tenor saxophone artistry of Brew Moore, ladies and gentlemen ... We promised you another appearance by Charlie Parker. Come on up here, Charlie, with that horn of yours. We seem to have got ourselves into the habit, Charlie, of asking our artists to introduce their own selections. How 'bout it? What are you going to do for your second one tonight?*

PARKER: Well, I think for our second one, we'll try another one of the Dial label's, released about 40... '48 – 1948 that is. Let's try 'Don't Blame Me'.

CAMERON: *It's all yours, boy ...*

PARKER: Okay ...

After the ballad, Brew Moore joins Charlie Parker and the quartet to play Benny Harris' 'Wahoo', based on the changes of 'Perdido'.

DON CAMERON: *Well, to the gentle strains of 'Perdido', we must unfortunately bring this particular program to a close. I think we created a small piece of musical history tonight here in Montreal, with featured work by Brew Moore, Charlie Parker, Buzzy Bley, Neil Michaud, let me see, Dick Garcia and Ted Paskert on drums ...*

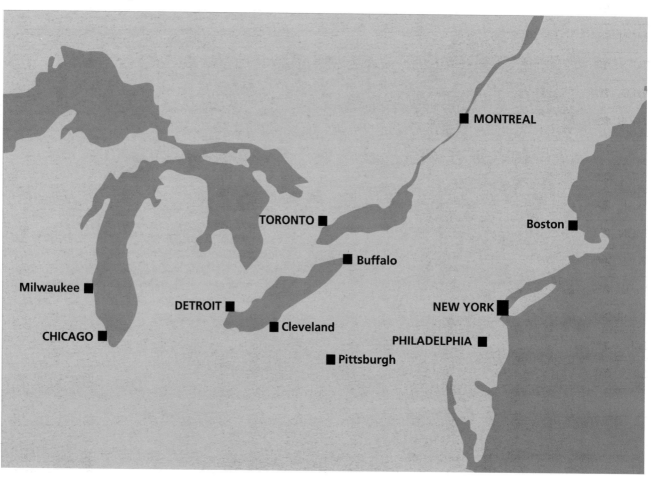

SUN	**1**
MON	**2**
TUES	**3**
WED	**4**
THUR	**5**
FRI	**6**
SAT	**7**
SUN	**8**
MON	**9**
TUES	**10**
WED	**11**
THUR	**12**
FRI	**13**
SAT	**14**
SUN	**15**
MON	**16**
TUES	**17**
WED	**18**
THUR	**19**
FRI	**20**
SAT	**21**
SUN	**22**
MON	**23**
TUES	**24**
WED	**25**
THUR	**26**
FRI	**27**
SAT	**28**

FRIDAY 6 FEBRUARY 1953
Bird has a day off in Montreal

SATURDAY 7 FEBRUARY 1953
A concert is arranged by the Jazz Workshop members to feature Charlie Parker at the Chez Paree. The concert is scheduled to run from 2pm until 5pm when the club has to be prepared for the evening performance by Frank Sinatra.
The concert kicks off at 2pm and Charlie Parker finally arrives, having made a connection, at 4pm. He borrows a necktie and at 4.30 Don Cameron introduces him.
Don Cameron: *Let me see now, we'd like to bring back, ah, Hal Gaylor and Dick Garcia on bass and guitar respectively. Gentlemen, are you out there? Hal? And Dick? Good. And let's bring back the fellow who helped us open the show. On drums, Mr Billy Graham. Billy! At last report, our pianist was Steep Wade. Steep, are you out there? Oh, now it's been changed to Valdo Williams, well... Every day something new ... Well, we have gathered, ah, what we consider, ah, as good a combination of musicians as we possibly can in order to background a gentleman, I suppose, that most of us consider way-up, number-one, top man on alto sax, CHARLIE PARKER!*

Charlie Parker: Thank you, thank you.
Cameron: *Ladies and gentlemen ... Man, they've been waiting! We asked Bird about what he'd like to say. He said, Man, I just don't talk, I wanna play 'How High The Moon'. So here it is.*

The concert is recorded by one of the Jazz Workshop members, despite Bird's protestations that he was exclusively under contract to Mercury.
Charlie Parker (alto sax), Valdo Williams (piano), Dick Garcia (guitar), Hal Gaylor (bass), Billy Graham (drums)
Ornithology (How High The Moon) / Cool Blues
Charlie Parker (alto sax), Steep Wade (piano), Dick Garcia (guitar), Bob Rudd (bass), Bobby Malloy (drums)
Moose The Mooche / Embraceable You / Now's The Time
In the evening, Charlie visits the Latin Quarter where there is a jam session. Charlie listens for a while from the bar, and later sits in.

Below: Bird, with plastic alto, at the Chez Paree in Montreal. Hal Gaylor is on bass and Billy Graham on drums.

SUN	**1**
MON	**2**
TUES	**3**
WED	**4**
THUR	**5**
FRI	**6**
SAT	**7**
SUN	**8**
MON	**9**
TUES	**10**
WED	**11**
THUR	**12**
FRI	**13**
SAT	**14**
SUN	**15**
MON	**16**
TUES	**17**
WED	**18**
THUR	**19**
FRI	**20**
SAT	**21**
SUN	**22**
MON	**23**
TUES	**24**
WED	**25**
THUR	**26**
FRI	**27**
SAT	**28**

FRIDAY 13 FEBRUARY 1953

Charlie Parker opens at the Bandbox, next door to Birdland, for a one-week engagement.

MONDAY 16 FEBRUARY 1953

Charlie signs a contract to appear at Club Kavakos in Washington on the following Sunday.
In the evening he broadcasts from the Bandbox with the Bill Harris-Chubby Jackson Herd.
CHARLIE PARKER (alto sax), CHARLIE MARIANO (alto sax), HARRY JOHNSON (tenor sax), BILL HARRIS (trombone), SONNY TRUITT (piano), CHUBBY JACKSON (bass), MOREY FELD (drums), LEONARD FEATHER (mc)
Your Father's Moustache

TUESDAY 17 FEBRUARY 1953

Charlie writes to the State Liquor Authority concerning his cabaret card:
My baby girl is a city case in the hospital because her health has been neglected since we hadn't the necessary doctor fees.
Charlie also pays the $100 fine imposed by the AF of M over the Say When affair.

THURSDAY 19 FEBRUARY 1953

Charlie Parker closes at the Bandbox.

SUNDAY 22 FEBRUARY 1953

Charlie travels to Washington DC where he appears at a 4–8pm concert at Club Kavakos with the Joe Theimer Orchestra for a flat fee of $50.
CHARLIE PARKER (alto sax), ED LEDDY, MARKY MARKOWITZ, CHARLIE WALP, BOB CAREY, JON EARDLEY (trumpet), JIM RILEY (alto sax), ANGELO TOMPROS, BEN LARY (tenor sax), JACK NIMITZ (baritone sax), EARL SWOPE, ROB SWOPE, DON SPIKER (trombone), JACK HOLLIDAY (piano), MERTON OLIVER (bass), JOE THEIMER (drums)
These Foolish Things / Thou Swell / Roundhouse / Light Green / Willis / Don't Blame Me / Fine And Dandy / Medley: Something To Remember You By, The Blue Room

WEDNESDAY 25 FEBRUARY 1953

Down Beat reviews Bird's latest album release:

CHARLIE PARKER
La Paloma / Tico Tico / Un Poquito de Tu Amor / Mama Inez / My Little Suede Shoes / Begin the Beguine / Estrellita / La Cucaracha
Album Rating: ***
Charlie Parker Plays South of the Border is the title of this LP, on which the music varies from two to four star value, with occasional one and five star moments. Bird is flanked by a small band: Walter Bishop Jr., Max Roach, Teddy Kotick, two of Machito's drummers, plus, on a couple of the sides, Little Benny Harris on trumpet.
   Some of the tunes seem to fit Charlie's style well, especially *Poquito* and *Tico*. Recording is too resonant, and the Parker tone lacks that intimate, supple quality we heard on the records that made him famous. (**Mercury MGC 513.**)

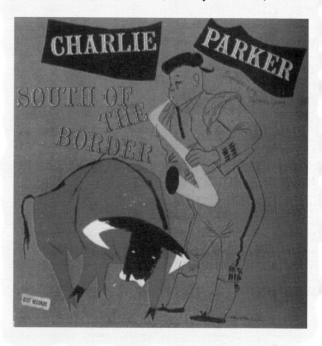

Down Beat also reports:

Bird Turns Teacher

New York—Charlie Parker, pianist Sanford Gold, guitarist Billy Bauer, and bassist Ed Safranski have all been recently added to the teaching staff at Hartnett Studios here. The New York Jazz Society also meets there and is holding Sunday afternoon jam sessions.

THURSDAY 26 FEBRUARY 1953

Charlie signs a contract to appear at George Wein's Storyville Club, Kenmore Square, Boston for 9 days (7–15 March).
$650 for first week, plus $186 for two extra days, total $936.00. $243.60 to be deducted for Shaw Artists Corporation, $692.40 to be paid to artist at the end of the engagement.

SUN	1	WED	1
MON	2	THUR	2
TUES	3	FRI	3
WED	4	SAT	4
THUR	5	SUN	5
FRI	6	MON	6
SAT	7	TUES	7
SUN	8	WED	8
MON	9	THUR	9
TUES	10	FRI	10
WED	11	SAT	11
THUR	12	SUN	12
FRI	13	MON	13
SAT	14	TUES	14
SUN	15	WED	15
MON	16	THUR	16
TUES	17	FRI	17
WED	18	SAT	18
THUR	19	SUN	19
FRI	20	MON	20
SAT	21	TUES	21
SUN	22	WED	22
MON	23	THUR	23
TUES	24	FRI	24
WED	25	SAT	25
THUR	26	SUN	26
FRI	27	MON	27
SAT	28	TUES	28
SUN	29	WED	29
MON	30	THUR	30
TUES	31		

SATURDAY 7 MARCH 1953

Charlie Parker opens at the Storyville Club in Boston. 8pm–1am nightly, Saturday 8–12, Sunday matinee 3–6pm.

SUNDAY 8 MARCH 1953

The Sunday matinee performance (3–6pm) at the Storyville Club is recorded.
CHARLIE PARKER (alto sax), RED GARLAND (piano), BERNIE GRIGGS (bass), ROY HAYNES (drums)
Moose The Mooche / I'll Walk Alone / Ornithology / Out Of Nowhere

SATURDAY 14 MARCH 1953

Charlie sends money to Chan with a cable:
MY ALL - THIS IS AN ADVANCE. BALANCE ON WAY. UNDIVIDED LOVE. BIRD.

SUNDAY 15 MARCH 1953

Charlie Parker closes at the Storyville Club in Boston.

MONDAY 23 MARCH 1953

Charlie Parker is interviewed by Leonard Feather on a broadcast from the Bandbox in New York City before playing with the Milt Buckner Trio
CHARLIE PARKER (alto sax), MILT BUCKNER (organ), BERNIE McKAY (guitar), CORNELIUS THOMAS (drums)
Groovin' High

MONDAY 30 MARCH 1953

Charlie Parker Quartet broadcast from the Bandbox in New York City
CHARLIE PARKER (alto sax), WALTER BISHOP (piano), KENNY O'BRIEN (bass), ROY HAYNES (drums), LEONARD FEATHER, BOB GARRITY (mc)
Caravan / Cool Blues / Star Eyes / My Little Suede Shoes / Ornithology / 52nd Street Theme / Diggin' Diz / 52nd Street Theme / Embraceable You / 52nd Street Theme

WEDNESDAY 22 APRIL 1953

The Financial Secretary of the Musicians' Protective Union, Local 208, Chicago, Illinois, writes to Charlie:

Dear Sir and Brother:

According to my records, your membership was terminated in this Local on Mar 31 - 53 for non-payment of dues.

If you wish to reinstate, you will have to pay $13.50, for the year 21.50. Kindly remit within ten (10) days, otherwise our record as above stated will become permanent, and recorded as such.

Thanking you for your cooperation.

Fraternally yours

Edward J. McCants, Fin. Sec.
Local 208, A.F. of M.

Down Beat reviews Bird's latest record release:

CHARLIE PARKER
**** **I Can't Get Started**
**** **Night And Day**
These feature Bird with a 17-piece swing band – brass, reeds, rhythm – and no strings. And the soloists aren't credited – they're Bill Harris, trombone; Bernie Privin, trumpet, and Oscar Peterson, piano. Bird plays excellently in this new setting; *Started* is a relaxed side, *Night* perhaps a little faster than necessary, but both superior Parker products. (**Mercury 11096.**)

FRIDAY 24 APRIL 1953

Charlie sends a Western Union Money Order message to Chan from Philadelphia:
FORGIVE ME MY MISTAKES. LOVE BIRD

SUNDAY 26 APRIL 1953

Bob Reisner launches the first of his Sunday jazz nights at the Open Door in Greenwich Village.

FRI	**1**
SAT	**2**
SUN	**3**
MON	**4**
TUES	**5**
WED	**6**
THUR	**7**
FRI	**8**
SAT	**9**
SUN	**10**
MON	**11**
TUES	**12**
WED	**13**
THUR	**14**
FRI	**15**
SAT	**16**
SUN	**17**
MON	**18**
TUES	**19**
WED	**20**
THUR	**21**
FRI	**22**
SAT	**23**
SUN	**24**
MON	**25**
TUES	**26**
WED	**27**
THUR	**28**
FRI	**29**
SAT	**30**
SUN	**31**

SATURDAY 9 MAY 1953

Charlie Parker Quartet broadcast from Birdland
CHARLIE PARKER (alto sax), JOHN LEWIS (piano), CURLEY RUSSELL (bass), KENNY CLARKE (drums), BOB GARRITY (mc)
Cool Blues / Star Eyes / Moose The Mooche / Lullaby Of Birdland (theme) / *Broadway* [CANDIDO (conga) added] / *Lullaby Of Birdland* (theme)

THURSDAY 14 MAY 1953

Joe Maini writes to Charlie from Los Angeles:
Dear Bird, Chan, Kim, Pree & Baird

I was so happy to hear that everything is so nice with "youse". I sure miss you. I am working pretty regularly. Disgustingly healthy! I'm deeply tanned from swimming. Teddy Kotick and Johnny Williams are out here with Stan Getz. I went to the beach with them yesterday. Nep is fine and going to City College here. I go sometimes. There's quite a few fellows from New York out here. I wish I were in New York taking lessons from you at Hartnett Studios. Although I took a lot from you when I was in N.Y. before, in a way.

I can't wait to see the Parker family again. I still feel you're like my almer pater, Bird. (Don't mind the sloppy penmanship, I should copy this letter over but I'm too lazy!)

If you get a chance, please send me some snapshots of yourselves and the new little ones. I'll do likewise.

All my love and wishes for crazy futures. (I'll write more neater next time)

Joe Maini(ac)

FRIDAY 15 MAY 1953

On the day of the Massey Hall Concert, the musicians gather at La Guardia Airport in New York for the flight to Toronto. Bud Powell is there with his legal guardian, Birdland manager Oscar Goodstein, Charlie Mingus with his wife Celia, Max Roach and Dizzy Gillespie, but Charlie Parker is missing. Dizzy eventually finds Charlie and they take a later flight to Buffalo. They arrive in Toronto and Charlie immediately disappears again. He turns up at Massey Hall at 8.30 p.m., as per contract.

The Hall is only half-full, due in no small measure to the clash with the postponed World Heavyweight Championship fight between Rocky Marciano and Jersey Joe Walcott. The concert is opened by Graham Topping and his 16-piece band.

FRI	**1**
SAT	**2**
SUN	**3**
MON	**4**
TUES	**5**
WED	**6**
THUR	**7**
FRI	**8**
SAT	**9**
SUN	**10**
MON	**11**
TUES	**12**
WED	**13**
THUR	**14**
FRI	**15**
SAT	**16**
SUN	**17**
MON	**18**
TUES	**19**
WED	**20**
THUR	**21**
FRI	**22**
SAT	**23**
SUN	**24**
MON	**25**
TUES	**26**
WED	**27**
THUR	**28**
FRI	**29**
SAT	**30**
SUN	**31**

GRAHAM TOPPING (trumpet/leader), DON JOHNSON, JULIUS PIEKARZ, BERNIE ROWE, ERICH TRAUGOTT (trumpets), ROSS CULLEY, RON HUGHES, RUSS MEYERS, STEVE RICHARDS (trombones), GORDIE EVANS, BERNIE PILTCH (alto saxes), JULIAN FILANOWSKI, HART WHEELER (tenor saxes), NORMAN SYMONDS (baritone sax), RALPH FRASER (piano), HOWIE MORRIS (bass), DOUG BENNETT (drums):
God Save The Queen / The Goof And I / Why Do I Love You? / All The Things You Are / Harvard Blues / Mambo / Beaver Junction / The Nearness of You / Fugue for Reeds and Brass / What's Schmoo? / Elevation
The band is well received, and the m.c. announces…
'Well, that's it for now. We'll be hearing from Graham a little bit later in the show. We've got some more boys to come along now…'

CHARLIE PARKER (alto sax), DIZZY GILLESPIE (trumpet), BUD POWELL (piano), CHARLES MINGUS (bass), MAX ROACH (drums)
Perdido / Salt Peanuts / All The Things You Are

INTERMISSION

Opposite page: The quintet on stage at Massey Hall. L to r: Bud Powell, Charlie Mingus, Max Roach, Dizzy Gillespie and Charlie Parker.

Below: Bird solos as the quintet join the Graham Topping Band for the finale.

FRI	**1**
SAT	**2**
SUN	**3**
MON	**4**
TUES	**5**
WED	**6**
THUR	**7**
FRI	**8**
SAT	**9**
SUN	**10**
MON	**11**
TUES	**12**
WED	**13**
THUR	**14**
FRI	**15**
SAT	**16**
SUN	**17**
MON	**18**
TUES	**19**
WED	**20**
THUR	**21**
FRI	**22**
SAT	**23**
SUN	**24**
MON	**25**
TUES	**26**
WED	**27**
THUR	**28**
FRI	**29**
SAT	**30**
SUN	**31**

During the 45-minute intermission, the musicians cross the street to the Silver Rail to watch the Marciano-Walcott fight. To Dizzy's dismay, Marciano knocks out Walcott in the first round. The second half of the concert begins with just Max on stage.

MAX ROACH (drums)
Drum Conversation
BUD POWELL (piano), CHARLES MINGUS (bass), MAX ROACH (drums)
Cherokee / Embraceable You / Jubilee / Sure Thing / Bassically Speaking / Lullaby of Birdland / I've Got You Under My Skin
CHARLIE PARKER (alto sax), DIZZY GILLESPIE (trumpet), BUD POWELL (piano), CHARLES MINGUS (bass), MAX ROACH (drums)
Wee / Hot House / A Night In Tunisia / 52nd Street Theme

*Below: Max, Dizzy and Bird on stage at Massey Hall.
Opposite page: Miles Davis sits in with Charlie at Birdland.
Curley Russell is on bass and Art Taylor on drums.*

GRAHAM TOPPING BAND:
Lover Come BackTo Me / Just Where You Are / Mambo Macocoa
Bird, Dizzy, Mingus and Roach join the band for the finale, a blues. In the aftermath, it transpires that the poor attendance has left the New Jazz Society with insufficient funds to pay the Quintet.

Mingus has taped the concert for his own Debut label, although most of his bass work has to be overdubbed in the ensuing weeks. The recordings are subsequently issued on three 10" albums as Jazz at Massey Hall. Parker, contracted to Mercury Records, has to be identified as Charlie Chan.

SATURDAY 16 MAY 1953
Cheques are issued to the musicians during the morning, despite there being insufficient funds to honour them. Charlie takes his cheque to the jazz-loving owner of Premier Radio, the company who had sold tickets for the concert, and he agrees to cash the cheque. Charlie returns to New York.

FRI	**1**
SAT	**2**
SUN	**3**
MON	**4**
TUES	**5**
WED	**6**
THUR	**7**
FRI	**8**
SAT	**9**
SUN	**10**
MON	**11**
TUES	**12**
WED	**13**
THUR	**14**
FRI	**15**
SAT	**16**
SUN	**17**
MON	**18**
TUES	**19**
WED	**20**
THUR	**21**
FRI	**22**
SAT	**23**
SUN	**24**
MON	**25**
TUES	**26**
WED	**27**
THUR	**28**
FRI	**29**
SAT	**30**
SUN	**31**

THURSDAY 21 MAY 1953

Charlie Parker Quartet open at Birdland opposite Dizzy Gillespie's Group and Bud Powell. Miles Davis substitutes for Dizzy on a couple of nights.

FRIDAY 22 MAY 1953

Charlie Parker Quartet broadcast from Birdland
CHARLIE PARKER (alto sax), BUD POWELL (piano), CHARLES MINGUS (bass), ART TAYLOR (drums)
Cool Blues / All The Things You Are / Lullaby Of Birdland

SATURDAY 23 MAY 1953

Charlie Parker joins Miles Davis and Dizzy Gillespie in a broadcast from Birdland
CHARLIE PARKER (alto sax), DIZZY GILLESPIE (trumpet), MILES DAVIS (trumpet), SAHIB SHIHAB (baritone sax), WADE LEGGE (piano), LOUIS HACKNEY (bass), AL JONES (drums), JOE CARROLL (vocal)
The Bluest Blues / On The Sunny Side Of The Street

FRI	**1**
SAT	**2**
SUN	**3**
MON	**4**
TUES	**5**
WED	**6**
THUR	**7**
FRI	**8**
SAT	**9**
SUN	**10**
MON	**11**
TUES	**12**
WED	**13**
THUR	**14**
FRI	**15**
SAT	**16**
SUN	**17**
MON	**18**
TUES	**19**
WED	**20**
THUR	**21**
FRI	**22**
SAT	**23**
SUN	**24**
MON	**25**
TUES	**26**
WED	**27**
THUR	**28**
FRI	**29**
SAT	**30**
SUN	**31**

MONDAY 25 MAY 1953

Recording session for Norman Granz in New York City with orchestra conducted by Gil Evans.
CHARLIE PARKER (alto sax), JUNIOR COLLINS (french horn), AL BLOCK (flute), HAL McKUSICK (clarinet), TOMMY MACE (oboe), MANNY THALER (bassoon), TONY ALESS (piano), CHARLES MINGUS (bass), MAX ROACH (drums), DAVE LAMBERT SINGERS (vocals), GIL EVANS (arranger/conductor)
In The Still Of The Night (7 takes) / *Old Folks* (9 takes) / *If I Love Again*

Gil Evans recalled the session in an interview with Charles Fox: *What happened that day made Norman Granz not one of my favourite people, because we had enough music for an album but we had to rehearse the music. I had a woodwind quintet and Dave Lambert had a vocal group and then Charlie's rhythm section... so we had to rehearse the numbers a little bit. Also, during the record date Max Roach had a concert, he had to dash off and play an hour concert somewhere, so there was a substitute drummer while that was going on, and Max came back. Well, Norman Granz was so impatient with it and had such poor musical equipment that he cancelled us out – right in the middle of the thing – he snapped the thing. He said, 'OK, that's all... goodnight!'*

THURSDAY 28 MAY 1953

Charlie Parker's week at Birdland is so successful that he is held over for a week to appear opposite Ella Fitzgerald.

SATURDAY 30 MAY 1953

Charlie Parker Quintet broadcast from Birdland
CHARLIE PARKER (alto sax), BUD POWELL (piano), CHARLES MINGUS (bass), ART TAYLOR (drums), CANDIDO (conga)
Moose The Mooche / Cheryl / Lullaby Of Birdland (theme)

Below: Sitting with guests at Birdland. L to r: Ahmet Ertegun, Rudi Blesh, Dizzy, Mr & Mrs Jorge Guinle from Argentina, and Bird. Sahib Shahib is the saxophonist at rear.

FRI **1**

SAT **2**

SUN **3**

MON **4**

TUES **5**

WED **6**

THUR **7**

FRI **8**

SAT **9**

SUN **10**

MON **11**

TUES **12**

WED **13**

THUR **14**

FRI **15**

SAT **16**

SUN **17**

MON **18**

TUES **19**

WED **20**

THUR **21**

FRI **22**

SAT **23**

SUN **24**

MON **25**

TUES **26**

WED **27**

THUR **28**

FRI **29**

SAT **30**

SUN **31**

MON	1
TUES	2
WED	3
THUR	4
FRI	5
SAT	6
SUN	7
MON	8
TUES	9
WED	10
THUR	11
FRI	12
SAT	13
SUN	14
MON	15
TUES	16
WED	17
THUR	18
FRI	19
SAT	20
SUN	21
MON	22
TUES	23
WED	24
THUR	25
FRI	26
SAT	27
SUN	28
MON	29
TUES	30

WEDNESDAY 3 JUNE 1953
Charlie Parker Quartet closes at Birdland.

MONDAY 8 JUNE 1953
Charlie Parker opens at the Hi Hat Club in Boston for a one-week engagement. He is backed by Herb Pomeroy (trumpet), Dean Earl (piano), Bernie Griggs (bass) and Bill Graham (drums).

The *Down Beat* review of the engagement is complimentary:

> Charlie Parker blew magnificently during his Hat engagement and was well complemented by trumpeter Herb Pomeroy.

SATURDAY 13 JUNE 1953
Charlie Parker is interviewed on Boston's Station WHDH by John McLellan, also known as John T. Fitch.

McLELLAN: *Welcome to Boston, Charlie, and more particularly to our show.*
PARKER: Thank you, John, it's a pleasure to be on this show.
McLELLAN: *We thought that with an unusual guest, perhaps we'd try a few unusual things this evening. So I've given you partly no indication of the sort of questions that I'm going to ask you, or, for that matter, the type of music that I'm going to play for you. Although, of course, in discussing it briefly last night over at the Hi-Hat where you're appearing – incidentally, through when?*
PARKER: Through Sunday.
McLELLAN: *... through Sunday, Sunday night, and you have an afternoon...*
PARKER: *...* afternoon session there, running from 4 to 8.
McLELLAN: *Well, I'm sure that many of our listeners will want to drop in and catch you either tonight, tomorrow afternoon or tomorrow evening at the Hi-Hat at Columbus and Massachusetts Avenue, because I know that they will be in for a very good show. Well, as I started to say, in the brief talk we did have a chance to have last night, I did find out a few of the artists that Charlie Parker himself listens to, including some of the music of a different nature... it may surprise some of our listeners. So, if you're game, I'm set to play something for you to get the ball rolling. You set to listen?*
PARKER: Alright Johnny, go ahead.
McLELLAN: *Alright, let's try this...*
[plays record by Bartok]
McLELLAN: *... hmm, I don't know quite what to ask you about that selection. Are you familiar with it?*
PARKER: Yes, it's one of Bartok's works, I forget the name, but, Bartok is my favourite, you know.
McLELLAN: *Well, that was one of the things I picked up yesterday in the brief chance we had to get together. That in particular was just a very small fragment from the... from one of my favourite works, the 'Concerto for...' ...no, no, it's not a concerto, it's 'Music for Stringed Instruments; Percussion and Celeste'.*
PARKER: Yes.
McLELLAN: *Well, the reason I chose that particular little portion of it was because of its violent rhythmic ideas that he brings out in that. And so, if you'd like to say a few words about your favourite composer, why, go right ahead.*

PARKER: Well, I mean, as far as his history is concerned, I mean, I've read that he was Hungarian born. He died an American exile in a General Hospital in New York, in 1945. At that time, I was just becoming introduced to modern classics, contemporary and otherwise, you know, and to my misfortune, he was deceased before I had the pleasure to meet the man. As far as I'm concerned, he is beyond a doubt, one of the most finished and accomplished musicians that ever lived.
McLELLAN: *Oh, now you made a very interesting point then when you said that you heard him in 1945...*
PARKER: Yeah.
McLELLAN: *... because this brings up a question that I'd like to ask you... and if some of these questions sound as though I wrote them out ahead of time, I did. At a certain point in our musical history, prior to 1945 as a matter of fact, you and a group of others evidently became dissatisfied with the stereotype form into which music had settled, so you altered the rhythm, the melody and the harmony...rather violently, as a matter of fact. Now, how much of this change that you were responsible for do you feel was spontaneous experimentation with your own ideas, and how much was the adaptation of the ideas of your classical predecessors, for example as in Bartok?*
PARKER: Oh, well... it was 100% spontaneous... 100%. Not a bit of the idiom of the music which travels today known as progressive music was adapted or even inspired by the older composers or predecessors.
McLELLAN: *It's rather strange we have this almost a progressive series of, not coincidences, but where one follows the other, for example... after Debussy, considerably after, you have piano players like Erroll Garner, who is respected, of course, by a great many people. But, even earlier than that, the trumpet playing of Bix Beiderbecke and his piano compositions was largely taken, I mean, from the Debussy form*
PARKER: Uh huh.
McLELLAN: *... very impressionistic, lush, rippling chords and clusters of chords, and even the titles of things like 'In A Mist', 'Clouds' remind you of Debussy. I just wondered if, in this case, it was partly the same thing, or whether this was actually spontaneous.*
PARKER: Well... I'm not too familiar with the Beiderbecke school of music, but the things which are happening now known as progressive music, or by the trade name Bebop, not a bit of it was inspired , or adapted, from the music of our predecessors Bach, Brahms, Beethoven, Chopin, Ravel, Debussy, Shostakovich, Stravinsky, etcetera.

MON	**1**
TUES	**2**
WED	**3**
THUR	**4**
FRI	**5**
SAT	**6**
SUN	**7**
MON	**8**
TUES	**9**
WED	**10**
THUR	**11**
FRI	**12**
SAT	**13**
SUN	**14**
MON	**15**
TUES	**16**
WED	**17**
THUR	**18**
FRI	**19**
SAT	**20**
SUN	**21**
MON	**22**
TUES	**23**
WED	**24**
THUR	**25**
FRI	**26**
SAT	**27**
SUN	**28**
MON	**29**
TUES	**30**

McLELLAN: *Then, whom do you feel were the really important persons, besides yourself, who evidently were dissatisfied with music as it was, and started to experiment?.*

PARKER: Well… let me make a correction here, please.It wasn't that we were dissatisfied with it, it was just that another conception came along, and this was just the way we thought it should go. During that time… this happened in 1938, just a little bit before '45… Dizzy Gillespie, Thelonious Monk, Kenny Clarke, there was Charlie Christian… '37 I guess… there was Bud Powell, Don Byas, Ben Webster… yours truly…

McLELLAN: *Ahh… the story-book names, the ones that we read about in our history, musical history books of that time. Well, now, I know it's difficult to sort of categorise musicians and schools of music, but in thinking this over I did sort of group what we hear today into seven different categories and I'd like to ask you what you feel, not only about the music, but about the future of each of these forms… for example, taking the earliest, just straight Dixieland, I mean, do you hear that today, it's featured in a lot of clubs… now, do the musicians who play that merely satisfy the demand of the college crowd or whoever it is that particularly wants to hear that, or do they honestly want to play that?*

PARKER: Well, I'd rather say they honestly wanted to play that. That's their conception, that's their idea. That's the way they think it should go, and so they render likewise.

McLELLAN: *And how often and how long will they continue to play 'High Society' and 'When the Saints go Marching in'?*

PARKER: There's no time… there's no way in the world you can tell how long that will go on, y'know.

McLELLAN: *With roughly the same solos, the same…*

PARKER: Yeah, roughly the same. Well, that's the skeleton, that's the way that music was set up, y'know, with certain… I guess you'd call them choruses, little ad-lib choruses that were remembered, and handed down from person to person, and they just respect the solos of the older age, you know, rather than improvisation… spontaneous improvisation that is.

McLELLAN: *But as I can probably gather, you have no interest in that subject at all.*

PARKER: Well, I like Dixieland…I like good Dixieland, you know. I just don't play it because… I most likely wouldn't make a good job at it, anyway… I just think it should go another way.

McLELLAN: *Sure. Now, what about the musicians who don't play Bebop, as you referred to it, and have also grown tired of Dixieland clichés. I don't even know what to call their music. But, I mean, people like Vic Dickenson, Doc Cheatham, Rex Stewart, many fine musicians who are not particularly Dixieland addicts, but who play… well, I just don't know what to call it?*

PARKER: Well, that came along during the Swing Era, say, for instance… Dixieland I think was introduced in '14 or '15, and then the Swing Era came in 1928 and lasted 'till 1935, 36. I guess you'd put them, say like, if you just had to categorise, you'd say that was the Swing Era, you know.

McLELLAN: *Of course, there are a lot of them still around and many of them, as Nat Hentoff has pointed out recently in Down Beat, are finding it pretty tough to work because people are, that is, the audiences are pretty violently split between Dixieland and Cool music, and there seems to be no room for these middle of the road swing musicians.*

PARKER: Oh, I'd like to differ… I beg to differ, in fact. There's always room for musicians, you know. There's no such thing as the middle of the road… it will be one thing or the other… good music or otherwise, you know. And it doesn't make any difference which idiom it might be in… Swing, Bebop, as you might want to call it, or Dixieland… if it's good it will be heard.

McLELLAN: *What about the musicians who were in on the growth of Bebop, but who quickly standardised a few clichés and now cater exclusively to the go-go-go crowd? Is that just a fad, or are we going to have that with us for some time?*

PARKER: That I wouldn't know either… since I don't cater for that particular thing, I wouldn't know. I mean, as far as I'm concerned, it's just more or less the way a man feels when he plays his instrument. I mean, if he feels that about it it will stay, if he's just trying to commercialise on it it will most likely vary from one thing to another.

McLELLAN: *Another group might be the experimenters and… I dreamed my own term… classical jazz… those who are well schooled and have adapted a number of things that they've been taught into their music. I'm speaking particularly of Dave Brubeck and Gerry Mulligan… Gerry Mulligan who is devoted almost entirely to a real contrapuntal music without even having a piano to lend any harmony to the things he plays… what about… what do you feel about them?*

PARKER: Well, the two men you mentioned being extremely good friends of mine, even if they weren't friends of mine I'd find their music very very interesting, not only from an intellectual standpoint… it's very intelligent music, and it's very well played… it's got a lot of feeling and it isn't missing anything… it's definitely music 100%.

McLELLAN: *Would you feel yourself fitting into a group like that if you played with them?*

PARKER: Oh, I imagine I could become acclimated, yes… I would like something like that.

McLELLAN: *Another group might be called the avant-garde, as primarily exemplified by Lennie Tristano.*

PARKER: Ah ha.

McLELLAN: *There we have what they try to do occasionally… complete collective improvisation with no theme, no chords, no chord changes on which to work, just six men, or whatever it may be, improvising together. It's that, er, it's always struck me as being extremely difficult to understand how it's possible in the first place.*

PARKER: Oh no, those are just like you said most improvisations, you know, and if you listen close enough you can find the melody travelling along within the chords, any series of chord structures, you know, and rather than to make the melody predominant. In the style used that Lennie and they present, it's more or less heard or felt.

McLELLAN: *Well, I refer particularly… they made one record called 'Intuition', and I heard them do it in concert, in which they started off with no key, no basic set of chord changes, or anything.*

PARKER: Ah ha… it must be a build up to… both the key signature and the chord structure tend to create the melody…

McLELLAN: *As they go along.*

PARKER: Yes.

McLELLAN: *Then there's a sort of a field apart, including mostly individuals who stick out… like Duke Ellington, Ralph Burns writing for Woody Herman and Stan Kenton, whom you expressed an interest*

MON	1
TUES	2
WED	3
THUR	4
FRI	5
SAT	6
SUN	7
MON	8
TUES	9
WED	10
THUR	11
FRI	12
SAT	13
SUN	14
MON	15
TUES	16
WED	17
THUR	18
FRI	19
SAT	20
SUN	21
MON	22
TUES	23
WED	24
THUR	25
FRI	26
SAT	27
SUN	28
MON	29
TUES	30

in. I think that before we go any further, I'd like to get your comments on a particular Stan Kenton record. If you'd like to listen to one now…

[plays Kenton record]

McLELLAN: *There you have Stan Kenton. Oh, I guess that's rather obvious, but I'll turn to Charlie Parker for at least the featured soloist on that record.*

PARKER: Yeah…it was Lee Konitz. Very fine alto work on that record, too. I hadn't heard that before, Johnny. What was the name of that?

McLELLAN: *It's called 'My Lady'.*

PARKER: Very beautiful.

McLELLAN: *I'm not sure, but I think perhaps Lee wrote it himself, I'm not sure of that.*

PARKER: It's a beautiful tune… very well done, too.

McLELLAN: *Well, now I'm giving you an opportunity to speak of Stan Kenton.*

PARKER: Yeah, well, as I was going on to say, Stan holds my definite interest. I mean, in lots of ways he has pioneered quite a bit in this progressive style of music. One particular record I was asking you about a few minutes ago… have you paid any attention, particular attention to 'House of Strings'?

McLELLAN: *We haven't played 'House of Strings'. We did play 'City of Glass' not too long ago, and we had a very interesting discussion here with Nat Hentoff and Rudolph Eley [?], the music critic of the Herald and Traveller but, adding a little more to that, I would like just to mention an article in this current edition of Down Beat magazine, written by Leonard Bernstein, in which in the course of discussing a number of things, he mentions this… I'd just like to read this to you for your comments…*

PARKER: Alright.

McLELLAN: *… 'pretentiousness means calling attention to oneself. It means the guy is saying "Look at me, I'm modern" and I think that's about the most old-fashioned attitude anyone can assume. I found that about Kenton: it's modernistic, like old-fashioned modern furniture which is just unbearable, it's moderne.' Composition is an important word, it means that somebody has to make a piece which is a work, which hangs together from beginning to end. Now, I think in particular he's referring to things of that nature…'House of Strings', 'City of Glass', which are completely scored, with perhaps little opening for improvisation by any soloist.*

PARKER: No… well, you had two factors moving there, you say Nat wrote that?

McLELLAN: *No, this is written by Leonard Bernstein.*

PARKER: Anyway, Leonard Bernstein, yeah, I can understand how he meant when he says the guy says 'Look at me, I'm modern'. That's strictly from the publicity agent's mouth. You know, Stan never has made such a statement, I know he hasn't…and most likely he never will. But he's still done many things, many good things, towards the pioneering of this music… introducing strings, different instrumentations, different chord structures and just pioneering in general… a definite asset to the music.

McLELLAN: *What do you feel about a longer piece of music, which is completely scored, which doesn't leave any opening for improvisation… is that still jazz?*

PARKER: Well, it depends on how it's written. It could be, yes.

McLELLAN: *I see. What about your own group, the people you work with, the other musicians who started with you? I've noticed that, for example, you play 'Anthropology' and '52nd Street*

Theme' perhaps, but they were written a long time ago. What is to take their place, and be the basis for your future?

PARKER: Mmm, that's hard to tell too, John, you see your ideas change as you grow older. Most people fail to realize that most of the things they hear coming out of a man's horn, ad-lib, or else things that are written, original things, they're just experiences, the way he feels… the beauty of the weather, the nice look of a mountain, or maybe a nice fresh cool breath of air, I mean all those things. You can never tell what you'll be thinking tomorrow. But I can definitely say that the music won't stop, you keep going forward.

McLELLAN: *And you feel that you, yourself, change continuously?*

PARKER: I do feel that way, yes.

McLELLAN: *And listening to your earlier recordings… you become dissatisfied with them? You feel that…*

PARKER: O.K., I still think that the best record is yet to be made, if that's what you mean.

McLELLAN: *That's about what I mean… I understand that you have something new in the offing.*

PARKER: Yes, we did it two weeks ago, Monday. Twelve voices… clarinet, flute, oboe, bassoon, French horn and three rhythm. I hope that they might sound O.K.

McLELLAN: *Well, we will be very much interested hearing them when they do come out. In the concluding moments of our show, I would like to play something else that I'm reasonably sure you haven't heard, which might be considered a salute to you. We won't have time to hear it all, but I'm sure you will be interested in, at least, hearing a bit of Stan Getz and his 'Parker 51'…*

[plays Getz record]

… and there we have about all we have time to hear of 'Parker 51'… Stan Getz from his 'Jazz at Storyville' album, and his obvious salute to you. Is that the first time you've heard that?

PARKER: Yes, that's the first time I've heard it, John.

McLELLAN: *Do you feel he captured your own mood?*

PARKER: Oh, yes… he's really too much. I sure like that… that was 'Cherokee'… a sad time 'Cherokee'.

McLELLAN: *Well, I'm afraid that our time has about run out. I certainly want to wish you a continuing good stay at the Hi-Hat… I did get the time to hear you play twice… I enjoyed it thoroughly. I feel that, if possible, you're playing better than ever. I hope that many of our listeners will take the opportunity to hear you, either tonight, or tomorrow afternoon at three, or your last night, Sunday night, and, Charlie, thank you very much for being with us on the Top Show this evening.*

PARKER: Thank you, John, it's always a pleasure to be on your show.

McLELLAN: *Thank you. And now, this is John McLellan hoping you've enjoyed our programme with recorded music, hoping too, you'll join us Saturday at seven with our music from the Top Show.*

SUNDAY 14 JUNE 1953

On their closing night, the Charlie Parker Quintet broadcast from the Hi Hat on station WCOP.

CHARLIE PARKER (alto sax), HERB POMEROY (trumpet), DEAN EARL (piano), BERNIE GRIGGS (bass), BILL GRAHAM (drums)

Cool Blues / Scrapple From The Apple / Laura / Ornithology / Cheryl / 52nd Street Theme

MON	1
TUES	2
WED	3
THUR	4
FRI	5
SAT	6
SUN	7
MON	8
TUES	9
WED	10
THUR	11
FRI	12
SAT	13
SUN	14
MON	15
TUES	16
WED	17
THUR	18
FRI	19
SAT	20
SUN	21
MON	22
TUES	23
WED	24
THUR	25
FRI	26
SAT	27
SUN	28
MON	29
TUES	30

THURSDAY 18 JUNE 1953

Charlie Parker Quartet opens at Birdland opposite Kai Winding and Slim Gaillard.

WINDING-PARKER at Birdland

By George T. Simon

KAI WINDING has one of the greatest small groups playing the small clubs these nights. (Why shouldn't it be great?" asked one of its flipper members on opening night. "After all, we had FOUR rehearsals.") But it's great nevertheless.

Sporting a book of good arrangements, many by Tommy Talbert, this low-voiced aggregation not only blows interesting stuff harmonically, but it also does what not enough of the small modern outfits do—it swings! The horns consist of Kai on trombone (playing lead on ensembles), the tenors of Brew Moore and Phil Urso, and the baritone of Cecil Payne. Backing them are pianist Walter Bishop, Jr., bassist Percy Heath and drummer "Philly" Joe Jones.

The soloists are all good, notably Kai who's boning with more guts than ever, and Brew Moore, who looks like a modern Pee Wee Russell, but who blows some mighty exciting, moving, well-toned horn. Urso keeps up with him some of the time (the two engage in cutting sessions now and then), but he has neither Brew's ideas nor his drive. Cecil Payne, who seems embarrassed everytime he's called upon to blow a solo, always does come through nicely. And as an anchor man in a section, he has few equals. As a matter of fact, the four-way section gets a great sound, an unusually good blend for a quartet of its variety and tonal depth, and despite its lack of tonal height, does manage to reach some exciting summits.

The rhythm section backs all this well, with Bishop feeding nicely on piano (his solos are light, modern and often quite interesting), Heath never allowing his beard to get in the way of the beat, and Philly Joe laying down steady time, though suffering from a tendency, as most bop drummers still do, to interfere with the rhythmic continuity.

CHARLIE PARKER appeared at Birdland on the same bill with Winding's group. He was blowing as wonderfully as ever, seemingly in thorough command of everything, blowing absolutely fabulous runs on his new alto, one of those plastic English jobs which has a very mellow tone but which doesn't permit the brilliance that comes out of the brass instrument.

Bird was backed by a rhythm trio of John Lewis on piano, Curley Russell on bass and Kenny Clarke on drums. John played some very nice things with his right hand, sort of an arranger's piano, but Curley and Kenny as a team were a big disappointment, for the former always seemed to be pulling ahead of the latter— or was the latter pulling back from the former? In any case, it was not a good, unified beat that they laid down, and I'm surprised that Bird was able to blow as well as he did. But then there's only one Bird, who, when he's as right as he was on this particular night, doesn't need anybody to show him the way!

Metronome reviews the opening night.

WED	**1**	SAT	**1**
THUR	**2**	SUN	**2**
FRI	**3**	MON	**3**
SAT	**4**	TUES	**4**
SUN	**5**	WED	**5**
MON	**6**	THUR	**6**
TUES	**7**	FRI	**7**
WED	**8**	SAT	**8**
THUR	**9**	SUN	**9**
FRI	**10**	MON	**10**
SAT	**11**	TUES	**11**
SUN	**12**	WED	**12**
MON	**13**	THUR	**13**
TUES	**14**	FRI	**14**
WED	**15**	SAT	**15**
THUR	**16**	SUN	**16**
FRI	**17**	MON	**17**
SAT	**18**	TUES	**18**
SUN	**19**	WED	**19**
MON	**20**	THUR	**20**
TUES	**21**	FRI	**21**
WED	**22**	SAT	**22**
THUR	**23**	SUN	**23**
FRI	**24**	MON	**24**
SAT	**25**	TUES	**25**
SUN	**26**	WED	**26**
MON	**27**	THUR	**27**
TUES	**28**	FRI	**28**
WED	**29**	SAT	**29**
THUR	**30**	SUN	**30**
FRI	**31**	MON	**31**

SUNDAY 26 JULY 1953

Charlie Parker plays at the Open Door in Greenwich Village.

A private recording is made:

CHARLIE PARKER (alto sax), BENNY HARRIS (trumpet), AL HAIG, BUD POWELL (piano), CHARLES MINGUS (bass), ART TAYLOR (drums)

Out Of Nowhere / Star Eyes / Cool Blues / East Of The Sun / The Song Is You / My Little Suede Shoes / 52nd Street Theme / Ornithology / Scrapple From The Apple / I Cover The Waterfront / This Time The Dream's On Me / I'll Remember April / My Old Flame / 52nd Street Theme / I Remember You / All The Things You Are / Hot House / Just You, Just Me / I'll Remember April / 52nd Street Theme / Scrapple From The Apple / 52nd Street Theme

THURSDAY 30 JULY 1953

Charlie Parker recording session for Mercury at the Fulton Recording Studios in New York.

CHARLIE PARKER (alto sax), AL HAIG (piano), PERCY HEATH (bass), MAX ROACH (drums)

Chi Chi (6 takes) / I Remember You / Now's The Time / Confirmation (3 takes)

SUNDAY 9 AUGUST 1953

Charlie Parker Quintet play a one-nighter at Sparrow's Beach Amusement Park in Annapolis, Maryland.

SUNDAY 16 AUGUST 1953

Charlie sends a Western Union Money Order message to Chan from St Louis, Missouri:

WILL CALL MONDAY HERES A LITTLE MONEY WITH A LOT OF SENTIMENT

THURSDAY 20 AUGUST 1953

Charlie sends a Western Union Money Order message to Chan from St Louis, Missouri:

HOLD ON TIGHT AND BE GOOD AND CALL ME

WEDNESDAY 26 AUGUST 1953

Charlie wins the Alto Sax award in the *Down Beat* Critics' Poll.

SATURDAY 29 AUGUST 1953

Charlie Parker's 33rd birthday.

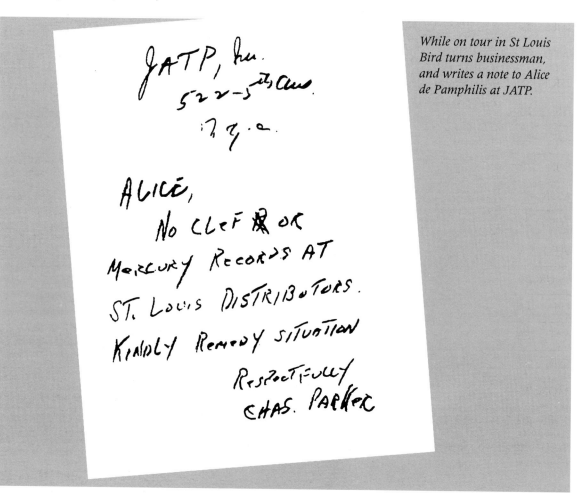

While on tour in St Louis Bird turns businessman, and writes a note to Alice de Pamphilis at JATP.

TUES **1**
WED **2**
THUR **3**
FRI **4**
SAT **5**
SUN **6**
MON **7**
TUES **8**
WED **9**
THUR **10**
FRI **11**
SAT **12**
SUN **13**
MON **14**
TUES **15**
WED **16**
THUR **17**
FRI **18**
SAT **19**
SUN **20**
MON **21**
TUES **22**
WED **23**
THUR **24**
FRI **25**
SAT **26**
SUN **27**
MON **28**
TUES **29**
WED **30**

SUNDAY 13 SEPTEMBER 1953

Charlie Parker appears at the Open Door (*above*) in Greenwich Village with Thelonious Monk (piano), Charles Mingus (bass) and Roy Haynes (drums).

Charlie sits in with Woody Herman's Band at the Bandbox, and mesmerizes both musicians and audience.

MONDAY 14 SEPTEMBER 1953

Irene Taverner writes to Bird from San Francisco:
Dear Bird,
A friend of yours Ted [Sturgis?] a bass player told me that Chan is ill in hospital. I wish you to know that many of your friends here feel for both of you and pray it will be a quick recovery. Bop City [the San Francisco club] no longer holds sessions the police being responsible however the doors are still open! A new club the Downbeat opened under the same management as the Black Hawk. Pettiford & his group also Buddy de Franco were there last week, unfortunately this brings me to a piece of bad news – Frank Morgan (alto) and Kenny Drew were picked up on a dope charge. Frank's father came up from LA and arranged for Frank to be sent to hospital under observation – the trial I understand comes up on Thursday.

Of myself there is little to tell. I have a showing at the Lucien Labaudt Galleries in October or November, then, I hope to consider returning to England.
All the very best to you & Chan
Sincerely, Irene.
P.S. Have you ever thought of recording Ave Maria?

MONDAY 21 SEPTEMBER 1953

Charlie Parker opens at the Storyville Club in Boston for a one-week engagement. He is backed by Herb Pomeroy (trumpet), Sir Charles Thompson (piano), Jimmy Woode (bass) and Kenny Clarke (drums)

TUESDAY 22 SEPTEMBER 1953

Charlie Parker Quintet broadcast from the Storyville Club in Boston.
CHARLIE PARKER (alto sax), HERB POMEROY (trumpet), SIR CHARLES THOMPSON (piano), JIMMY WOODE (bass), KENNY CLARKE (drums)
Now's The Time / Don't Blame Me / Dancing On The Ceiling / Cool Blues / Groovin' High

MONDAY 28 SEPTEMBER 1953

Charlie Parker closes at the Storyville Club.

THUR	**1**
FRI	**2**
SAT	**3**
SUN	**4**
MON	**5**
TUES	**6**
WED	**7**
THUR	**8**
FRI	**9**
SAT	**10**
SUN	**11**
MON	**12**
TUES	**13**
WED	**14**
THUR	**15**
FRI	**16**
SAT	**17**
SUN	**18**
MON	**19**
TUES	**20**
WED	**21**
THUR	**22**
FRI	**23**
SAT	**24**
SUN	**25**
MON	**26**
TUES	**27**
WED	**28**
THUR	**29**
FRI	**30**
SAT	**31**

SUNDAY 4 OCTOBER 1953

Charlie Parker Quintet with Benny Harris, Horace Silver, Charlie Mingus and Liaquat Salaam (Kenny Clarke) play a one-nighter at the Memorial Auditorium in Buffalo, N.Y..

WEDNESDAY 7 OCTOBER 1953

Billy Shaw writes to Chan at 151 Ave B:

Dear Chan:

Thanks for your nice letter relative to the telegram from the union.

After checking on Charlie Parker's bookings and the kind of money he has been earning, I sincerely believe that the small amount of money that we have agreed to accept from him is very insignificant and yet, coming in in weekly payments, this would have long since cleared up his indebtedness to us. We have yet to receive anything on account of the debt and he has completely ignored his obligation to us.

At the time that Charlie asked for his release in order to be booked by another agency, we could have held him. However, we didn't want to hurt him in any way, so we agreed to let another agency book him with the understanding that we would get 10% of his salary on account.

He has other bookings coming up and has been working consistently and with this in mind, we're looking forward to and shall expect monies from his current and future bookings, otherwise I am sorry, we'll have to take further steps through the proper channels to get our moneys back.

Sincerely SHAW ARTISTS CORP.
Billy Shaw

FRIDAY 9 OCTOBER 1953

Charlie sends a money order to Chan from Los Angeles with the message:

I LOVE YOU BELIEVE IN ME.

MONDAY 12 OCTOBER 1953

Charlie Parker opens a one-week engagement at Latin Quarter in Montreal with Benny Harris (trumpet), Harry Biss (piano), Conrad Henry (bass) and Art Mardigan (drums)

The management at the club complain about the musicians. In a letter of complaint to the AFM, Latin Quarter owner Morton Berman complains: *'Their performance was pitiful; Mr Parker personally did his best but the others, especially the pianist, didn't match him at all; the*

piano player was always in a fog; half of the time he didn't play ... Customers walked out disgusted and our business suffered during the three days we had to put up with this group.'

WEDNESDAY 14 OCTOBER 1953

Charlie Parker Quintet close after only three days at the Latin Quarter.
The band is only paid for three days.

A contract is drawn up for Charlie to appear on a one night tour with the West Coast in Jazz Concert Package, 30 October 1953 thru 9 November 1953 for $1000 plus transportation. $400 deposit on signing contract, balance at end of engagement.

MONDAY 19 OCTOBER 1953

Charlie Parker lodges an appeal with the AFM for the balance of the salary due to him from the Latin Quarter.

TUESDAY 20 OCTOBER 1953

James C. Petrillo, President of AF of M writes to Charlie at 151 Ave B:

Dear Sir and Brother:

This is to acknowledge receipt of your communication of October 19th which is in reality a claim for balance of salaries due in the amount of $743.04, the money now being held in escrow in the Montreal local.

We are mailing your claim to Secretary Cluesmann's office where it rightfully belongs and you will hear from him shortly.

Fraternally yours, James C. Petrillo President

SUNDAY 25 OCTOBER 1953

Charlie Parker and Strings play a one-nighter at Jordan Hall, Boston for jazz disc jockey John McLellan.

FRIDAY 30 OCTOBER 1953

Charlie Parker begins a one-nighter tour with 'West Coast in Jazz' concert package.

SATURDAY 31 OCTOBER 1953

Charlie sends a money order to Chan from Los Angeles with the message:

LOVE MISS AND NEED YOU WILL WRITE SOON.

SUN	**1**
MON	**2**
TUES	**3**
WED	**4**
THUR	**5**
FRI	**6**
SAT	**7**
SUN	**8**
MON	**9**
TUES	**10**
WED	**11**
THUR	**12**
FRI	**13**
SAT	**14**
SUN	**15**
MON	**16**
TUES	**17**
WED	**18**
THUR	**19**
FRI	**20**
SAT	**21**
SUN	**22**
MON	**23**
TUES	**24**
WED	**25**
THUR	**26**
FRI	**27**
SAT	**28**
SUN	**29**
MON	**30**

SUNDAY 1 NOVEMBER 1953

Charlie sends a Western Union Money Order message to Chan from Seattle:

LOVE YOU MORE EACH DAY

WEDNESDAY 4 NOVEMBER 1953

Down Beat publishes an article on the Open Door with a picture of Charlie.

THURSDAY 5 NOVEMBER 1953

The West Coast in Jazz package plays at the University of Oregon in Eugene, Oregon.
A private recording is made of Charlie Parker's part of the programme.
CHARLIE PARKER (alto sax), CHET BAKER (trumpet), JIMMY ROWLES (piano), CARSON SMITH (bass), SHELLY MANNE (drums)
How High The Moon / Barbados / Cool Blues

SATURDAY 7 NOVEMBER 1953

The West Coast in Jazz package plays in Portland, Oregon.

Left and below: Bird on the West Coast in Jazz tour with Carson Smith on bass and Chet Baker on trumpet. The obscured members of the quintet are Jimmy Rowles (piano) and Shelly Manne (drums).

SUN	**1**
MON	**2**
TUES	**3**
WED	**4**
THUR	**5**
FRI	**6**
SAT	**7**
SUN	**8**
MON	**9**
TUES	**10**
WED	**11**
THUR	**12**
FRI	**13**
SAT	**14**
SUN	**15**
MON	**16**
TUES	**17**
WED	**18**
THUR	**19**
FRI	**20**
SAT	**21**
SUN	**22**
MON	**23**
TUES	**24**
WED	**25**
THUR	**26**
FRI	**27**
SAT	**28**
SUN	**29**
MON	**30**

SUNDAY 8 NOVEMBER 1953

The West Coast in Jazz package plays a second night in Portland, Oregon.
Charlie sends a Western Union Money Order message to Chan from Los Angeles:

HAVE JOE MARSOLAIS CONTACT ME WATKINS HOTEL IMMEDIATELY YOUR HUSBAND

MONDAY 9 NOVEMBER 1953

The West Coast in Jazz package tour ends.

FRIDAY 13 NOVEMBER 1953

Morton Berman, owner of the Latin Quarter in Montreal, writes to the AFM in response to Charlie Parker's claim for the balance of his salary.

Montreal, November 13th, 1953
Mr Leo Cluesmann,
Secretary,
American Federation of Musicians,
220 Mt.Pleasant Avenue,
Newark, N.J.

Re: Case 829-1953-54

Dear Sir,
Herewith is our reply relative to claim filed by Mr Charlie Parker member of the American Federation of Musicians. On October 6th, 1953, we signed a contract with the Gale Agency hiring Mr.Charlie Parker and his band for one week's engagement at the "Latin Quarter" which we operate. The contract price was $1250.00. One of the reasons we hired this band was because of the reputation enjoyed by Mr.Parker and his group which, when negotiations were carried on, was sold to us as a set band. We were even given the names of the personnel of the orchestra and the assurance that all these men were good and in the habit of playing with Mr. Parker. However, when the musicians arrived, we found out that they were not the ones whose names had been given to us; except for Mr Benny Harris, trumpet player, none of them had ever worked with or for Parker. Mr Harris "remembered" having worked with him about two years previous. After listening to the group, we soon realised that it was not a set band and that the musicians had been recruited at the last moment possibly "around 52nd Street". They had no routine whatsoever, as a matter of fact, they were not rehearsed at all, so much so, that Parker had to delay the opening of the first show to set a routine and rehearse the numbers he wanted to play. The band was definitely a pick-up band, nothing else, and didn't meet with expectations; that for their musicianship. Now for their appearance. When they arrived at the club, they looked anything but musicians, at least, those who have been in the habit of engaging. They were shabbily dressed, torn shirts, even on Mr. Parker's back; they were unshaven, dirty looking and not fit to be presented to any public. We send them away to get cleaned up before they were allowed to start the performance which was delayed because Mr. Parker was trying to set a routine. The drummer came to Montreal, without even an outfit; if it hadn't been for one of our patrons who offered to loan him a set of drums, he wouldn't have been able to go on the opening night; yet the group had been sold to us as a set band, with routine and all. Their performance was pitiful; Mr. Parker personally did his best but the others, especially the pianist, didn't match him at all; the piano-player was always in a fog; half of the time he didn't play; didn't know where he was; one of the men in the band remarked "the pianist is way off...is bad". This can be verified by the Montreal Union investigators, the Sergeant-at-Arms, and Mr. C.J. Lewis who were sent to ascertain whether or not our complaints were founded. They have admitted to us and their officers that the band was really bad.
The patrons were disgusted and many of them thought we were pulling a gag on them by putting on some amateur talent; after they found out the truth, they felt sorry for Parker because "he was alright ... but his men..." etc.etc. Needless to say that we were terribly disappointed. Customers walked out disgusted and our business suffered during the three days we had to put up with this group. It also hurt the reputation of the house which is known for the quality of its shows and the talent it presents. The week previous we had Earl Hines orchestra, an excellent group which we paid $1500.00. It was lucky for us that he had not left town; after the poor performance of Parker's band, we begged him to take over for the balance of the week; after he surveyed the situation and found out our predicament and the mess we were in, he finished the week; we offered Parker to play for the remainder of the week in Hines' band as we felt sorry for him; he refused our offer which was made more than once, even in front of the officials of the Montreal Union. Of course, we assume that he had to save face with his men, but why at our expense? We didn't mind paying for good services, but certainly not the type given by the group he had with him.
Mr. Parker was uncooperative on more than one occasion. On the opening night, for instance, he was asked to play a little theme song in order to give our M.C., Mr. Al Cowans, a chance to start his show; he was arrogant and told the latter: "don't get excited... I'm running my band... I'll start when I'm ready..." Mr. Al Cowans, also colored, is the leader of the local band which has been working here for over two years; he is one of the finest gentlemen we ever had working for us; he took a lot of abuse from Parker, but managed to refrain from being tricked into an argument which, it was evident, Parker was seeking; as a matter of fact, he threatened to strike Mr. Cowans in front of the Union Representative, Mr. Lewis, because he resented the fact that at the Union's request, he (Cowans) had given an account of what was taking place.
Here is another incident which we resented very much, as well as was resented by our patrons. When terminating a thirty-minute set, Parker didn't even finish the number, but stopped cold and announced to the customers that "his time was up. If they wanted to hear the rest of the number he would be back in thirty minutes". When we remonstrated to him he tried to make it appear that this was one of his jokes and that he meant no harm; that may be but the joke was not relished by those present and we think it was very uncalled for.
His continuous chewing on lemon peels and spitting them back on the band-stand in full view of the customers, is another indication of his spiteful disposition towards us. A great number of our patrons, many of them musicians, had been attracted by the reputation of this band. It was a dire disappointment when they heard it; we were the

SUN	**1**
MON	**2**
TUES	**3**
WED	**4**
THUR	**5**
FRI	**6**
SAT	**7**
SUN	**8**
MON	**9**
TUES	**10**
WED	**11**
THUR	**12**
FRI	**13**
SAT	**14**
SUN	**15**
MON	**16**
TUES	**17**
WED	**18**
THUR	**19**
FRI	**20**
SAT	**21**
SUN	**22**
MON	**23**
TUES	**24**
WED	**25**
THUR	**26**
FRI	**27**
SAT	**28**
SUN	**29**
MON	**30**

laughing stock of the customers who have been in the habit of listening to the excellent bands presented in our night-club.

Right after the first day, we filed a protest with the Union who told us that the contract must be respected; we made it clear however that, while we wanted to abide by the Union's decision, a contract is a deal between two people and once that deal is not in accordance with the terms agreed upon we felt there is no deal. We were willing to pay the boys for the work done up till then and pay their fare back home. However, the Union insisted upon first communicating with your Headquarters and the Agency before canceling the contract. We followed their suggestion to deposit in escrow the amount of the balance of the contract pending your decision. We were of the impression, and still are, that you will not stand for unfairness and that we can rely fully on the integrity and justice of your judgement. We have deposited with the Montreal Union a cheque for $534.06, amount which remains after paying Parker on a pro rata basis, and $117.00 to the Gale Agency.

Ever since we are in operation, we have dealt with Union musicians, whom we always pay more than scale. Since the start of these operations, we have been on most friendly terms with the Montreal Union and we feel that we have their respect and confidence inasmuch as we always consult them and follow their advice and suggestions. In this instance, it is not a question of money but one of business; we bought an article which was mis-represented and didn't live up to expectations; we feel we have the right to receive value for our money. We are willing to pay the services of these men, and have paid them, for the time they worked even though we feel that doing so is an imposition on us as it is our conviction that in view of the poor showing of the orchestra, we could have cancelled it after the first performance, however, we have given our word to the Montreal Union that we would follow their suggestions, which we have.

We now rest our case in your hands in the hope and with the assurance of the Union that you will give us a fair treatment. If you need further particulars, we will be pleased to furnish them to you.

Yours very truly,
LATIN QUARTER LIMITED

Morton Berman
Secretary-Treasurer

MONDAY 16 NOVEMBER 1953

AF of M secretary Leo Cluesmann sends a copy of the Latin Quarter Letter to Charlie telling him he may submit a rebuttal within 10 days.

WEDNESDAY 18 NOVEMBER 1953

Charlie Parker writes to the AFM in reply to the charges made by Morton Berman:

151 Avenue B
New York, New York
November 18, 1953

Mr Leo Cluesmann,
Secretary,
American Federation of Musicians,
220 Mt.Pleasant Avenue,
Newark, New Jersey

Dear Sir and Brother:

Following is my answer to the reply of the management of the Latin Quarter Night Club in Montreal, Canada, in regard to Case 829-1953-54. I am going to endeavour to reply to your document paragraph by paragraph.

In the first paragraph, the management of the Latin Quarter state that one of the reasons they hired myself and orchestra was that it was sold to them as a set band. This statement in itself is completely wrong inasmuch as I know that my Agency offered to sell me to this Club as a single musician at a salary of $750.00 per week. I normally play many engagements in this way. I know that the Latin Quarter turned this arrangement down and insisted that I bring an orchestra with me. Although it doesn't happen very often, I happened to be sitting in my Agent's office at the time the negotiation occurred and the agreement was made, and I know that due to the fact that I had not been appearing previously with a set band, that my Agency advised the Latin Quarter of this, but did say that as the Club insisted on a band, that I would appear with four other men at a salary of $1250.00, and these four men would be selected from a number of musicians that had worked with me previously and who, I believed, were available for the date. This, of course, in my mind, has nothing to do with the claim, actually, as I did appear with five men as per contract. I only wish to clarify the fact that I was not sold to the Club in anything but an honest manner. The fact remains that I did open at the Latin Quarter in Montreal as per schedule with five men, the number of men that appeared on the contract. Naturally, under these conditions, there only being five days to present a band, it was not easy.

I also wish to state that inasmuch as I am personally, proud of my reputation, I try to play with the finest musicians that I possibly can, and in the band that I took to Montreal, were men I have played with time and time again over a long period of my being a musician and a leader. I most certainly was not rehearsing a band in Montreal. I went up there to perform and do a good job for the Latin Quarter, and, frankly, was not allowed to do so.

In paragraph two in which Mr. Berman states that my band had terrible appearance, please be advised that he is correct about this, but he is not correct about the time at which the boys were unshaven, dirty looking, and frankly not in a presentable appearance. For explanation: It is an overnight ride on a train from New York to Montreal, and the men who arrived in the early evening went immediately, as soon as they got off the train, to the Latin Quarter to ascertain what the requirements of the engagement were, and naturally, this being in the neighbourhood of 7.30 in the

SUN	**1**
MON	**2**
TUES	**3**
WED	**4**
THUR	**5**
FRI	**6**
SAT	**7**
SUN	**8**
MON	**9**
TUES	**10**
WED	**11**
THUR	**12**
FRI	**13**
SAT	**14**
SUN	**15**
MON	**16**
TUES	**17**
WED	**18**
THUR	**19**
FRI	**20**
SAT	**21**
SUN	**22**
MON	**23**
TUES	**24**
WED	**25**
THUR	**26**
FRI	**27**
SAT	**28**
SUN	**29**
MON	**30**

evening, and we not scheduled to play until 10 o'clock, and having ridden all day on a very dirty train, all of us certainly admit we were definitely not dressed to make a professional appearance. Mr. Berman did not have to send us away to get cleaned up to start a performance, as this naturally, would be a normal thing for us to do, and we did it, and had every intention of doing it without Mr. Berman requesting it. When we appeared on his band stand at the prescribed time of 10:00 p.m., my entire band wore dark blue suits, were cleanly shaven, and were ready to perform in a professional manner.

In paragraph three, Re: My Drummer: While Mr. Berman is correct that one of his patrons loaned my drummer a set of drums, that is not the complete story. The complete story is, my drummer having his drums repaired at a Drum establishment called Manny's, in New York City, and due to the fact the repairs were not completed on time, he could not take them with him to Montreal. It was my intention to rent for my drummer, a complete set of instruments in Montreal. However, when my drummer and I arrived at the Club, before securing the drums, (and incidentally, my drummer and I arrived in Montreal early the morning of the engagement) waiting in the Club for me was a man who is a fan of mine. When he heard that we were en route to secure a set of drums, he very kindly offered to loan my drummer, his particular set of drums and this eliminated the necessity of our securing them elsewhere. Most certainly, I have been a band leader long enough to know that a drummer without a set of drums is of no value to me.

In paragraph four, Mr. Berman attacks the quality of my musicians and especially my pianist. Following is a list of the orchestras with whom my pianist has worked for varying periods of time during the last two years. My pianist's name is HARRY BISS, and he has been employed by the following orchestra leaders: SHEP FIELDS, GEORGIE AULD, TOMMY DORSEY, TEX BENEKE, NEAL HEFTI, LOUIS PRIMA, SONNY DUNHAM, ART MOONEY, BILLY BUTTERFIELD, BOYD RAEBURN, INA RAY HUTTON, and TERRY GIBBS. I do not wish to cast any aspersions on whoever made the alleged comments to Mr. Berman, but following is the personnel of the band I had in Montreal, and after each name is a list of orchestra leaders that each has worked for during the past few years. In addition to HARRY BISS, who was mentioned above, I had with me, ART MARDIGAN, drummer, who has worked with WOODY HERMAN, TOMMY REYNOLDS, GEORGIE AULD, CHUBBY JACKSON, and ALLEN EAGER. I had CONRAD HENRY on bass fiddle who has been employed consistently by many of the top jazz combos and has appeared with such musicians as, COLEMAN HAWKINS, MILES DAVIS, SONNY STITT, BULLMOOSE JACKSON, and GENE AMMONS, all recognized groups. On trumpet, I had BENNIE HARRIS, who has appeared with COLEMAN HAWKINS, BOYD RAEBURN, DIZZY GILLESPIE, HERBIE FIELDS, CHARLIE VENTURA, BENNY CARTER, DON REDMAN, and EARL HINES.

To say that I had delivered poor musicians to Montreal, which I did not, would be to say that all the above mentioned orchestra leaders also had very poor taste in their employment of musicians, which I am certain they do not have. Because I feel that I have advanced a great deal in the field of music, in a musical manner, I cannot afford to, nor do I have the inclination to, appear with amateur musicians, and none of the above men who have played with such outstanding musicians were amateurs.

In regard to paragraph five in which Mr. Berman states his patrons were disgusted, and that they were lucky to have available the EARL HINES orchestra, and about the fact that he offered me the opportunity to play in HINES' orchestra, I did refuse the offer to play with EARL HINES as I felt that first, EARL HINES would have had to agree to this, and secondly it was not only unfair to me to be offered a job as a side man in another leader's orchestra when I am already a leader on an engagement, but, I also had a duty to the members of my orchestra, each of whom I had hired for a full week of work, and I felt, and still feel responsible to them for the money due them. I did, however, offer to work personally, with my band at the club, with no pay for myself, if the Latin Quarter would retain my band for the week and pay the men in my band the salary I had guaranteed them. This offer was refused by the management of the Latin Quarter. I do not have to save face with my men because they all understood that I was definitely trying to do the job that I and my orchestra had been contracted for, and running into unheard of difficulty, set up by a Night Club. They also understood that I would not terminate a contract without making certain that they were to be paid for the full week as per agreement.

In regard to the paragraph regarding Mr. AL COWANS, I have very little to say about this with the exception that AL COWANS has worked for the Latin Quarter for a period of two years, and probably his feelings in any matter would naturally be colored by this length of engagement, and that he had difficulty in presenting a picture that would be favourable to the management. In regard to the statements about a theme song, I do have a theme song which the Montreal orchestra did not know, and the reason for the delay of starting the show was the fact that I changed my theme song to one that would be easier for the Montreal band to catch on to, and I was teaching this new theme song to AL COWANS so that he would recognize it when he heard it during the evening and during the week, and after that the theme was played, but it did take a little time to familiarize Mr. COWANS with the number.

In regard to the next paragraph in which they objected to my terminating the set with the remark that my time was up and if they wanted to hear the rest of the number, I would be back in thirty minutes to finish it, the wording of this is not exactly correct. To explain: I have used a gimmick for years, along with a number of other orchestra leaders in Jazz Clubs, and that is at the end of any set I start a number, go halfway through it and stop cold, and say to the audience, "I will be back in thirty minutes to finish this tune". Most Night Club owners appreciate this gimmick as it has a basic business reason, which is obvious. If the public likes you, it is a cute gimmick to keep them sitting in the Night Club spending their money, and extends the time a person spends in a Night Club. Mr. Berman, who is new in the business of presenting jazz groups, had evidently never heard of this business gatherer. I most certainly do this in many other Night Clubs in the United States without having it tossed back at me as being a bad thing to do. Usually, it is appreciated.

In regard to the next paragraph regarding lemon peels, I have a stomach condition, and have been advised to chew occasionally on lemon peels. What they do for me, I do not know. However, I most certainly did not spit them out on the band stand in full view of the customers, and certainly, there was nothing spiteful toward Mr. Berman or his customers in my chewing lemon peels. In this paragraph, Mr. Berman admits that a great number of patrons had been

SUN **1**

MON **2**

TUES **3**

WED **4**

THUR **5**

FRI **6**

SAT **7**

SUN **8**

MON **9**

TUES **10**

WED **11**

THUR **12**

FRI **13**

SAT **14**

SUN **15**

MON **16**

TUES **17**

WED **18**

THUR **19**

FRI **20**

SAT **21**

SUN **22**

MON **23**

TUES **24**

WED **25**

THUR **26**

FRI **27**

SAT **28**

SUN **29**

MON **30**

attracted to hear me. I wish to say that I think the dire disappointment he mentioned was in his own mind as I received many good remarks about my playing, and again, I say that because Mr.Berman is new in presenting modern jazz orchestras, he became unhappy with something that he did not understand, but most certainly, his customers who came to hear me, did.

In the next paragraph, Mr. Berman advises that he feels a contract must be respected. Of course, I do too, and I am also willing to abide by the Union's decision and I also agree that a contract is a deal between two people, and once that deal is not in accordance with the terms agreed upon, that it is no deal. My contract with Mr. Berman read that I should open on October 12, 1953 for a period of seven consecutive days, and that I should deliver five musicians, including myself, to play during this time at a salary of $1250.00 per week. I did deliver the five men, as stated on the contract, arrived on time, opened the engagement, and was perfectly willing to finish it. In Mr.Berman's paragraph he states that he was willing to pay the boys for the time they had worked up until then, and pay their fare back home. That definitely was not the contract I had with Mr. Berman. I believe that Mr. Berman is wrong in stating that he has deposited with the Musician's Union $534.06 inasmuch as he had deposited over $700.00 and he did forward to the Gale Agency, $117.00.

In Mr. Berman's last paragraph he states that he has been on most friendly terms with the Musician's Union, and I appreciate this and I believe that the Latin Quarter does have the respect and confidence of the Union. He states that this is not a question of money but a question of business. I know that I was not misrepresented as I was in the office of my Agency at the time I was sold to Mr. Berman. I do not know what Mr. Berman's expectations were but I do know that I appeared in Montreal as per the contract, and I feel that I should be paid as per contract, inasmuch as I did, in no way, break said contract. I did however, agree to close the engagement at the end of the third day of the engagement upon the suggestion of the representative of the Montreal Local, who advised me that I would receive from the Club, personally, at that time, the pro rata salary due my orchestra for the three days worked, and that the balance of the $1250.00 would be placed in escrow with the National office until such time as the facts of this situation could be presented to the National office.

The facts of the situation are, that I was engaged by the Latin Quarter Club in Montreal for a period of seven consecutive days at a salary of $1250.00. On this engagement, I was to deliver five musicians, including myself, which I did do. I arrived on time, I opened the engagement and performed for the hours specified, up until the time that the Montreal Union representative advised me as stated above. Inasmuch as I am a member of the American Federation of Musicians, I must abide by the suggestions and decisions of this organization, and I did do this. I feel that I am entitled to the balance of the money held in escrow by the National office, because, by no fault of mine, or my orchestra, I was not allowed to complete the full weeks engagement. At the moment, I am obliged to pay the members of my orchestraa full weeks salary and the round trip transportation, New York to Montreal. The $743.04 now in escrow will enable me to do this.

If I may add a personal note to this answer, I wish to say that I believe the reason for this situation is that the

Latin Quarter management recently started to play what might be termed, name jazz musicians and their orchestras and at the time I appeared there for them, they were not fully aware of the various types of jazz that is being played today in America. Preceding me, they employed two very fine organizations led by EARL HINES, and JOHNNY HODGES, whose orchestras play an excellent brand of jazz, entirely different from the type my orchestra plays, and Mr. Berman was comparing my type of music to the type he had been listening to, and because he was not familiar with it, he did not like it. However, this is only due to the fact that my type of music has not appeared in Montreal too often. There are Night Clubs in America , where I am at times, a little more successful than the above named orchestra leaders, because my type of music is more well known in these places and owners know about the music.

I respectfully submit this reply to you for your consideration and trust that this case shall be decided in my favor, as it is plainly a question of contract obligation, in my mind.

Sincerely yours,

Charlie Parker

SUN	**1**
MON	**2**
TUES	**3**
WED	**4**
THUR	**5**
FRI	**6**
SAT	**7**
SUN	**8**
MON	**9**
TUES	**10**
WED	**11**
THUR	**12**
FRI	**13**
SAT	**14**
SUN	**15**
MON	**16**
TUES	**17**
WED	**18**
THUR	**19**
FRI	**20**
SAT	**21**
SUN	**22**
MON	**23**
TUES	**24**
WED	**25**
THUR	**26**
FRI	**27**
SAT	**28**
SUN	**29**
MON	**30**

FRIDAY 20 NOVEMBER 1953

Charlie Parker opens at the Bee Hive in Chicago for a three-week engagement.

SUNDAY 22 NOVEMBER 1953

Charlie sends a Western Union Money Order message to Chan from Chicago:

MY DARLING SORRY FOR DELAY MORE LATER ILL CALL YOU ALL MY LOVE

TUESDAY 24 NOVEMBER 1953

Charlie sends a money order to Chan from Chicago with the message:

DARLING THERE ARE NO WORDS TO DESCRIBE THE VASTNESS OF MY LOVE FOR YOU AND ETERNALLY WILL LOVE YOU HAPPY THANKSGIVING.

SATURDAY 28 NOVEMBER 1953

Charlie Parker appears in two shows at the Regal Theatre, Chicago with Ben Webster and T-Bone Walker at 8pm and 12 midnight as well as his stint at the Bee Hive Lounge.

TUES	1
WED	2
THUR	3
FRI	4
SAT	5
SUN	6
MON	7
TUES	8
WED	9
THUR	10
FRI	11
SAT	12
SUN	13
MON	14
TUES	15
WED	16
THUR	17
FRI	18
SAT	19
SUN	20
MON	21
TUES	22
WED	23
THUR	24
FRI	25
SAT	26
SUN	27
MON	28
TUES	29
WED	30
THUR	31

Above: Bird at the Bee-Hive Lounge in Chicago with Israel Crosby on bass.

THURSDAY 10 DECEMBER 1953

Charlie Parker closes at the Bee Hive Lounge in Chicago.

SATURDAY 19 DECEMBER 1953

Charlie Parker opens at the Club Tijuana in Baltimore for a two-week engagement using local sidemen.

SATURDAY 26 DECEMBER 1953

Charlie Parker sends a Western Union Money Order message to Chan from Baltimore:
A KISS COMES WITH THIS WIRE

SUNDAY 27 DECEMBER 1953

Charlie Parker closes at the Club Tijuana in Baltimore.

WEDNESDAY 30 DECEMBER 1953

Charlie Parker wins the 1953 Alto Sax award in the 17th Annual Down Beat Poll. The magazine also reviews the Massey Hall albums:

Jazz at Massey Hall

Vol. 1
Perdido / Salt Peanuts / All the Things You Are
Rating: ****
Vol. 2
Embraceable You / Sure Thing / Cherokee / Jubilee / Lullaby Of Birdland / Bass-ically Speaking
Rating: *****

Massey Hall is in Toronto, and the Toronto Jazz Society assembled Dizzy, Bud Powell, Max Roach, Charlie Mingus, and Charlie Chan there in May of this year for its first annual jazz festival. Mr. Chan is known to ornithologists the world over as an exceedingly rare species unto himself. Vol. 1, except for Bud's solos, is a little uneven. *Perdido* is marred by the hornmen's tendency toward exhibitionism. The extended *Peanuts* is a five-way delight. The exhibitionism returns in *Things*, with Bird tossing in a Kerry Dance figure and Dizzy digging into the *Grand Canyon Suite* for a couple of seconds. Otherwise, the solos are good until the performance collapses. To use an understatement, there was tension even before that between Bud and the horns.

Vol. 2 has some of the most fabulous Powell on records. (It's an all-trio set with Billy Taylor on *Bass-ically*). This can stand an enormous number of replays, for there's more to hear and learn each time. Charlie Mingus and Max Roach are equal to the exacting task of keeping up with Bud's unpredictable explorations. Max's solo on *Cherokee* builds like the *Twelve Days of Christmas*, and Mingus is peerless in *Bass-ically*. Even Herman Leonard's cover portrait of Bud wails. (**Debut DLP-2, DLP-3**)

FRI	**1**
SAT	**2**
SUN	**3**
MON	**4**
TUES	**5**
WED	**6**
THUR	**7**
FRI	**8**
SAT	**9**
SUN	**10**
MON	**11**
TUES	**12**
WED	**13**
THUR	**14**
FRI	**15**
SAT	**16**
SUN	**17**
MON	**18**
TUES	**19**
WED	**20**
THUR	**21**
FRI	**22**
SAT	**23**
SUN	**24**
MON	**25**
TUES	**26**
WED	**27**
THUR	**28**
FRI	**29**
SAT	**30**
SUN	**31**

MONDAY 4 JANUARY 1954

Charlie Parker opens at the Blue Note in Philadelphia for a one-week engagement with Clifford Brown on trumpet.

SUNDAY 10 JANUARY 1954

Charlie Parker writes to the AF of M Local 274 in Philadelphia:

Dear Sir and Brother;

Some time ago I wrote to you about a debt of $350 incurred by Herb Gordy of your Local for services rendered by me during a concert engagement October 21, 1952 in Philadelphia. In my letter to you I enclosed the contract from this engagement. Could you please write to me and let me know if you received my letter and contract.

Since quite some time has passed since this engagement, and I feel it only right that I should be paid for my services, I know that you will look into the matter immediately and see if you can't collect my money for me.

Respectfully, Charlie Parker.

Charlie Parker closes at the Blue Note in Philadelphia.

MONDAY 11 JANUARY 1954

Charlie Parker writes to the union:

Dear Sir and Brother:

I am enclosing three contracts for three separate engagements which I played for and did not get paid; and I wish to file claim against these promoters.

The first: Against James LaRue, 49 W99 St, NYC for the sum of $350 due me on a $500 guarantee, for services rendered him on January 4, 1952 at Chateau Gardens on Houston St. in NYC. I was not paid for this job except for a $150 advance, although I played overtime for this man. The four other men in my band who worked this job with me filed claim against me and received their money out of my pocket. I would appreciate being reimbursed by Mr LaRue. I know he still runs dances ... some at the same Chateau Gardens, and I feel it only fair that I be paid for my services before Mr LaRue is permitted to continue running dances.

The second claim is against Albert Bryan, 382 Bainbridge St, B'klyn, NY for a balance of $300 on a $500 guarantee. I worked on the excursion boat S.S. Peter Stuyvesant on September 12, 1952 along with several other musicians. No one got paid on this job. In fact the entrepreneur skipped out with all our salaries, and when we tried to claim our money, we found that Mr. Bryan was out on bail. Could you please take action against this man?

The third claim is against Mr. N.R. Wattam, 12 Tyndall Ave, Toronto, Ont. Canada, who is president of the New Jazz Society, for the sum of $200 plus 21.7% of the musicians share of the net profit, for services rendered by me on May 15, 1953 at Massey Hall in Toronto. No one got paid on this job either.

There is also a $15 balance due me by Eugene Riley, 2734

3rd Ave, NYC for a job I played for him at Hunts Point Palace on Dec 7, 1953. I have an IOU for this amount. I know this is quite an order, but I would truly appreciate it if you would kindly take action against these four people as I rendered my services to them and I feel I am entitled to be paid the amount they agreed upon.

MONDAY 18 JANUARY 1954

Charlie Parker opens at the Hi Hat Club in Boston for a one-week engagement.
Private recording features
CHARLIE PARKER (alto sax), HERB POMEROY (trumpet), UNKNOWN (piano), CHARLIE MINGUS (bass), UNKNOWN (drums)
Ornithology / Out Of Nowhere / My Funny Valentine / Cool Blues

During the Hi-Hat engagement Charlie appears on a Boston radio programme with Paul Desmond and John McLellan:
[record]
DESMOND: *That music, because there's many good people playing in that record, but the style of the alto is so different from anything else that's on the record, or that went before. Did you realise at that time the effect you were going to have on jazz… that you were going to change the entire scene in the next ten years?*
PARKER: Well… let's put it like this… no. I had no idea that it was that much different.
MCLELLAN: *I'd like to stick in a question, if I may. I'd like to know why there was this violent change, really. After all, up until this time the way to play the alto sax was the way that Johnny Hodges and Benny Carter played alto, and this seems to be an entirely different conception, not only of how to play that particular horn, but of music in general.*
DESMOND: *Yeah… how to play any horn.*
PARKER: I don't think there's any answer to…
DESMOND: *… it's like the way you eat.*
PARKER: That's what I said when I first started talking, that's my first conception, man, that's the way I thought it should

FRI	1
SAT	2
SUN	3
MON	4
TUES	5
WED	6
THUR	7
FRI	8
SAT	9
SUN	10
MON	11
TUES	12
WED	13
THUR	14
FRI	15
SAT	16
SUN	17
MON	18
TUES	19
WED	20
THUR	21
FRI	22
SAT	23
SUN	24
MON	25
TUES	26
WED	27
THUR	28
FRI	29
SAT	30
SUN	31

go, and I still do. I mean, music can stand much improvement. Most likely, in another 25, maybe 50 years, some youngster will come along and take this style and really do something with it, you know, but I mean, ever since I've ever heard music I've always thought it should be very clean, very precise... as clean as possible, anyway... you know, and more or less to the people, you know, something they could understand, something that was beautiful, you know... there's definitely stories and stories and stories that can be told in the musical idiom, you know... you wouldn't say idiom, but it's so hard to describe music other than the basic way to describe it... music is basically melody, harmony and rhythm... but, I mean, people can do much more with music than that. It can be very descriptive in all kinds of ways, you know, all walks of life. Don't you agree, Paul?

DESMOND: *Yeah... and you always do have a story to tell... it's one of the most impressive things about everything I've ever heard of yours.*

PARKER: That's more or less the object, that's what I thought it should be.

DESMOND: *Uh huh. Another thing that's a major factor in your playing, is this fantastic technique, that nobody's quite equalled. I've always wondered about that, too... whether there was... whether that came behind practising or whether that was just from playing... whether that evolved gradually.*

PARKER: Well... you make it so hard for me to answer you, you know... because I can't see where there's anything fantastic about it all. I put quite a bit of study into the horn, that's true. In fact, the neighbours threatened to ask my mother to move once. We were living out West. She said I was driving them crazy with the horn. I used to put in at least 11 to 15 hours a day.

DESMOND: *Yes... that's what I wondered.*

PARKER: That's true, yes. I did that for over a period of 3 or 4 years.

DESMOND: *... because that's the answer.*

PARKER: That's the facts, anyway.

DESMOND: *I heard a record of yours a couple of months ago that somehow I've missed up to date, and I heard a little 2 bar quote from the Closé book that was like an echo from home...* [hums the quote]

PARKER: Yeah, yeah... well, that was all done with books, you know, naturally it wasn't done with mirrors this time, it was done with books.

DESMOND: *Well, that's very reassuring to hear, because somehow I got the idea that you were just sort of born with that technique, and you never had to worry too much about it... about keeping it working.*

McLELLAN: *You know, I'm very glad that he's bringing up this point, because I think that a lot of young musicians tend to think that...*

DESMOND: *Yeah, they do. They just go out...*

McLELLAN: *... it isn't necessary to do this.*

DESMOND: *... and make those sessions and live the life, but they don't put in those 11 hours a day with any of the books.*

PARKER: Oh, definitely... study is absolutely necessary, in all forms. It's just like any talent that's born within somebody, it's like a good pair of shoes when you put a shine on it, you know, like schooling just brings out the polish, you know, of any talent, it happens anywhere in the world. Einstein had schooling, but he has a definite genius, you know, within himself... schooling is one of the most wonderful things there's ever been.

McLELLAN: *I'm glad to hear you say this.*

PARKER: That's absolutely right.

DESMOND: *Yeah..*

PARKER: Well...

DESMOND: *What other record?*

PARKER: Which one should we take this time?

McLELLAN: *I want to skip a little while. We... Charlie, picked out 'Night and Day', that's one of his records. Is this with a band or with strings?*

PARKER: No, this is with the live band... I think there's about 19 pieces on this.

McLELLAN: *Why don't we listen to it, then... and talk about it.* [record: 'Night and Day']

DESMOND: *Charlie, this brings us kind of up to when you and Diz started joining forces... the next record we have coming up. When did you first meet Dizzy Gillespie?*

PARKER: Well... the first time... our official meeting I might say, was on the bandstand of the Savoy Ballroom in New York City in 1939. McShann's band first came to New York... I'd been in New York previously, but I went back West and rejoined the band and came back to New York with it. Dizzy came by one night... I think at the time he was working with Cab Calloway's band... and he sat in on the band and I was quite fascinated by the fellow, and we became very good friends and until this day we are, you know... and that was the first time I ever had the pleasure to meet Dizzy Gillespie.

DESMOND: *Was he playing the same way then... before he played with you?*

PARKER: I don't remember precisely. I just know he was playing... what you might call, in the vernacular of the streets, a beaucoup of horn, you know?

DESMOND: *Beaucoup?*

PARKER: Yeah.

DESMOND: *O.K.*

PARKER: You know, just like all of the horns packed up in one, you know.

DESMOND: *Right.*

PARKER: And we used to go around different places and jam together... and we had quite a bit of fun in those days, and shortly after the McShann band went out West again, I went out with them and I came back to New York again... I found Dizzy again, in the old Hines organisation in 1941, and I joined the band with him. I was in New York... I, we... both stayed on the band about a year. It was Earl Hines... and Dizzy Gillespie, Sarah Vaughan, Billy Eckstine, Gail Brockman, Thomas Crump, Shadow Wilson... quite a few names that you'd recognise in the music world today, you know, were in that band.

DESMOND: *That's quite a collection.*

PARKER: And then that band broke up in '41. In '42 Dizzy was in New York and formed his own new combination in the Three Deuces, in New York City, and I joined his band there, and that's when these records you're about to play now... we made these in '42 in New York.

DESMOND: *Yeah... I guess the first time I heard that group was...*

FRI	**1**
SAT	**2**
SUN	**3**
MON	**4**
TUES	**5**
WED	**6**
THUR	**7**
FRI	**8**
SAT	**9**
SUN	**10**
MON	**11**
TUES	**12**
WED	**13**
THUR	**14**
FRI	**15**
SAT	**16**
SUN	**17**
MON	**18**
TUES	**19**
WED	**20**
THUR	**21**
FRI	**22**
SAT	**23**
SUN	**24**
MON	**25**
TUES	**26**
WED	**27**
THUR	**28**
FRI	**29**
SAT	**30**
SUN	**31**

you came out to Billy Berg's?

PARKER: Oh, yes… but that was '45, that was later… we'll get to that.

DESMOND: *I'm just illustrating how far I was behind all this.*

PARKER: Oh, don't be that way… modesty will get you nowhere.

DESMOND: *I'm hip.*

McLELLAN: *So, shall we spin this 1942 one… Groovin' High?*

DESMOND: Yes.

McLELLAN: *O.K. This is Dizzy and Charlie…*

[play record]

McLELLAN: *I guess this is Slam Stewart and Remo Palmieri… I guess I don't know who it is on piano.*

PARKER: Yes, I think that was Clyde Hart.

McLELLAN: *Yes, I think so.*

PARKER: And Big Sid Catlett, deceased now.

DESMOND: *You said at that time… New York was jumping in '42.*

PARKER: Yeah, New York was… well, those were what you might call the good old days, you know Paul… gay youth.

DESMOND: *Tell me about it.*

PARKER: Well, descriptively, just like I was going to say… gay youth… lack of funds…

DESMOND: *Listen at grandfather Parker talking here.*

PARKER: There was nothing to do but play, you know, and we had a lot of fun trying to play, you know… I did plenty of jam sessions… meant much late hours, plenty good food… nice clean living, you know, but basically speaking, much poverty.

DESMOND: *That's always good, too… no worries.*

PARKER: It had it's place, definitely, in life.

DESMOND: *Would you like that sort of situation to have continued indefinitely?*

PARKER: Well, whether I liked it or not, it really did Paul… I'm glad it finally blew over of a sort… and I do mean of a sort.

DESMOND: *Yes.*

PARKER: Yeah, I enjoy this a little… much more, in fact…having the pleasure to work with the same guys of the sort that I've met… and I've met other young fellows, you know, that come along and I enjoy working with them when I have the pleasure to. If I might say… you, yourself Paul.

DESMOND: *Oh, thanks.*

PARKER: Sure, I've had lots of fun working with you, man… that's a pleasure in a million. And David, Dave Brubeck… David Brubeck, lots of other fellows have come along, you know, since that era… that particular era. It makes you feel that everything you did wasn't for nought, you know, that you really tried to prove something, and…

DESMOND: *Well, man, you really did prove it. I think you did more than anybody in the last 10 years to leave a decisive mark on the history of jazz.*

PARKER: Well… not yet, Paul, but I intended to. I'd like to study some more, I'm not quite through yet, I'm not quite… I don't consider myself too old to learn.

DESMOND: *No, I know many people are watching you at the moment, with the greatest of interest, to see what you're going to come up with next, in the next few years… myself among the front row of them. And what have you got in mind? What are you going to be doing?*

PARKER: Well, seriously speaking, I mean, I'm going to try to go to Europe to study. I had the pleasure to meet one Edgar Varese in New York City… he's a classical composer from Europe… he's a Frenchman, very nice fellow, and he wants to teach me… in fact, he wants to write for me, because he thinks I'm more for… more or less on a serious basis, you know… and if he takes me on, I mean, when he finishes with me, I might have a chance to go to the Academie Musicale in Paris itself, and study, you know. My prime interest still is learning to play music, you know.

McLELLAN: *Would you study playing or composition, or everything?*

PARKER: I would study both… never want to lose my horn.

DESMOND: *Yeah, and you never should. That would be a catastrophe.*

PARKER: I don't want to do that. That wouldn't work.

BROADCASTER: *Well, we're kind of getting ahead of the record sequence here, but it's been most fascinating. Do you want to say something about Miles Davis?*

PARKER: Yeah, well…I'll tell you how I met Miles. In 1944, Billy Eckstine formed his own organisation… Dizzy was on that band also… Lucky Thompson… there was Art Blakey, Tommy Potter… a lot of other fellows, and last and least… yours truly.

DESMOND: *Modesty will get you nowhere, Charlie.*

PARKER: I had the pleasure to meet Miles, for the first time, in St Louis, when he was a youngster… he was still going to school. Later on he came to New York. He finished Juilliard, Miles did, he graduated from Juilliard and, at the time, I was just beginning to get my band together, you know… five pieces here… five pieces there. So I formed a band and took it into the Three Deuces for maybe seven to eight weeks, and at the time, Dizzy… after the next time the organisation broke up… Dizzy was about to form his own band. There was so many things taking place then, I mean, it's hard to describe it, because it happened in a matter of months. Nevertheless, I went to California in 1945 with Dizzy, after I broke up my band… the first band I had… then I came again back to New York in '47, the early part of '47, and that's when I decided to have a band of my own permanently, and Miles was in my original band. I had Miles… I had Max… I had Tommy Potter and Al Haig in my band. Another band I had, I had Stan Levey… I had Curley Russell… I had Miles and George Wallington… but I think you have a record out there, one of the records that we made with Max and Miles, I think, and yours truly, Tommy and Duke Jordan… What is it? I think it's 'Perhaps'. Is it not so? Well, this came along in the years of say '47… '46, '47. These particular sides were made in New York City, WOR 1440 Broadway, and this is the beginning of my career as a bandleader.

McLELLAN: *O.K. Well, let's listen to 'Perhaps'.*

[plays record 'Perhaps']

FRI	**1**
SAT	**2**
SUN	**3**
MON	**4**
TUES	**5**
WED	**6**
THUR	**7**
FRI	**8**
SAT	**9**
SUN	**10**
MON	**11**
TUES	**12**
WED	**13**
THUR	**14**
FRI	**15**
SAT	**16**
SUN	**17**
MON	**18**
TUES	**19**
WED	**20**
THUR	**21**
FRI	**22**
SAT	**23**
SUN	**24**
MON	**25**
TUES	**26**
WED	**27**
THUR	**28**
FRI	**29**
SAT	**30**
SUN	**31**

FRIDAY 22 JANUARY 1954
Charlie Parker sends a Western Union Money Order message to Chan from Boston:
LOVE YOU AND MISS YOU

SATURDAY 23 JANUARY 1954
Charlie Parker Quintet broadcast from the Hi Hat Club in Boston on station WCOP.
CHARLIE PARKER (alto sax), HERBIE WILLIAMS (trumpet), JAY MIGLIORI (tenor sax), ROLLINS GRIFFITH (piano), JIMMY WOODE (bass), GREGG SOLANO (drums), SYMPHONY SID TORIN (mc)
Now's The Time / Out Of Nowhere / My Little Suede Shoes / Jumpin' With Symphony Sid

SUNDAY 24 JANUARY 1954
Charlie Parker closes at the Hi Hat Club in Boston.

MONDAY 25 JANUARY 1954
Norman Granz writes to Charlie Parker at 151 Ave B:

THURSDAY 28 JANUARY 1954
Charlie Parker joins the Festival of Modern American Jazz Tour with the Stan Kenton Orchestra, Dizzy Gillespie, Erroll Garner Trio, Lee Konitz, June Christy and Candido.
The first concert is at Wichita Falls, Texas.
The musicians stay at the Green Acre Courts Hotel.

FRIDAY 29 JANUARY 1954
The tour continues at the Coliseum in San Antonio, Texas.
The musicians stay at the Ritz Hotel.

SATURDAY 30 JANUARY 1954
The tour appears at the City Auditorium in Houston, Texas.
The musicians stay at the Crystal Hotel in Houston.

SUNDAY 31 JANUARY 1954
The tour appears at the Auditorium in New Orleans.
The musicians stay at the Patterson Hotel.

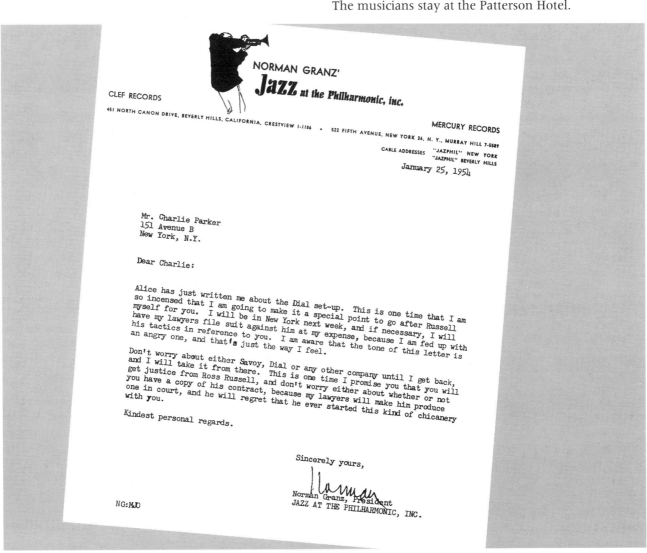

MON	**1**
TUES	**2**
WED	**3**
THUR	**4**
FRI	**5**
SAT	**6**
SUN	**7**
MON	**8**
TUES	**9**
WED	**10**
THUR	**11**
FRI	**12**
SAT	**13**
SUN	**14**
MON	**15**
TUES	**16**
WED	**17**
THUR	**18**
FRI	**19**
SAT	**20**
SUN	**21**
MON	**22**
TUES	**23**
WED	**24**
THUR	**25**
FRI	**26**
SAT	**27**
SUN	**28**

On the road: Bird, June Christy and Stan Kenton.

MON **1**
TUES **2**
WED **3**
THUR **4**
FRI **5**
SAT **6**
SUN **7**
MON **8**
TUES **9**
WED **10**
THUR **11**
FRI **12**
SAT **13**
SUN **14**
MON **15**
TUES **16**
WED **17**
THUR **18**
FRI **19**
SAT **20**
SUN **21**
MON **22**
TUES **23**
WED **24**
THUR **25**
FRI **26**
SAT **27**
SUN **28**

MONDAY 1 FEBRUARY 1954
The Festival of Modern American Jazz appears at Fort Whiting, Mobile, Alabama.

TUESDAY 2 FEBRUARY 1954
The Festival of Modern American Jazz appears at the Municipal Auditorium, Atlanta, Georgia. The musicians stay at the Walgrave Hotel in Atlanta.

WEDNESDAY 3 FEBRUARY 1954
The Festival of Modern American Jazz appears at the Ryman Auditorium, Nashville, Tennessee. The musicians stay at the Brown Hotel in Nashville.

THURSDAY 4 FEBRUARY 1954
The Festival of Modern American Jazz appears at the Memorial Auditorium, Spartanburg, South Carolina.

MON	1
TUES	2
WED	3
THUR	4
FRI	5
SAT	6
SUN	7
MON	8
TUES	9
WED	10
THUR	11
FRI	12
SAT	13
SUN	14
MON	15
TUES	16
WED	17
THUR	18
FRI	19
SAT	20
SUN	21
MON	22
TUES	23
WED	24
THUR	25
FRI	26
SAT	27
SUN	28

Mary Lou Williams writes to Charlie from Paris:

Dear Charlie,

I have written Klook, Art Blakey and others I know to try and help situation that has been brought on by certain people in the States through their writing for foreign musical magazines. They're trying to change the public as far as negro musicians. I will have to see you and show you, however please strengthen yourselves. Miles, Art Blakey, Max Roach, you and the beginners of the modern trend have almost disappeared as far as record sales etc. over here. Am having fights with musicians who .... in all papers. .... broke it up and opened new work for everyone in Africa – I didn't know that he was in Europe until I came to Paris. He broke all records – ask Curley or some of the other musicians. Give Chan and your family my best.

Mary Lou

FRIDAY 5 FEBRUARY 1954

The Festival of Modern American Jazz appears at the Memorial Auditorium, Raleigh, North Carolina. The musicians stay at the Eckers Hotel in Raleigh.

SATURDAY 6 FEBRUARY 1954

Charlie receives an advance of $80 from the Gale Agency.

The Festival of Modern American Jazz appears at the Paramount Theatre, New York City.

SUNDAY 7 FEBRUARY 1954

The Festival of Modern American Jazz appears at the National Guard Armory in Washington, D.C.

MONDAY 8 FEBRUARY 1954

The Festival of Modern American Jazz appears at Upper Darby, Pennsylvania.

TUESDAY 9 FEBRUARY 1954

The Festival of Modern American Jazz appears in Worcester, Massachusetts.

WEDNESDAY 10 FEBRUARY 1954

The Festival of Modern American Jazz appears at the Civic Center, White Plains, NY.

WEDNESDAY 10 FEBRUARY 1954

Down Beat reviews Charlie's latest record release:

CHARLIE PARKER
***** **She Rote**
** **   K.C. Blues**

Rote, on the changes of *Beyond the Blue Horizon*, flashes a fiery pair of opening choruses from Bird that should chase quite a few altoists back to the woodshed. He's superb, both here and later in the record. Between, there's a solo from Miles Davis in which he plays confidently and movingly, obviously inspired by Parker's opening lance, and a piano contribution from Walter Bishop. Max Roach and bassist Teddy Kotick give unwavering backing.

Flip side is a throw away, once-through blues of only mild interest. (**Clef 11101**)

CHARLIE PARKER Alternate Masters, Vol. 2

Ornithology / Yardbird Suite / Moose the Mooche / A Night in Tunisia / The Famous Alto Break / This Is Always / Bird's Nest / Drifting On A Reed / Charlie's Wig / Crazeology / Dexterity / Dewey Square / Home Cooking, I / Home Cooking, II

Rating: ****

Another issue of the famous Hollywood sessions made in 1946 and 1947, along with some made later that year in New York. With five exceptions, all these bands are the original 78 rpm releases that were never put out on LP (though a number of alternate masters have been). The other five are being released for the first time on any speed and include other masters of *Bird's Nest*, *Crazeology*, two of *Home Cooking* and a fabulous alto break from *A Night in Tunisia*. The label distinguishes between the two categories.

No personnel is listed but as you recall, Bird was joined on these by musicians like Miles, Lucky Thompson, Dodo Marmarosa, Erroll Garner, Red Callender, Harold West, Jay Jay Johnson, Duke Jordan, Tommy Potter, Max Roach, and others. Aside from the high musical value of a number of the original 78s, this is another absorbing opportunity to compare masters and thereby to study the morphology of improvisation. (**Dial LP 905**)

MON	1
TUES	2
WED	3
THUR	4
FRI	5
SAT	6
SUN	7
MON	8
TUES	9
WED	10
THUR	11
FRI	12
SAT	13
SUN	14
MON	15
TUES	16
WED	17
THUR	18
FRI	19
SAT	20
SUN	21
MON	22
TUES	23
WED	24
THUR	25
FRI	26
SAT	27
SUN	28

THURSDAY 11 FEBRUARY 1954

The Festival of Modern American Jazz appears at Ann Arbor, Michigan.

FRIDAY 12 FEBRUARY 1954

The Festival of Modern American Jazz appears at Massey Hall in Toronto.
Charlie receives a $98 advance from the Gale Agency for rent.

SATURDAY 13 FEBRUARY 1954

The Festival of Modern American Jazz appears in Detroit, Michigan.

SUNDAY 14 FEBRUARY 1954

The Festival of Modern American Jazz appears at the Rainbo in Chicago.

Between shows, Charlie sends a Western Union Valentine greeting to Chan

WHILE SEARCHING MENTALLY FOR WORDS IN MY VOCABULARY I CHOSE THE MEANING OF THE BIRDS. IM PROUD ITS YOU I MARRIED. IM ALSO GLAD TO LET YOU KNOW IN WORDS THAT GENTLY RHYME IM VERY MUCH IN LOVE WITH YOU SO BE MY VALENTINE.
CHARLIE PARKER.

TUESDAY 16 FEBRUARY 1954

The AF of M write to Charlie to advise him that his claim against Albert Bryan for $300 has been upheld and that Mr. Bryan has been advised to make payment of the award through the AF of M.

WEDNESDAY 17 FEBRUARY 1954

TheAF of M write to Charlie to advise him that his claim against Eugene Riley for $15 has been upheld and that Mr. Riley has been advised to make payment of the award through the AF of M.
They also write to advise Charlie that his claim against James LaRue for $350 has been upheld.

WEDNESDAY 24 FEBRUARY 1954

Charlie sends a cable to Chan from Seattle:

SENDING YOU SMALL PRESENT HEARD YOU DID NOT GET MY TELEGRAM HAVE PRESENT FOR YOU WHEN YOU ARRIVE. FINALLY REACHED SEATTLE LANTHEIE BROKE HIS OLD LADIES NECK LAST NIGHT AFTER WE TALKED TO YOU ON PHONE GETZ OUT ON SUSPENDED SENTENCE LOOKING FOR HIM TO KILL HIM IN A CERTAIN TOWN. DARLING HAVE HUNDRED DOLLARS SENDING YOU RIGHT AWAY CALL ME IMMEDIATELY OLYMPIC HOTEL BY THE WAY HAVING A WONDERFUL TIME THANK YOU FOR MAKING A MAN OF ME I WILL ALWAYS LOVE YOU
=GUESS WHO=

THURSDAY 25 FEBRUARY 1954

The Festival of Modern American Jazz appears at the Civic Auditorium in Portland, Oregon. A private recording is made of Charlie with the Kenton Band.
CHARLIE PARKER (alto sax), SAM NOTO, VIC MINICHELLI, BUDDY CHILDERS, DON SMITH, STU WILLIAMSON (trumpet), MILT GOLD, JOE CIAVARDONE, BOB FITZPATRICK, FRANK ROSOLINO (trombone), GEORGE ROBERTS (bass trombone), CHARLIE MARIANO, DAVE SCHILDKRAUT (alto sax), MIKE CICCHETTI, BILL PERKINS (tenor sax), TONY FERINA (baritone sax), STAN KENTON (piano), BOB LESHER (guitar), DON BAGLEY (bass), STAN LEVEY (drums)
Night And Day / My Funny Valentine / Cherokee

FRIDAY 26 FEBRUARY 1954

The Festival of Modern American Jazz appears at the Paramount Theatre in San Francisco.

SATURDAY 27 FEBRUARY 1954

The Festival of Modern American Jazz appears at the Auditorium Arena in Oakland.

SUNDAY 28 FEBRUARY 1954

The Festival of Modern American Jazz tour ends at the Shrine Auditorium in Los Angeles.
Jack Tucker, manager of the Tiffany Club, visits Charlie at the concert to arrange a rehearsal for the next morning, prior to Charlie's scheduled opening at the Tiffany. Charlie at first refuses to appear, but Tucker calls the Gale Agency in New York.

MON	**1**
TUES	**2**
WED	**3**
THUR	**4**
FRI	**5**
SAT	**6**
SUN	**7**
MON	**8**
TUES	**9**
WED	**10**
THUR	**11**
FRI	**12**
SAT	**13**
SUN	**14**
MON	**15**
TUES	**16**
WED	**17**
THUR	**18**
FRI	**19**
SAT	**20**
SUN	**21**
MON	**22**
TUES	**23**
WED	**24**
THUR	**25**
FRI	**26**
SAT	**27**
SUN	**28**
MON	**29**
TUES	**30**
WED	**31**

MONDAY 1 MARCH 1954

Charlie attends a midday rehearsal at the Tiffany Club (3260 West 8th Street, Los Angeles) with the Joe Rotondi Trio. After only a quarter of an hour, Charlie says no more rehearsals are necessary.
Charlie Parker opens at the Tiffany Club in the evening. Al Hibbler is also on the bill. Charlie plays only two short sets and leaves the club at 11 o'clock during intermission to get a sandwich. He makes a long distance telephone call to Chan. He is picked up by the LAPD and held overnight on suspicion of being a narcotics user.

TUESDAY 2 MARCH 1954

Charlie Parker is booked on a drunk and disorderly charge but after Charles Carpenter of the Gale Agency pays a $10 fine Charlie is released at 7 p.m. Carpenter accompanies Charlie to the Tiffany Club and re-negotiates his contract. Parker plays four short sets.

WEDNESDAY 3 MARCH 1954

During the course of the third night at the Tiffany Club, Charlie has a few drinks with George Hoefer of *Down Beat* magazine and Norman Granz' brother. A row ensues with the management and Charlie is fired. Charlie hears from Chan that their baby, Pree, is to be put into an oxygen tent in a last effort to save her life.

THURSDAY 4 MARCH 1954

Charlie reappears at the Tiffany Club and plays three sets before another row develops with the management and Charlie is fired again.

FRIDAY 5 MARCH 1954

Charlie advises the Gale Agency of the situation at the club and is advised to go back to the Tiffany and offer his services. The management of the Tiffany reject the offer and refuse to negotiate a settlement.

SATURDAY 6 MARCH 1954

Pree Parker dies in the evening.

SUNDAY 7 MARCH 1954

When Charlie hears the news of his daughter's death it is early Sunday morning. He fires off three confused telegrams to Chan.
4.11 am:
MY DARLING MY DAUGHTER'S DEATH SURPRISED ME MORE THAN IT DID YOU DON'T FULFILL FUNERAL PROCEEDINGS UNTIL I GET THERE I SHALL BE THE FIRST ONE TO WALK INTO OUR CHAPEL FORGIVE ME FOR NOT BEING THERE WITH YOU WHILE YOU WERE AT THE HOSPITAL YOURS MOST SINCERELY YOUR HUSBAND CHARLIE PARKER

4.13 am:
MY DARLING FOR GOD'S SAKE HOLD ON TO YOURSELF
CHAS PARKER

4.15 am:
CHAN, HELP
CHARLIE PARKER

A few hours later, after gathering his thoughts, Charlie sends another cable to Chan.
7.58 am
MY DAUGHTER IS DEAD. I KNOW IT. I WILL BE THERE AS QUICK AS I CAN. MY NAME IS BIRD. IT IS VERY NICE TO BE OUT HERE. PEOPLE HAVE BEEN VERY NICE TO ME OUT HERE. I AM COMING IN RIGHT AWAY TAKE IT EASY. LET ME BE THE FIRST ONE TO APPROACH YOU. I AM YOUR HUSBAND. SINCERELY, CHARLIE PARKER.

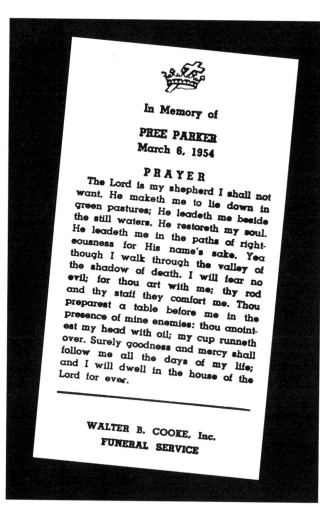

In Memory of
PREE PARKER
March 6, 1954

PRAYER

The Lord is my shepherd I shall not want. He maketh me to lie down in green pastures; He leadeth me beside the still waters. He restoreth my soul. He leadeth me in the paths of righteousness for His name's sake. Yea though I walk through the valley of the shadow of death. I will fear no evil; for thou art with me; thy rod and thy staff they comfort me. Thou preparest a table before me in the presence of mine enemies: thou anointest my head with oil; my cup runneth over. Surely goodness and mercy shall follow me all the days of my life; and I will dwell in the house of the Lord for ever.

WALTER B. COOKE, Inc.
FUNERAL SERVICE

TUESDAY 9 MARCH 1954

Charlie receives a $25 advance from the Gale Agency

MON	**1**
TUES	**2**
WED	**3**
THUR	**4**
FRI	**5**
SAT	**6**
SUN	**7**
MON	**8**
TUES	**9**
WED	**10**
THUR	**11**
FRI	**12**
SAT	**13**
SUN	**14**
MON	**15**
TUES	**16**
WED	**17**
THUR	**18**
FRI	**19**
SAT	**20**
SUN	**21**
MON	**22**
TUES	**23**
WED	**24**
THUR	**25**
FRI	**26**
SAT	**27**
SUN	**28**
MON	**29**
TUES	**30**
WED	**31**

THURSDAY 11 MARCH 1954

Charlie receives a $25 advance from the Gale Agency

Jack Tucker, manager of the Tiffany Club writes to Joe Marsolais of the Gale Agency:

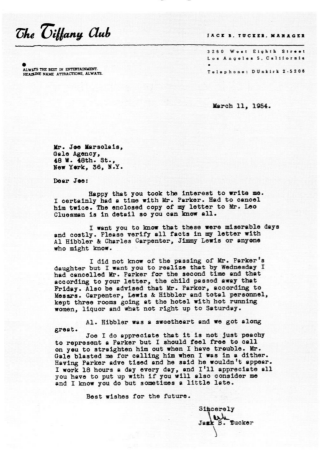

Enclosed with this letter is a copy of the letter of complaint to the Union:

Mr. Leo Cluesmann, Sec'y,
American Federation of Musicians,
220 Mt.Pleasant,
Newark 4, N.J.

Dear Mr.Cluesmann,

I negotiated a contract for Charlie Parker to appear at the Tiffany Club March 1st., through his agent, Joe Marsolais of the Gale Agency, New York, via mail and telephone. He was closing in L.A. with Gene Norman concert at the Shrine Auditorium, February 28th. I went to the concert to introduce myself and to give Charlie Parker a rehearsal call and he said he would not appear the next day. I explained that he was already advertised in the newspapers that evening, but he said that didn't matter to him. I went back to my club and called New York again. Not being able to reach Mr. Marsolais, I did reach Tim Gale. His reply was, that if Mr. Marsolais arranged the date, Parker would play it. Monday morning, I called a rehearsal for 12 o'clock. Mr.Parker played with the trio less than fifteen minutes and said no more rehearsal was necessary. That evening Mr. Parker appeared but would not sign his contract until the Union official, Mr. Elmer

Fain demanded it. I also had on my bill, Al Hibbler, so I asked Mr. Parker to play 25 minutes. Mr. Parker was to leave the stand so that Al Hibbler could sing 15 minutes with the trio, rounding out the trio's 40 minutes. Mr. Parker played two sets and left the Club about 11 o'clock and didn't return. I have a policy, $1.25 per person admission. I had to make refunds the balance of the evening and also turn away people who would not come in when they found out Charlie Parker was not appearing. I also had to try to cancel ads.

Tuesday, March 2nd, Mr. Parker came in with Mr. Charles Carpenter and asked to re-negotiate because the Union would bar him from ever playing anywhere in the Country. We re-negotiated and Mr. Parker played four sets instead of five, consisting of 17-14-18-20 minutes each. During these short sessions, Mr. Parker played very little. He leaned on the piano and weaved from side to side, obviously intoxicated. His eyes were shut for three and four minutes at a time and he didn't play a note. He sweat profusely, and wiped his brow with his forefinger and thrust sweat to the floor, unbecoming to a performer. His stage behavior was the most deplorable I have ever witnessed. Patrons laughed and giggled and wondered what next.

He rarely called his numbers and on the second show asked me if he could use a drummer friend for that set and I told him we weren't having a Jam Session and had no permission from the Union to do that. However, he announced the other drummer and after the set, asked the audience if that wasn't a good replacement, causing embarrassment to the regular drummer. During this evening he had a bottle stashed, without my knowledge, which is against the law in California and at the bar drank triple Brandy Alexanders with double Scotch on the side. Also made one appearance with lipstick all over him.

Wednesday, March 3rd Mr. Parker arrived 9:50 p.m., and I announced him at 9:55 p.m. At 10:03 p.m. and only playing about 3 minutes of the 8, Mr. Parker proceeded to introduce Mr. Hibbler. I walked to the dais and reminded him that I would do that when the time came to play more. Again he announced Mr. Hibbler, so I told him to either play or leave the stand. He left and while I was announcing Mr. Hibbler, Mr. Parker went to the bar and ordered another triple alexander and scotch. My bartender refused to serve him. When I came off stage, my bartender explained Mr. Parker was too intoxicated to serve and that he would be subject to fine or arrest or both himself. Mr. Parker then stated that he would finish that night but I said not to wait any longer that he was through the last time he got off stage.

I now hereby file claim against Mr. Parker for:

Advertising (newspaper and radio)	$315.32
Refunded admissions	423.75
Cash advance on salary	55.00
Bar bill	34.40
Loss of club prestige	1,000.00
Loss of business & profit (people who came but left when told Parker was not appearing)	1,000.00
Total claim	$2,828.47

I respectfully ask that steps be taken so that club operators will not be faced with the same situation and loss in the future.

Kindly respond as soon as possible. If I am not compensated, I intend to file civil action against Mr. Parker.

With many thanks, for your consideration, I am,

Respectfully, Jack B. Tucker

MON	1
TUES	2
WED	3
THUR	4
FRI	5
SAT	6
SUN	7
MON	8
TUES	9
WED	10
THUR	11
FRI	12
SAT	13
SUN	14
MON	15
TUES	16
WED	17
THUR	18
FRI	19
SAT	20
SUN	21
MON	22
TUES	23
WED	24
THUR	25
FRI	26
SAT	27
SUN	28
MON	29
TUES	30
WED	31

FRIDAY 19 MARCH 1954

Leo Cluesmann, Secretary of the AF of M writes three letters to Charlie:

Dear Sir and Brother:

This is to officially advise you that the name of Eugene Riley, New York City, has been placed on the National Defaulters List of the Federation for failure to make payment of your claim for $15.00 as allowed by the International Executive Board. The April International Musician will contain notice to that effect.

Local 802, New York City has been so advised.

Fraternally yours, Leo Cluesmann.

Dear Sir and Brother:

This is to officially advise you that the name of Albert Bryan, Brooklyn, NY, has been placed on the National Defaulters List of the Federation for failure to make payment of your claim for $300.00 as allowed by the International Executive Board. The April International Musician will contain notice to that effect.

Local 802, New York City has been so advised.

Fraternally yours, Leo Cluesmann.

Dear Sir and Brother:

This is to officially advise you that the name of James LaRue, New York City, has been placed on the National Defaulters List of the Federation for failure to make payment of your claim for $350.00 as allowed by the International Executive Board. The AprilInternational Musician will contain notice to that effect.

Local 802, New York City has been so advised.

Fraternally yours, Leo Cluesmann.

MONDAY 22 MARCH 1954

Charlie receives a $25 advance from the Gale Agency.

WEDNESDAY 24 MARCH 1954

Charlie receives a $20 advance from the Gale Agency.

FRIDAY 26 MARCH 1954

Charlie writes to Norman Granz in reply to the letter of 25 January:

...I hereby give permission to Norman Granz to sue Ross Russell and Dial Record Co. for monies owed to me for composer's royalties and any other royalties from Dial Recordings ...

He also writes to James C. Petrillo, president of the AF of M, in pursuit of his claim against Herb Gordy:

Dear Sir and Brother:

I have written several letters and sent the original contract to Local 274 in Philadelphia, filing claim against Herb Gordy of that Local, for wages owed me since October 21, 1952. I played an engagement for Mr. Gordy and he owes me $350 since that time.

I have received no acknowledgement from the Local of either of my letters and I wonder if you could look into this for me.

Sincerely, Charlie Parker

MONDAY 29 MARCH 1954

The American Federation of Musicians write to Charlie with the outcome of his case against the Latin Quarter in Montreal:

Mr. Charlie Parker
151 Avenue B
New York, New York

March 29, 1954

Re: Case 829, 1953-54

Dear Sir and Brother:

The following is the decision of the International Executive Board in the above numbered case:

This constitutes the official award of the International Executive Board of the American Federation of Musicians on the demand of Charlie Parker against Morton Berman, employer and The Latin Quarter, Montreal, Que., Canada, dated October 19, 1953.

The International Executive Board denies the claim of Charlie Parker against Morton Berman, employer and The Latin Quarter, Montreal, Que., Canada for $743.04 alleged salary due him.

Fraternally yours,

Leo Cluesmann,
Secretary, A. F. of M.

James C. Petrillo, President of the AF of M also writes to Charlie, concerning the Herb Gordy affair:

Dear Sir and Brother:

This will acknowledge your letter of March 26th, re money due you by Mr. Herb Gordy of Local 274 in Philadelphia. I presume that this was for services rendered as a travelling musician.

I would therefore sincerely advise you to place a claim against Herb Gordy for the amount due you, with Secretary Leo Cluesmann.

Fraternally yours,

James C. Petrillo
President

WEDNESDAY 31 MARCH 1954

Recording session as the Charlie Parker Quintet for Mercury/Verve at the Fine Studios in New York City. CHARLIE PARKER (alto sax), WALTER BISHOP (piano), JEROME DARR (guitar), TEDDY KOTICK (bass), ROY HAYNES (drums)
I Get A Kick Out Of You (7 takes) / *Just One Of Those Things* / *My Heart Belongs To Daddy* (3 takes) / *I've Got You Under My Skin*

THUR	**1**
FRI	**2**
SAT	**3**
SUN	**4**
MON	**5**
TUES	**6**
WED	**7**
THUR	**8**
FRI	**9**
SAT	**10**
SUN	**11**
MON	**12**
TUES	**13**
WED	**14**
THUR	**15**
FRI	**16**
SAT	**17**
SUN	**18**
MON	**19**
TUES	**20**
WED	**21**
THUR	**22**
FRI	**23**
SAT	**24**
SUN	**25**
MON	**26**
TUES	**27**
WED	**28**
THUR	**29**
FRI	**30**

THURSDAY 8 APRIL 1954

Charlie Parker sends a Western Union Money Order message to Chan from Detroit:

MORE MONEY PLUS CONTINUED LOVE EN ROUTE THURS SUSAPHONE

FRIDAY 9 APRIL 1954

Charlie Parker writes to Leo Cluesmann, secretary of the AF of M:

Dear Sir and Brother:

I was advised by the office of the President to file a claim with you against Mr. Herb Gordy of Local 274 in Philadelphia for services rendered by me as a traveling musician.

Mr. Gordy owes me a balance of $350 on an engagement I played for him quite some time ago. I advised the Philadelphia Local of this twice and I sent them the original contract, but my letters were never acknowledged.

I trust you will give this matter your kind attention as it has been in long standing.

Fraternally yours, Charlie Parker.

MONDAY 12 APRIL 1954

Charlie Parker opens a one-week engagement at the Blue Note Club in Philadelphia.

SATURDAY 17 APRIL 1954

Charlie Parker closes at the Blue Note, Philadelphia.

WEDNESDAY 21 APRIL 1954

Charlie Parker writes to the AF of M Local 274 in Philadelphia:

Dear Sir and Brother:

Almost a year ago I wrote to you to file claim against Herb Gordy of your local for money due me on an engagement I played there for him. At the time I enclosed the original of the contract.

This case is now in the hands of the Federation, and Leo Cluesmann's office requested that I write to you for my contract. If you would be so kind as to send it back immediately to the above address, I would appriciate [sic] it.

Thank you in advance for your prompt attention I remain

Sincerely yours,

Charlie Parker

THURSDAY 22 APRIL 1954

Leo Cluesmann, secretary of the American Federation of Musicians, writes to Charlie about the charges made by Jack B. Tucker of the Tiffany Club in Los Angeles.

THURSDAY 29 APRIL 1954

Jazz at the Philharmonic send Charlie a cheque for $79.45:

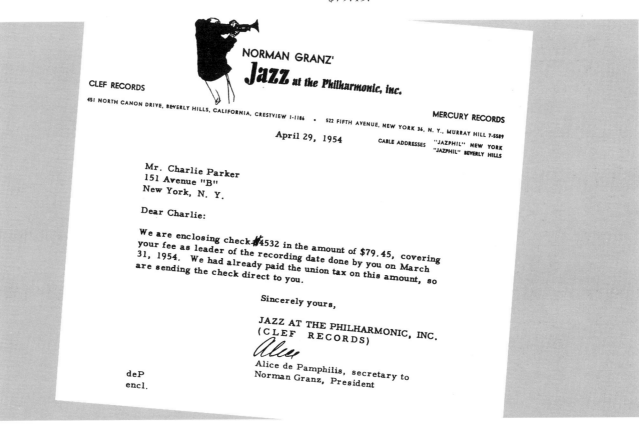

NORMAN GRANZ'
Jazz at the Philharmonic, inc.

CLEF RECORDS
451 NORTH CANON DRIVE, BEVERLY HILLS, CALIFORNIA, CRESTVIEW 1-1186 • 522 FIFTH AVENUE, NEW YORK 36, N. Y., MURRAY HILL 7-5589

MERCURY RECORDS

CABLE ADDRESSES "JAZPHIL" NEW YORK "JAZPHIL" BEVERLY HILLS

April 29, 1954

Mr. Charlie Parker
151 Avenue "B"
New York, N. Y.

Dear Charlie:

We are enclosing check #4532 in the amount of $79.45, covering your fee as leader of the recording date done by you on March 31, 1954. We had already paid the union tax on this amount, so are sending the check direct to you.

Sincerely yours,

JAZZ AT THE PHILHARMONIC, INC.
(CLEF RECORDS)

Alice de Pamphilis, secretary to
Norman Granz, President

deP
encl.

SAT	**1**
SUN	**2**
MON	**3**
TUES	**4**
WED	**5**
THUR	**6**
FRI	**7**
SAT	**8**
SUN	**9**
MON	**10**
TUES	**11**
WED	**12**
THUR	**13**
FRI	**14**
SAT	**15**
SUN	**16**
MON	**17**
TUES	**18**
WED	**19**
THUR	**20**
FRI	**21**
SAT	**22**
SUN	**23**
MON	**24**
TUES	**25**
WED	**26**
THUR	**27**
FRI	**28**
SAT	**29**
SUN	**30**
MON	**31**

WEDNESDAY 5 MAY 1954

Down Beat reviews the third Massey Hall album:

Jazz at Massey Hall, Vol. 3
Wee / Hot House / A Night in Tunisia
Rating: *****

Here we go again. A third set taken from the May, 1953, concert at Massey Hall presented by the New Jazz Society of Toronto. The giants that crossed the border that night were Dizzy Gillespie, Charlie Chan (everybody knows who *he* is by now), Bud Powell, Charlie Mingus, and Max Roach. Not only is the general level of performance more sustained than on volume one (volume two was that astonishing set by Bud), but this is the best recorded of the series.

Rather than dissect the performances, let me recommend your getting the set and digging the cabinet level conference yourselves. A prominent critic wrote the liner notes and provides another contribution to my campaign to get musicians rather than critics to annotate jazz recordings. Dig this: "... laminating firmly one the bottom of the bop boxes a supporting layer of fresh modernity strictly of his own carpentering." Axe, anyone? **(Debut DLP-4)**

SUNDAY 9 MAY 1954

Charlie plays at the Open Door in Greenwich Village using his plastic alto. For a fee of $161 Charlie plays from 4pm to 7pm and from 10pm to 2am.

THURSDAY 13 MAY or FRIDAY 14 MAY 1954
Herb Gordy replies to Leo Cluesmann:

Dear Sir:

I am writing to you in reply to a letter I received from you concerning Mr. Charlie Parker Case #29.

I am with a band which is working a series of one nighters and my mail just caught up with me, otherwise I would have answered you sooner. I hope I did not cause you any inconvenience by answering you at this time, because I am having a hard enough time with my creditors as it is, and I don't want to have any confusion with the Union.

Sometime ago I gave a concert here in Philadelphia, November 21, 1953 [sic]. The night of the concert we had a terrible rain-storm here and 2 of my backers left me holding the bag and I had to pay all of the people in the show including the Union taxes, City taxes. The fellows put in a claim and took my car and all of my personal valuables to get their money and I am still paying everyone off. I am only a sideman who is working irregularly, but I am definitely going to pay Charlie Parker next. It is true I owe Mr. Parker money for an engagement at the Met Hall, Broad and Poplar Sts,. November 21, 1953 [sic]. I have receipts and stubs and the signatures of Mr. Parker on various occasions that he was paid at different times after the concert. I also have a letter that Mr. Parker sent to me stating that he had made mis-calculations in the money I owed him. I will send you this letter and the receipts and telegram stubs proving Mr. Parker has been paid some of the money.

I owe Mr. Parker a balance of $187.00 and I will pay him the money within 45 days starting next week, I will send you a check for $25.00 because it seems Mr. Parker doesn't believe in my receipts. If you want my evidence in the case I will send you my receipts at your convenience. I will pay Mr. Parker weekly until the $187.00 is paid up within 45 days.

Awaiting your reply,

Herb Gordy (sgd.)

Herb Gordy also writes direct to Charlie Parker:

42 East Collom Street
Philadelphia, PA

Mr Charlie Parker:

I just got a job with a band and we are on a series of one nighters so my mail just caught up with me. I just got a letter from Mr Cluesmann and I answered him today. You know it is not fair about the way you are telling the Union I owe you $350 so I am sending Mr Cluesmann all of my receipts and your signature and the telegram that I sent you for transportation money. Also the letter you sent me stating that your mis-calculations were wrong.

1) You were payed some money the night of the concert in that little back room behind the stage of the Met. I have 2 witnesses and your signature.

2) I have a Western Union stub here stating I sent you $8 dollars for train fare to make a rehearsal that you <u>DID NOT MAKE</u> the whole band will testify to that? I have your signature that you were paid in Baltimore when you were working with Fats Wright at the Tiajuana Club on Pennsylvania Ave. I am sending Mr Cluesmann everything today I wrote to him telling him that I owe you $187 <u>NO MORE AND NO LESS</u>

SAT	**1**
SUN	**2**
MON	**3**
TUES	**4**
WED	**5**
THUR	**6**
FRI	**7**
SAT	**8**
SUN	**9**
MON	**10**
TUES	**11**
WED	**12**
THUR	**13**
FRI	**14**
SAT	**15**
SUN	**16**
MON	**17**
TUES	**18**
WED	**19**
THUR	**20**
FRI	**21**
SAT	**22**
SUN	**23**
MON	**24**
TUES	**25**
WED	**26**
THUR	**27**
FRI	**28**
SAT	**29**
SUN	**30**
MON	**31**

That is what I am paying Charlie no more!!

I told him I would pay you within 45 days. I am sending him your checks weekly. You will receive your first check next week. I am sending all of your checks to Mr Cluesmann and he will forward them to you.

Herb Gordy

P.S. The 45 days was the limit I will do my best to pay you much sooner than that so this case will be closed. I am sorry you and I could have not made this more pleasant. But £350 is the last straw. It is $187..

SUNDAY 16 MAY 1954

Charlie again plays at the Open Door.

MONDAY 17 MAY 1954

Leo Cluesmann writes to Charlie Parker enclosing Herb Gordy's reply (undated but received May 14, 1954):

Case No. 29 1954-55

Mr. Charlie Parker
151 Avenue B
New York, New York

Dear Sir:

Enclosed herewith please find the reply of Member Herb Gordy in the matter of your claim against him for $350.00 alleged balance salary due you.

In accordance with the rules of the International Executive Board, you may submit a rebuttal which must contain no new issues but must be confined to statements or evidence in answer to the statements or evidence contained in the reply.

Failure on your part to forward such rebuttal within ten (10) days from this date will result in the consideration of the case by the International Executive Board in its present form.

Very truly yours

Leo Cluesmann
Secretary, A.F. of M.

WEDNESDAY 19 MAY 1953

Down Beat reviews Charlie's latest record release:

SATURDAY 22 MAY 1954

Charlie writes to the Union about the Tiffany affair:

*** Almost Like Being In Love
**** What Is This Thing Called Love?

Recorded in 1952, the full band behind Charlie has, I believe, a rhythm section of Lou Stein, Bob Haggart, Remo Palmieri, and Don Lamond. Toots Mondello leads the saxes; the trumpets include Al Porcino, Bernie Privin, and Billy Butterfield; and Will Bradley and Bill Harris are in the trombone section. The arrangements are by Joe Lipman. Bird blows well on both, with the best fusing on *Thing*. The band kicks especially well on that one, with short solos by Privin, Harris, and Stein. There's some distortion at the beginning of the side. (**Clef 11102**)

Mr. Leo C. Cluesmann,
Secretary, American Federation of Musicians
220 Mt. Pleasant Avenue
Newark 4, New Jersey

RE: Case No 28, 1954-55

Tiffany Club, Los Angeles,California
                 vs
CHARLIE PARKER, Local 802

Dear Sir:

I have your letter dated April 22, 1954 relative to charges made by Jack B.Tucker of the Tiffany Club in Los Angeles, California. I am herewith submitting my answers to the allegations made in his claim. As you know, I was given an extension of time to deliver this answer.

I opened the Tiffany Club in Los Angeles as per contract on Monday night, March 1, 1954, and performed as per contract up to about 11 P.M. and at that time, I left the Club during my intermission to get a sandwich, and also to make a long distance telephone call to my wife in New York. While I was out of the Club, I was picked up by Los Angeles Police Officers, and taken to a Los Angeles Police Station on suspicion of being a user of narcotics. I was held there over night, and after it was found out that the charges could not be substantiated, as a substitute, I was booked on a drunken and disorderly charge which was unfounded. Mr.Charlie Carpenter (who works out of the Gale Agency) paid a $10.00 fine for me, and I was released at 7 P.M. on Tuesday evening, March 2nd. All during the time I was being held by the Police Department, I was not allowed to call the Tiffany Club to explain why I never returned after leaving the Club at 11 o'clock Monday night, and no one else contacted the Club to explain my absence.

This was later explained to Mr. Tucker, and due to the fact that he was aware of why I did not return on Monday, we renegotiated a contract to start on Tuesday evening, March 2nd, at a salary of $450.00, which was accepted by the Los Angeles local representative. I reopened the Club on March 2nd, and played all of the sets I was instructed to play under local house policy. Mr. Carpenter remained with me at the Club for most of the evening, and if necessary, I will forward a statement from him that I was not intoxicated during the time he was there. I deny having a bottle statched [sic] away, as claimed by Mr. Tucker, on that night or any other night that I was in the Club, as if I desired intoxicants of any kind, they were available to me in the Club. His comments about my behavior on the stage are purely a matter of opinion and conjecture. All I can say is that the people seemed satisfied with my performance and applauded the performance.

His comments as to whether or not I could use a drummer friend for one set, are not correct due to the fact that the sitting in of the drummer was done with the permission of Mr.Fain of the Los Angeles local, and with the permission of the regular drummer inasmuch as his equipment was used. I have been a member of the American Federation of Musicians for many years, and I surely understand the laws regarding musicians sitting in on other people's engagements, and this was done with complete accord.

On Wednesday, March 3rd, I worked throughout the night and played all the sets I was instructed to play under local house policy. I did have a few drinks with Norman Granz' brother and George Hoefer of Down Beat Magazine, who were in the Club, but I was most certainly not intoxicated.

SAT	1
SUN	2
MON	3
TUES	4
WED	5
THUR	6
FRI	7
SAT	8
SUN	9
MON	10
TUES	11
WED	12
THUR	13
FRI	14
SAT	15
SUN	16
MON	17
TUES	18
WED	19
THUR	20
FRI	21
SAT	22
SUN	23
MON	24
TUES	25
WED	26
THUR	27
FRI	28
SAT	29
SUN	30
MON	31

Mr. Tucker's comments about the introduction of AL HIBBLER, the other artist on the show with me, are absolutely wrong due to the fact that it was the scheduled time for MR. HIBBLER to appear, and MR. HIBBLER'S manager was insisting that HIBBLER sing as per schedule. Mr. Tucker should know this. While I should probably not have announced MR. HIBBLER at the time, I only did this to save Mr.Tucker the time, and to satisfy MR. HIBBLER'S personal manager, who was correct.

Mr. Tucker keeps repeating the fact that I drank triple Brandy Alexanders, and that I was supposed to have walked over to the bar after announcing HIBBLER, and ordered another of these drinks. He explains that his bartender explained that I was too drunk to be served and that the bartender would be subject to fine or arrest himself. The true story of this is that I could not have been drinking triple Brandy Alexanders and Scotch and become so completely intoxicated while I was in the Club, buy other people drinks, and only run up a bar bill for three days of $34.40 (which Mr. Tucker acknowledges) inasmuch as you undoubtedly know, Brandy and Scotch are normally expensive drinks in any Club, and the Tiffany Club is not one that one would consider a cheap Club. The bartender simply refused to serve me because Mr. Tucker had taken the attitude that I should not be served or have any courtesy shown me in the Club, and he was an employee, only following Mr. Tucker's instructions. It had nothing to do with the fact that I had one drink, or any drinks, or that I was intoxicated.

In Mr.Tucker's claim, I wish to point out that he admits several times that he "fired me", and he did this, of course, without permission of any authority of the Los Angeles local union. On Thursday night, March 4th, I reported to the Club before 9 o'clock and played three sets, according to house policy, and again an altercation with Mr. Tucker took place, and again he "fired me" without offering to pay for my services up to that point, or offering any negotiable settlement of any kind. I advised my Agency of this, and upon their instructions, went back to the Tiffany Club again on Friday, March 5th and offered my services to Mr. Tucker. He refused them and did not offer any negotiable settlement of any type.

I received from Mr. Tucker, during the four days I worked for him, the sum of $55.00 and I will also acknowledge and admit the bar bill of $34.40, but I deny that I was the cause of any of the alleged losses listed in his claim. Mr.Tucker admits that I played on Monday night, Tuesday night, Wednesday night, and part of Thursday night, and he admits that he "fired me" without consultation with me or any union representative. I feel that I am entitled to the sum of $450.00, the price of the renegotiated contract, less $89.50, or, $365.50.

In Mr. Tucker's claim, he lists various alleged losses as follows:

a) Advertising - $315.32. I feel that inasmuch as Mr. Tucker "fired me" without any approved reason that this alleged loss is strictly his own as I was perfectly willing to continue and finish the engagement.

b) Refunded admissions - $423.75. This, of course, cannot be checked by me, and if he did refund this number of admissions during the time I was in the Club, please bear in mind that I did not perform on Friday, Saturday, and Sunday of the engagement due to the fact that Mr.

Tucker "fired me", and this must also be his own loss because of this fact.

c) Cash advance on salary - $55.00

Bar bill - $34.40. These two items I admit receiving.

d) Loss of Club prestige - $1000.00. I do not think that this is a loss to the fact that the Tiffany Club continued to operate after I left, with MISS JUNE CHRISTY as an attraction. Other attractions followed, and the Club is operating now, and I do not believe that any prestige was lost by the Club. If Mr.Tucker feels that it did lose prestige by my not being there, may I again point out that I was not there due to Mr. Tucker terminating my engagement himself.

e) Loss of business and profit - $1000.00. This alleged loss I also answer as I did with item (d), I was not in the Club due to Mr. Tucker terminating my engagement himself.

To sum all of this up:

1) I was fired by Mr. Tucker.

2) If Mr. Tucker thought my behavior was erratic during the part of the engagement I played with him, I wish to state for the record that I was aware all of the time, that my three year old daughter was extremely ill, and I was completely worried about this. On Wednesday night, I learned that she was to be put into an oxygen tent in a last effort to save her life. This was unsuccessful, and my baby died on Friday evening. Even though I knew the condition of my baby, I voluntarily offered my services to Mr. Tucker for Friday and Saturday night, which, of course, he refused. I feel that not only should Mr. Tucker's alleged claim be denied, but that I should receive from Mr. Tucker, the sum of $365.50 for the balance of the money due me on the renegotiated contract which he terminated without the approval of anyone. I point out that if Mr.Tucker did have all of these alleged difficulties with me that he should have called upon the Local Union to come down to the Club and discuss this with him and with me, and if the Local Union had decided that I was conducting myself as Mr. Tucker alleges, and had advised me close, I would have done so. However, Mr. Tucker did not do this. He took it upon himself to fire me, and now wishes me to pay for alleged damages to him which he created himself, if there were any at all.

Thanking you for your kind consideration, I remain, Respectfully,

CHARLES PARKER

SAT	**1**
SUN	**2**
MON	**3**
TUES	**4**
WED	**5**
THUR	**6**
FRI	**7**
SAT	**8**
SUN	**9**
MON	**10**
TUES	**11**
WED	**12**
THUR	**13**
FRI	**14**
SAT	**15**
SUN	**16**
MON	**17**
TUES	**18**
WED	**19**
THUR	**20**
FRI	**21**
SAT	**22**
SUN	**23**
MON	**24**
TUES	**25**
WED	**26**
THUR	**27**
FRI	**28**
SAT	**29**
SUN	**30**
MON	**31**

SUNDAY 23 MAY 1954
Charlie again plays at the
Open Door.

TUESDAY 25 MAY 1954
Charlie opens at Basin Street in
New York City for a two week
engagement opposite Ella
Fitzgerald. Charlie sends Ella
a cable.

*Below: Charlie spends time with Baird
and Chan in the spring sunshine in
Washington Square Park.*

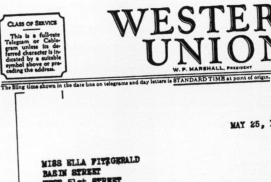

WESTERN
UNION

W. P. MARSHALL, PRESIDENT

MAY 25, 1954

MISS ELLA FITZGERALD
BASIN STREET
WEST 51st STREET
NEW YORK, NEW YORK

IF YOU'LL FORGIVE THE PUN, ELLA FITZGERALD IS STRICTLY FOR "THE BIRD".

YARDBIRD PARKER

TUES	1
WED	2
THUR	3
FRI	4
SAT	5
SUN	6
MON	7
TUES	8
WED	9
THUR	10
FRI	11
SAT	12
SUN	13
MON	14
TUES	15
WED	16
THUR	17
FRI	18
SAT	19
SUN	20
MON	21
TUES	22
WED	23
THUR	24
FRI	25
SAT	26
SUN	27
MON	28
TUES	29
WED	30

SUNDAY 6 JUNE 1954
Charlie again plays at the Open Door.

MONDAY 7 JUNE 1954
Charlie closes at Basin Street.

SATURDAY 12 JUNE 1954
Charlie plays a one-nighter at the Sparrow Beach Amusement Park in Annapolis, Maryland.

MONDAY 14 JUNE 1954
Charlie Parker Quartet opens at the Blue Note in Philadelphia for a one-week engagement. Clifford Brown is added on trumpet.

SATURDAY 19 JUNE 1954
Charlie closes at the Blue Note.

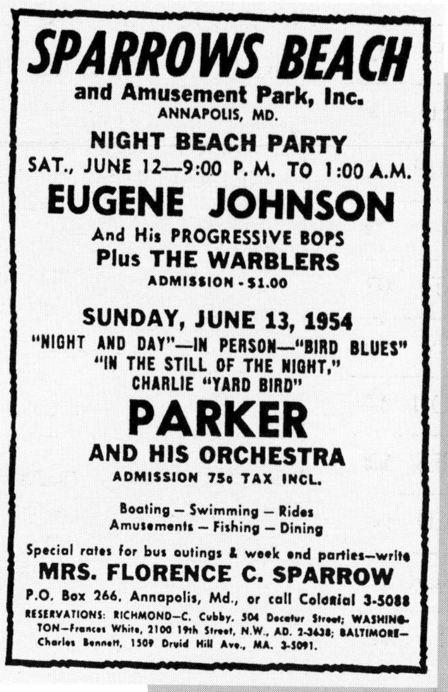

BOB REISNER Presents
"BIRD"
CHARLIE PARKER
AND HIS ALL STARS

BREW MOORE — Tenor   WALTER BISHOP JR. — Piano
ART MADIGAN — Drums   TED KOTICH — Bass

Sunday, June 6
9.30 P. M. to 2 A. M.
OPEN DOOR
55 WEST 3rd STREET

SPARROWS BEACH
and Amusement Park, Inc.
ANNAPOLIS, MD.
NIGHT BEACH PARTY
SAT., JUNE 12—9:00 P. M. TO 1:00 A.M.
EUGENE JOHNSON
And His PROGRESSIVE BOPS
Plus THE WARBLERS
ADMISSION - $1.00

SUNDAY, JUNE 13, 1954
"NIGHT AND DAY"—IN PERSON—"BIRD BLUES"
"IN THE STILL OF THE NIGHT,"
CHARLIE "YARD BIRD"
PARKER
AND HIS ORCHESTRA
ADMISSION 75¢ TAX INCL.

Boating — Swimming — Rides
Amusements — Fishing — Dining

Special rates for bus outings & week end parties—write
MRS. FLORENCE C. SPARROW
P.O. Box 266, Annapolis, Md., or call Colonial 3-5088
RESERVATIONS: RICHMOND—C. Cubby, 504 Decatur Street; WASHING-
TON—Frances White, 2100 19th Street, N.W. AD. 2-3638; BALTIMORE—
Charles Bennett, 1509 Druid Hill Ave., MA. 3-5091.

THUR	**1**
FRI	**2**
SAT	**3**
SUN	**4**
MON	**5**
TUES	**6**
WED	**7**
THUR	**8**
FRI	**9**
SAT	**10**
SUN	**11**
MON	**12**
TUES	**13**
WED	**14**
THUR	**15**
FRI	**16**
SAT	**17**
SUN	**18**
MON	**19**
TUES	**20**
WED	**21**
THUR	**22**
FRI	**23**
SAT	**24**
SUN	**25**
MON	**26**
TUES	**27**
WED	**28**
THUR	**29**
FRI	**30**
SAT	**31**

FRIDAY 9 JULY 1954

Charlie Parker sends a telegram to Chan in East Brewster, Massachusetts from St Louis, Missouri:

CALL ME STATLER HOTEL DETROIT TUES THE 13TH COLLECT FONDEST ADORATIONS YOUR HUSBAND BIRD=

MONDAY 12 JULY 1954

Charlie Parker opens at the Crystal Lounge in Detroit.

Anita O'Day remembers :

> I WAS APPEARING AT THE FLAME SHOW BAR IN DETROIT, AND IN BETWEEN SETS, I WENT OVER TO A PLACE CALLED THE CRYSTAL LOUNGE WHERE PARKER WAS PLAYING. WHEN HE SPOTTED ME, HE MADE THE FOLLOWING LITTLE SPEECH – ALTHOUGH HE DID NOT KNOW ME. "I WOULD LIKE TO ACKNOWLEDGE THE PRESENCE OF MY GOOD FRIEND ANITA O'DAY, BUT PLEASE DO NOT ASK HER TO SING BECAUSE SHE IS UNDER CONTRACT TO ANOTHER ESTABLISHMENT IN THIS CITY." I CAME BACK TO HEAR HIM A SECOND TIME THAT EVENING, AND THIS TIME I SANG A FEW NUMBERS WITH HIS GROUP.

FRIDAY 23 JULY 1954

Charlie Parker sends a telegram to Chan in East Brewster, Massachusetts from Detroit:

DEAREST. YOUR RENT. HOLD GEORGIE'S MONEY OFF UNTIL SATURDAY. CALL ME IF YOU NEED ME BEFORE THEN. ALL MY LOVE EVERY BIT OF IT. YOUR HUSBAND BIRD =

SUNDAY 25 JULY 1954

Charlie closes at the Crystal Lounge, Detroit.

WEDNESDAY 28 JULY 1954

Down Beat reports:

> New York—In recent weeks, pleased customers at the Record Collectors Shop on 47th Street have been able to hear hours of Miles Davis, Art Farmer, and Charlie Parker for free. Not on the demonstration machines— but in live Thursday night concerts.
>
> It's a uniquely effective move—with application possibilities all over the country—to advertise the extensive jazz department at the Shop. For 17 years, the Record Collectors Shop was primarily a classical operation, but like many other record retailers, owner-violist Herman Lemberg has been discovering that even when the rest of the record field is in a temporary decline, "jazz pays the rent."

Down Beat also reviews Charlie's latest album release:

CHARLIE PARKER
Now's The Time / I Remember You / Confirmation / Chi Chi / I Hear Music / Laird Baird / Kim / Cosmic Rays
Rating: *****
Bird's best session in some time and one of the best recording jobs he's been given. His thoroughly outstanding accompaniment is by Max Roach, Percy Heath, and Al Haig. All six of the originals are Parker's. Not all these are Bird at his most stratospheric, but there's enough superior work to make this one of the improvisatory highpoints of the year— particularly with the added premium of solos by the other three. Dig especially Roach's kaleidoscopic drum breaks, but don't miss Haig or Heath either. When Bird is right, to follow his blazing idea patterns is one of the greatest kicks in jazz. (**Clef LP MGC-157**)

SUN	**1**
MON	**2**
TUES	**3**
WED	**4**
THUR	**5**
FRI	**6**
SAT	**7**
SUN	**8**
MON	**9**
TUES	**10**
WED	**11**
THUR	**12**
FRI	**13**
SAT	**14**
SUN	**15**
MON	**16**
TUES	**17**
WED	**18**
THUR	**19**
FRI	**20**
SAT	**21**
SUN	**22**
MON	**23**
TUES	**24**
WED	**25**
THUR	**26**
FRI	**27**
SAT	**28**
SUN	**29**
MON	**30**
TUES	**31**

Left: Charlie on stage at the Apollo Theatre in front of a 17-piece big band. Benny Harris can be seen on trumpet.

MONDAY 2 AUGUST 1954
Charlie Parker opens at Midtown in St Louis for a one week engagement.

TUESDAY 10 AUGUST 1954
Charlie closes at Midtown, St Louis.

THURSDAY 12 AUGUST 1954
Charlie Parker rehearses with a 17-piece Orchestra for a one-week engagement at the Apollo Theatre. The Orchestra includes Charlie Rouse, Sahib Shihab, Gerry Mulligan, Benny Green and Benny Harris.

FRIDAY 13 AUGUST 1954
Charlie Parker and the 17-piece Orchestra open at the Apollo Theatre.

WEDNESDAY 18 AUGUST 1954
At 4.08 am on Wednesday morning, Charlie sends a telegram to Chan at 7 West 52nd Street:
MY DARLING I JUST WANTED TO LET YOU KNOW REGARDLESS OF THE THINGS WE HAVE TO EXPERIENCE IN LIFE I WANT YOU TO KNOW THAT I AM IN THE GROUND NOW I WOULD SHOOT MYSELF FOR YOU IF I HAD A GUN BUT I DONT HAVE ONE TELL MY WIFE THE MOST HORRIBLE THING IN THE WORLD IS SILENCE AND AM EXPERIENCING SAME. IM TIRED AND GOING TO SLEEP
CHARLES PARKER

THURSDAY 19 AUGUST 1954
Charlie Parker and the 17-piece Orchestra close at the Apollo Theatre.

SUN	1
MON	2
TUES	3
WED	4
THUR	5
FRI	6
SAT	7
SUN	8
MON	9
TUES	10
WED	11
THUR	12
FRI	13
SAT	14
SUN	15
MON	16
TUES	17
WED	18
THUR	19
FRI	20
SAT	21
SUN	22
MON	23
TUES	24
WED	25
THUR	26
FRI	27
SAT	28
SUN	29
MON	30
TUES	31

FRIDAY 20 AUGUST 1954

The Herb Gordy affair is settled in favour of Charlie.

WEDNESDAY 25 AUGUST 1954

Down Beat announces the results of the 1954 Critics' Poll. Charlie again wins the Alto Sax Award.

THURSDAY 26 AUGUST 1954

Charlie Parker and Strings open at Birdland for a three-week residency opposite Dizzy Gillespie and Dinah Washington.

FRIDAY 27 AUGUST 1954

Charlie Parker and Strings broadcast from Birdland over station WABC.
CHARLIE PARKER (alto sax), TEDDY BLUME (violin), WALTER BISHOP (piano), TEDDY KOTICK, TOMMY POTTER (bass), ROY HAYNES (drums), unknown oboe and string section
Theme / What Is This Thing Called Love? / Repetition / Easy To Love / East Of The Sun / Theme

SUNDAY 29 AUGUST 1954

Charlie Parker's 34th birthday.

At Birdland, Charlie is at odds with the string section. He behaves strangely, playing one tune while the strings play another. After an altercation he fires the whole orchestra. The Birdland management fire Parker, but not before having a camera girl take a photograph of him in action.

MONDAY 30 AUGUST 1954

After a row with Chan in the early hours of Monday morning, Parker swallows iodine in a suicide attempt. Chan calls an ambulance at 5 am and he is rushed to Bellevue Hospital.

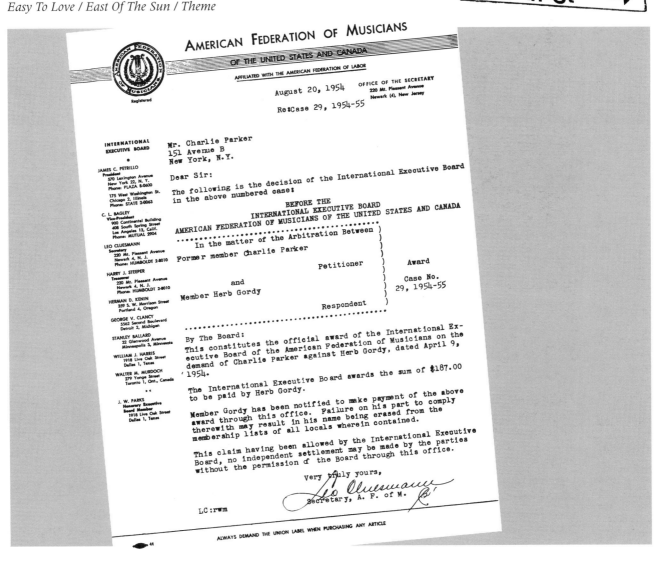

WED	1
THUR	2
FRI	3
SAT	4
SUN	5
MON	6
TUES	7
WED	8
THUR	9
FRI	10
SAT	11
SUN	12
MON	13
TUES	14
WED	15
THUR	16
FRI	17
SAT	18
SUN	19
MON	20
TUES	21
WED	22
THUR	23
FRI	24
SAT	25
SUN	26
MON	27
TUES	28
WED	29
THUR	30

WEDNESDAY 1 SEPTEMBER 1954

Charlie Parker is admitted to the Psychiatric Division of Bellevue Hospital.

SATURDAY 4 SEPTEMBER 1954

Britain's Melody Maker announces that Bird is to play in Britain.

WEDNESDAY 8 SEPTEMBER 1954

Leo Cluesmann writes to Charlie Parker:

Re Case No. 29, 1954-55

Mr. Charlie Parker
151 Avenue B
New York, New York

Dear Sir and Brother:

Member Herb Gordy has made payment of $50.00 to apply on your claim against him in the above numbered case and, inasmuch as the Money Order has been made payable to you, it is enclosed herewith. Kindly acknowledge receipt.

We have notified Gordy that all future remittances to apply on this claim are to be made payable to the American Federation of Musicians in order that same may clear our books.

Fraternally yours,
Leo Cluesmann,
Secretary, A.F. of M.

THURSDAY 9 SEPTEMBER 1954

Leo Cluesmann writes again to Charlie Parker:

Re Case No. 29, 1954-55

Dear Sir and Brother:

We are today in receipt of another Money Order from Herb Gordy, in the sum of $25.00, and since this remittance has also been made payable to you it is enclosed herewith. Same represents payment on account in above case.

This reduces the balance now due on your claim against Gordy to $112.00.

Please acknowledge receipt.

Fraternally yours,
Leo Cluesmann,
Secretary, A.F. of M.

FRIDAY 10 SEPTEMBER 1954

Charlie Parker is discharged from Bellevue Hospital.

SATURDAY 18 SEPTEMBER 1954

The Melody Maker reports on Bird's suicide attempt on the eve of the British tour.

WED	1
THUR	2
FRI	3
SAT	4
SUN	5
MON	6
TUES	7
WED	8
THUR	9
FRI	10
SAT	11
SUN	12
MON	13
TUES	14
WED	15
THUR	16
FRI	17
SAT	18
SUN	19
MON	20
TUES	21
WED	22
THUR	23
FRI	24
SAT	25
SUN	26
MON	27
TUES	28
WED	29
THUR	30

SATURDAY 25 SEPTEMBER 1954
Charlie Parker appears at Carnegie Hall with the Birdland Stars of '54 package which also includes the Count Basie Orchestra, The Modern Jazz Quartet, Stan Getz, Lester Young, Billie Holiday and Sarah Vaughan. The MC is Bob Garrity. There are two shows, at 8.30 and Midnight. Charlie is backed by members of the MJQ and part of his set is recorded.
CHARLIE PARKER (alto sax), JOHN LEWIS (piano), PERCY HEATH (bass), KENNY CLARKE (drums)
The Song Is You / My Funny Valentine / Cool Blues

SUNDAY 26 SEPTEMBER 1954
The package does two shows, at 3.30 and 8.30, at the Boston Arena in Boston. Charlie Parker is billed but does not feature in the review.

TUESDAY 28 SEPTEMBER 1954
Charlie voluntarily re-commits himself to Bellevue stating that he has been severely depressed since his previous discharge, is drinking again, and fears for his own safety. The admitting diagnosis is: acute alcoholism and undifferentiated schizophrenia.

FRI	1
SAT	2
SUN	3
MON	4
TUES	5
WED	6
THUR	7
FRI	8
SAT	9
SUN	10
MON	11
TUES	12
WED	13
THUR	14
FRI	15
SAT	16
SUN	17
MON	18
TUES	19
WED	20
THUR	21
FRI	22
SAT	23
SUN	24
MON	25
TUES	26
WED	27
THUR	28
FRI	29
SAT	30
SUN	31

SATURDAY 2 OCTOBER 1954
Coleman Hawkins replaces Bird on a 3-week European tour.

FRIDAY 15 OCTOBER 1954
Charlie Parker is released from Bellevue as an out patient, reporting daily for psychotherapy. He moves with Chan and the kids to Chan's mothers house in New Hope, Pennsylvania. He travels in to Bellevue each day by train.

Charles Colin writes a cheque to Chan for $150 as payment for five songs that Charlie had been commissioned to write. Chan is so insulted by the meagre sum that she never cashes the cheque.

TUESDAY 19 OCTOBER 1954
Charlie Parker sends a Western Union Money Order message to Chan in New Hope, from New York:
WILL TUESDAY 4PM NEVER FORGET ME MY LOVE

WEDNESDAY 20 OCTOBER 1954
Down Beat reviews Charlie's latest record release:

> **CHARLIE PARKER**
> *** Si Si
> *** Swedish Schnapps
> Recorded in August, 1951, these Bird sides have Red Rodney, John Lewis, Ray Brown, and Kenny Clarke. On *Si Si*, Bird is not at his best, but blows acceptably enough. Rodney is rather erratic. Rhythm section is fine and there's a good John Lewis solo plus alert breaks by Clarke and Brown. On the other side Bird's alto is equally casual, and Red Rodney's trumpet is somewhat better. There's also another worthwhile Lewis solo.
> **(Clef 11103)**

TUESDAY 26 OCTOBER 1954
The AFM judgement over the Tiffany Club affair goes against Charlie and he is fined $500:
AFM awards the sum of $500.00 to be paid by Charlie Parker and denies the counter-demand of Charlie Parker against the Tiffany Club for $365.50 alleged to be due him.
Payable ($500) on or before 5 Nov 1954.

SATURDAY 30 OCTOBER 1954
Charlie Parker appears at a Town Hall concert produced by Bob Reisner. Also featured on the concert are Sonny Rollins, Thelonious Monk, Art Farmer, Horace Silver, Jimmy Raney, Gigi Gryce and Wynton Kelly. The concert is poorly publicised and poorly attended. During intermission, a share of Charlie's earnings are impounded by a union patrolman.

Charlie tells Leonard Feather that he is commuting between New Hope, Pennsylvania and Bellevue Hospital where he is undergoing psychiatric treatment.

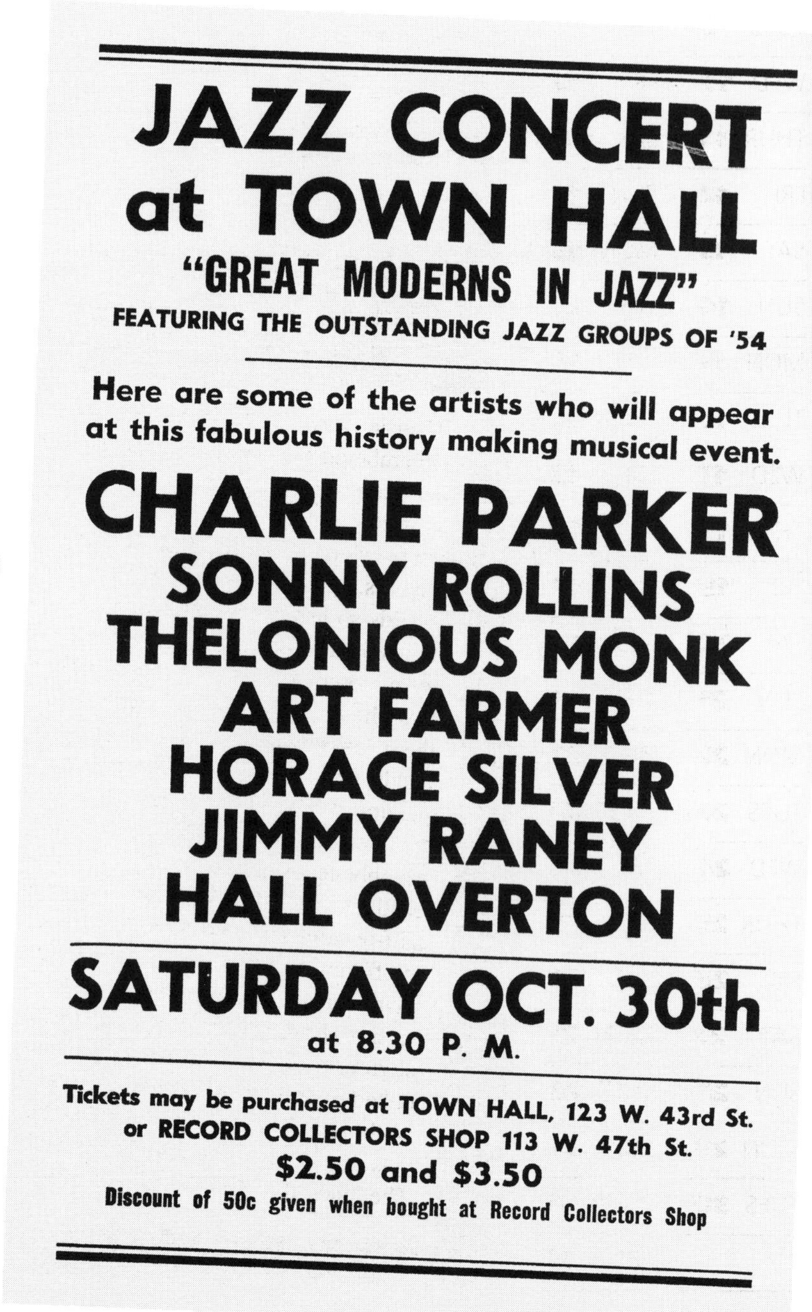

MON	1	WED	1
TUES	2	THUR	2
WED	3	FRI	3
THUR	4	SAT	4
FRI	5	SUN	5
SAT	6	MON	6
SUN	7	TUES	7
MON	8	WED	8
TUES	9	THUR	9
WED	10	FRI	10
THUR	11	SAT	11
FRI	12	SUN	12
SAT	13	MON	13
SUN	14	TUES	14
MON	15	WED	15
TUES	16	THUR	16
WED	17	FRI	17
THUR	18	SAT	18
FRI	19	SUN	19
SAT	20	MON	20
SUN	21	TUES	21
MON	22	WED	22
TUES	23	THUR	23
WED	24	FRI	24
THUR	25	SAT	25
FRI	26	SUN	26
SAT	27	MON	27
SUN	28	TUES	28
MON	29	WED	29
TUES	30	THUR	30
		FRI	31

FRIDAY 5 NOVEMBER 1954

Hot Lips Page dies of a heart attack, aged 46.

Charlie takes young altoist Jackie McLean to the funeral and spends a long time studying the body in the casket. 'They fixed Lips up real nice. His wig sure does look good.'

THURSDAY 18 NOVEMBER 1954

Leo Cluesmann, Secretary of AF of M writes to Charlie:

I have received no reply to mine of October 26th wherein I requested you forward payment to this office on your account in the above case.

Your failure to give this matter your attention may place your membership in jeopardy.

Kindly give this your immediate attention and forward proper remittance by return mail.

Fraternally yours,
Leo Cluesmann.

Dave Brubeck's portrait appears on the front cover of *Time* magazine.
When Charlie Parker is asked why he isn't on the cover, he answers: 'My clock doesn't work – I don't come on time!'

FRIDAY 10 DECEMBER 1954

Charlie makes his final recording for Norman Granz and Verve at the Fine Sounds Studio in New York City.
CHARLIE PARKER (alto sax), WALTER BISHOP (piano), BILLY BAUER (guitar), TEDDY KOTICK (bass), ART TAYLOR (drums)
Love For Sale (5 takes) / *I Love Paris* (2 takes)

MONDAY 13 DECEMBER 1954

Charlie Parker opens a one-week engagement at the Blue Note in Philadelphia.

SATURDAY 18 DECEMBER 1954

Charlie closes at the Blue Note, Philadelphia.

During Christmas week Charlie appears at Le Club Downbeat on Eighth Avenue near 48th Street. Ross Russell sees him there and remembers:

'Charlie was shabbily dressed in a suit I remembered from earlier years. The suit had not been to a cleaner in weeks. Dirt creases showed on the cuffs and collar of a rumpled white shirt. Charlie was wearing carpet slippers. His face was bloated and his eyelids so heavy that only half of the pupils showed. The first five minutes of the set were spent in slowly assembling the saxophone while fellow musicians, all of them unknowns, stood nervously on the bandstand. When Charlie got around to playing it was evident that he was having trouble getting air through the horn. The saxophone tone, normally so clear and brilliant, had flabby spots. The club was half-occupied and the management indifferent to the music. The musicians were trying hard to organize an old-fashioned jam session, Kansas City style, but the effort was obviously a failure. At tables customers talked over their drinks and cast vexed looks at the bandstand, indicating that the music was too loud, or unmusical for their tastes. The lines that Charlie played were strange and exciting, as if he were trying to press forward into a new and unexplored area of his music. The performance was painfully reminiscent of the Lover Man date in California....

An attempt to talk after the set proved futile. He sat at the table, sullen and barely coherent, full of hostility, staring at me with heavy-lidded eyes. He demanded the usual large sum of money, and I gave him the few extra dollars I had with me. He dug into his pocket and brought out a huge white pill and began munching it slowly, explaining that it was codeine and helped control the pain of his stomach ulcers. He launched into recriminations about the release of Lover Man and the arm twisting that he claimed had taken place before he was permitted to leave Camarillo State Hospital. During the next set a club employee came to the table to say that Charlie was carrying a gun and had threatened to shoot me and that it would be in everyone's best interest if I left the premises. That was the last time I saw Charlie Parker.'

SAT	1
SUN	2
MON	3
TUES	4
WED	5
THUR	6
FRI	7
SAT	8
SUN	9
MON	10
TUES	11
WED	12
THUR	13
FRI	14
SAT	15
SUN	16
MON	17
TUES	18
WED	19
THUR	20
FRI	21
SAT	22
SUN	23
MON	24
TUES	25
WED	26
THUR	27
FRI	28
SAT	29
SUN	30
MON	31

SATURDAY 1 JANUARY 1955

Bob Reisner meets Charlie on the street in Greenwich Village. Charlie says: 'You know, Bobby, I never thought I'd live to see 1955.' He then quotes a stanza he has memorized from the Rubaiyat of Omar Khayyam.

Come, fill the cup, and in the fire of Spring,
Your Winter garment of Repentance fling;
The Bird of Time has but a little way
To flutter – and the Bird is on the Wing.

Reisner offers him a gig at the next Sunday afternoon Open Door concert.

SUNDAY 9 JANUARY 1955

Charlie Parker appears at the Open Door in Greenwich Village.

SATURDAY 22 JANUARY 1955

Charlie Parker opens at the Comedy Club, Baltimore for a one-week engagement.

THURSDAY 27 JANUARY 1955

Leo Cluesmann writes to Charlie Parker:

Cases 28 and 29 1954-55

Mr. Charlie Parker
151 Avenue B
New York, New York

Dear Sir:

This is to inform you that HERB GORDY paid the balance of $92.00 due on your claim against him in Case No 29.

This sum is being transferred to the claim of the Tiffany Club, Los Angeles, Cal. against you for $500.00 in Case No28.

You stand erased for failure to clear the balance and surcharge due the National Treasurer's office.

Very truly yours,

Leo Cluesmann
Secretary, A.F. of M.

SATURDAY 29 JANUARY 1955

Charlie Parker closes at the Comedy Club, Baltimore.

Charlie then moves on to Detroit for his next engagement.

Bird On The Wing

New York—Charlie Parker has hit the road as a single with, in most cases, the clubs he plays supplying the sidemen during his stay. After brief engagements in Detroit, Chicago, and Detroit again, Charlie was scheduled to go into the Blue Note in Philadelphia for a week, starting Feb. 21. He also has a week at Storyville in Boston, beginning March 10.

THURSDAY 10 FEBRUARY 1955

Charlie flies from Detroit to Chicago. He takes out an insurance policy for $2,500 at the airport for a premium of $2.50.

FRIDAY 11 FEBRUARY 1955

Charlie Parker opens at the Bee Hive in Chicago for a 4-night engagement backed by Ira Sullivan (trumpet), Norman Simmons (piano), Victor Sproles (bass) and Bruz Freeman (drums).

Joe Segal, now a well-known Chicago club-owner, is working as a host at the Bee Hive. He remembers:
He had arrived late from Detroit for the four-day engagement. Some of us knew he had just been through a severe illness, and when he showed us the great swelling at the back of his tongue, we knew he was very ill, perhaps deathly so.

On opening night, Bird retired to a back room, spent most of his time resting, and didn't emerge very often to play. *The first time he was really ready to play, African drummer Guy Warren, in full regalia, breezed in and cornered Charlie in the back room and talked about music and Africa. Bird played no more that night.*

The next night, Saturday, began fairly cool because the musicians' union had warned Parker to play or he would be fined. But by midnight Bird had retired to the back room and passed out. Several of us repeatedly tried to awaken him, but every time we'd get him to his feet, he would push

CHARLIE (YARD BIRD) PARKER
4 DAYS ONLY
FEB. 11, 12, 13 & 14th.
SUNDAY MATINEE 4 P. M.
MONDAY JAZZ SESSIONS
BEE HIVE LOUNGE
1503 E. 55th St. ● 1 Block West of Lake Park

Bird backstage at the Bee Hive wearing the African regalia brought in by drummer Guy Warren (front). Ira Sullivan is second from the left, with Victor Sproles behind him.

TUES	**1**
WED	**2**
THUR	**3**
FRI	**4**
SAT	**5**
SUN	**6**
MON	**7**
TUES	**8**
WED	**9**
THUR	**10**
FRI	**11**
SAT	**12**
SUN	**13**
MON	**14**
TUES	**15**
WED	**16**
THUR	**17**
FRI	**18**
SAT	**19**
SUN	**20**
MON	**21**
TUES	**22**
WED	**23**
THUR	**24**
FRI	**25**
SAT	**26**
SUN	**27**
MON	**28**

us away mumbling, "One moment, please," and would collapse again, one time thunderously hitting the floor before we could grab him. He was very strong and very heavy and very sick.

At the end of the night when six of us put him immobile in a car, I didn't think he would be alive in the morning. But when I anxiously arrived early for the Sunday matinee, Bird was sitting at the end of the bar with a drink, eyes sparkling and looking dapper.

On one of those nights a friend and I were catching a breath of air in front of the club when Charlie came storming out, with no overcoat, shouting, "Why does he tell me about it? I don't do that!" When we asked what was the matter he said the owner had told him to be cool because the narcotics man was around. After we advised him to put on a coat, he said, "I don't want to see another winter – pneumonia's next for me!"

He had begun playing better Sunday afternoon, and by the time the gig was over Monday night, he was wailing as of old. Everyone felt much better. But I'll always remember the last thing he said to me as he was leaving, though I still don't quite understand what he meant – he said, "I'd tell you a joke, but you're too hip."

Norman Simmons is the pianist at the Bee Hive and, in a 1970 interview with Mark Gardner, he remembers:

But that first set was really the one. J.J. Johnson and Kai Winding preceded Bird and before they left J.J. told us to watch out for Bird because he was a tricky showman. I selected Bruz Freeman to play drums on this gig. He had played with Bird before, been to New York and on the road with Sarah Vaughan etc. Bruz is from a musical family of brothers out of Chicago and was responsible for dropping my name in the hat when pro gigs came around. Bird came and he was a sick man at that time but it was hard to tell when he was ill and when he was faking. He was a slick showman! They sent the musicians' union delegate to his room to bring him to work the first night while a throng of people waited. He got on the stand, played a tune and the next one was a blues (about then I decided I'd try to breathe). I even tried to get into something on my solo but about the middle somewhere, as I had my head buried into the keyboard, I heard this banging on the music stand. I looked up and Bird was waving me off the stand. I wished he had said the magic word so I could disappear. He then turned to Victor who was now looking worried as he walked the bass. Bird then lifted Victor's fingers from the bass finger board one by one and told him to leave the stand. You could hear a pin drop in the Bee Hive. You could hear Bruz swinging all alone as Bird stared at him. Then Bird picked up his horn, took a couple of choruses of fours with Bruz, put the horn down and left the stage, leaving Bruz to finish alone. That was one intermission gimmick!

Another was one which J.J. had tipped us on. Bird never informed the band about his little tricks etc. We were always startled and the audience was paralysed every minute. Right in the middle of anywhere in a song, Bird would raise his hand and give the cut off to stop. He would raise his hand and give a down beat to start the same tune, same spot in the tune and same tempo! We had him that time, thanks to J.J. Another of Bird's acts: When he was not playing he would rest his elbow on the top of the piano which was tilted in his direction, and nod. The stage was behind the bar, just about a foot or more off the floor level. One of the bartenders would be patrolling nearby and keeping a watch as Bird would let his elbow, which was also resting his head, slide slowly towards the end of the piano which reached to the edge of the stage. Just when Sam, the bartender, thought Bird was falling off the piano and the stage and would reach up to grab him, Bird would have straightened up and turned away as if nothing had happened, leaving Sam there with his arms stretched up into the air. Bird was a comedian too!

CHARLIE (YARD BIRD) PARKER
4 DAYS ONLY
FEB. 11, 12, 13 & 14th.
SUNDAY MATINEE 4 P. M.
MONDAY JAZZ SESSIONS
BEE HIVE LOUNGE
1503 E. 55th St. • 1 Block West of Lake Park

TUES	**1**
WED	**2**
THUR	**3**
FRI	**4**
SAT	**5**
SUN	**6**
MON	**7**
TUES	**8**
WED	**9**
THUR	**10**
FRI	**11**
SAT	**12**
SUN	**13**
MON	**14**
TUES	**15**
WED	**16**
THUR	**17**
FRI	**18**
SAT	**19**
SUN	**20**
MON	**21**
TUES	**22**
WED	**23**
THUR	**24**
FRI	**25**
SAT	**26**
SUN	**27**
MON	**28**

Bird in a series of poses at the Bee Hive. Opposite page with Norman Simmons (piano) and Ira Sullivan (trumpet).

MONDAY 14 FEBRUARY 1955
Charlie Parker closes at the Bee Hive in Chicago.

TUESDAY 15 FEBRUARY 1955
Charlie Parker opens at the Rouge Lounge in Detroit for a one-week engagement opposite the Johnny Smith Quartet.

SUNDAY 20 FEBRUARY 1955
Charlie Parker closes at the Rouge Lounge in Detroit.

MONDAY 21 FEBRUARY 1955
Charlie Parker opens at the Blue Note in Philadelphia for a one-week engagement.

WEDNESDAY 23 FEBRUARY 1955
Charlie Parker writes to Chan in Lumberville, PA:
Wensday [sic]
Chan
You still seem to underestimate me.
The only reason I stopped By the house in N.H. that night was to bring you the money. Not to Ball.
It is a known fact that I not only adore you – But, in front of that, I respect you.
I have many reasons to take care of myself – and shall do so. You can help.
It isn't necessary for me to know where you are – But Please Write me
Please never
Forget
Me.

SUNDAY 27 FEBRUARY 1955
Charlie Parker closes at the Blue Note in Philadelphia.

TUES	**1**
WED	**2**
THUR	**3**
FRI	**4**
SAT	**5**
SUN	**6**
MON	**7**
TUES	**8**
WED	**9**
THUR	**10**
FRI	**11**
SAT	**12**
SUN	**13**
MON	**14**
TUES	**15**
WED	**16**
THUR	**17**
FRI	**18**
SAT	**19**
SUN	**20**
MON	**21**
TUES	**22**
WED	**23**
THUR	**24**
FRI	**25**
SAT	**26**
SUN	**27**
MON	**28**
TUES	**29**
WED	**30**
THUR	**31**

FRIDAY 4 MARCH 1955

Charlie Parker opens at Birdland for a two-night 'comeback' engagement opposite Kai Winding's group. Charlie leads Kenny Dorham (trumpet), Bud Powell (piano), Charles Mingus (bass) and Art Blakey (drums).

SATURDAY 5 MARCH 1955

Charlie Parker arrives late to find the first set underway without him. Bud Powell is drunk. Oscar Goodstein, the manager of Birdland, orders Charlie to get up on stage and start playing. Charlie sees the state of Bud Powell and retreats to the dressing room. When Pee Wee Marquette introduces the band for the second set only Bud Powell appears, and drunkenly attempts to play *Little Willie Leaps*. Mingus and Dorham attempt to support him and then Parker and Blakey appear. Charlie announces, "Ladies and gentlemen, the management of Birdland has gone to enormous expense to bring you our all-star band." He then leads the band into *Hallucination*, but Bud Powell plays *Little Willie Leaps*. Parker stops the band and they restart with the same result.

"Come on, Baby!" Charlie pleads with Bud. Powell demands "What key, motherfucker?"

"The key of S, mother," replies Charlie, angrily. Powell smashes the keyboard with his elbow and leaves the stage. Charlie takes the mike: "Ladies and gentlemen, I'm sorry to say our most brilliant member has deserted us. Bud Powell! Bud Powell! Bud Powell! Bud Powell!" He repeats the name over and over.

Mingus takes the mike: "Ladies and gentlemen, please don't associate me with any of this. This is not jazz. These are sick people."

Below: Bird's last night at Birdland, just one week before his death. Kenny Dorham can just be seen at right.

TUES	**1**
WED	**2**
THUR	**3**
FRI	**4**
SAT	**5**
SUN	**6**
MON	**7**
TUES	**8**
WED	**9**
THUR	**10**
FRI	**11**
SAT	**12**
SUN	**13**
MON	**14**
TUES	**15**
WED	**16**
THUR	**17**
FRI	**18**
SAT	**19**
SUN	**20**
MON	**21**
TUES	**22**
WED	**23**
THUR	**24**
FRI	**25**
SAT	**26**
SUN	**27**
MON	**28**
TUES	**29**
WED	**30**
THUR	**31**

WEDNESDAY 9 MARCH 1955

Charlie Parker sets off for Boston to play an engagement at Storyville where he is due to open on Thursday. He stops off at the Stanhope Hotel on Fifth Avenue to visit Baroness Pannonica de Koenigswarter, known to her many musician friends as Nica. When he refuses a drink, Nica realises something is wrong and she calls a doctor. This is Nica's account:

He had stopped by that evening before leaving for Boston where he had a gig at Storyville. His horn and bags were downstairs in his car. The first thing that happened which was unusual was when I offered him a drink, and he said no. I took a look at him, and I noticed he appeared quite ill. A few minutes later he began to vomit blood. I sent for my doctor, who came right away. He said that Bird could not go on any trip, and Bird, who felt better momentarily, started to argue the point and said that he had a commitment to play this gig and that he had to go. We told him that he must go to the hospital. That, he said, was the last thing he was going to do. He said he hated hospitals, that he had had enough of them. I then said to the doctor, "Let him stay here." We agreed on that, and my daughter and I took shifts around the clock watching and waiting upon him and bringing ice water by the gallon, which he consumed. His thirst was incredible; it couldn't be quenched. Sometimes he would bring it up with some blood, and then he lay back and had to have more water. It went on like this for a day or two. When the doctor first came, he asked Bird the routine questions and some others. "Do you drink?" he asked. This brought a sidelong wink from Bird. "Sometimes," he said ironically, "I have a sherry before dinner."

The doctor came three times a day and any other times we would call him. The doctor knew how serious it was. Before he left the first time, he told me, "I have to warn you that this man may die at any moment. He has an advanced cirrhosis and stomach ulcers. He must not leave, except in an ambulance."

The doctor liked Bird, and Bird, when he wasn't racked by seizures, was in wonderful spirits. He made me swear not to tell anybody where he was. The third day he was a lot better. Dr. Freymann said he might be able to leave in a little while.

Left: Baroness Pannonica de Koenigswarter – Nica. Below: the Stanhope Hotel in 1990.

TUES	1
WED	2
THUR	3
FRI	4
SAT	5
SUN	6
MON	7
TUES	8
WED	9
THUR	10
FRI	11
SAT	12
SUN	13
MON	14
TUES	15
WED	16
THUR	17
FRI	18
SAT	19
SUN	20
MON	21
TUES	22
WED	23
THUR	24
FRI	25
SAT	26
SUN	27
MON	28
TUES	29
WED	30
THUR	31

SATURDAY 12 MARCH 1955

Nica continues:

At first, Charlie Parker was just a name to the doctor; he didn't know of Bird's genius, nor did he know of Bird's weaknesses. Bird wanted the doctor, who had been a musician, to listen to some of his records, and the doctor developed an interest in his patient and wanted to hear Bird's work. Bird and I spent a considerable time mapping out a program. First we played the album with strings, "Just Friends" and "April in Paris." The doctor was very impressed. Bird got a great charge out of that. That was on Saturday, about 7:30 p.m. Bird was so much better that the doctor agreed that he could get up and watch the Tommy Dorsey program on TV.

We braced him up in an easy chair, with pillows and wrapped in blankets. He was enjoying what he saw of the program. Bird was a fan of Dorsey's, and he didn't see anything strange in that. "He's a wonderful trombonist," he said. Then came part of the show consisting of jugglers who were throwing bricks around that were stuck together. My daughter was asking how they did it, and Bird and I were being very mysterious about it. Suddenly in the act, they dropped the bricks, and we all laughed. Bird was laughing uproariously, but then he began to choke. He rose from his chair and choked, perhaps twice, and sat back in the chair. I was on the phone immediately, calling the doctor. "Don't worry, Mummy," my daughter said. "He's all right now."

I went over and took his pulse. He had dropped back in the chair, with his head falling forward. He was unconscious. I could feel his pulse still there. Then his pulse stopped.

I didn't want to believe it. I could feel my own pulse. I tried to believe my pulse was his. But I really knew that Bird was dead.

At the moment of his going, there was a tremendous clap of thunder.

The time was 8:45 p.m.

SUNDAY 13 MARCH 1955

The body is taken to the city morgue. Nica is concerned with telling Chan about Charlie's death before it hits the newspapers. She searches the Greenwich Village clubs for news of Chan, talking with many musicians, but saying nothing of Bird's death.

TUESDAY 15 MARCH 1955

The daily newspapers print the story of Bird's death.

CHARLIE PARKER, JAZZ MASTER, DIES

Bop King Dies in Heiress Flat

BARE DEATH OF BOP KING PARKER

TUES	**1**
WED	**2**
THUR	**3**
FRI	**4**
SAT	**5**
SUN	**6**
MON	**7**
TUES	**8**
WED	**9**
THUR	**10**
FRI	**11**
SAT	**12**
SUN	**13**
MON	**14**
TUES	**15**
WED	**16**
THUR	**17**
FRI	**18**
SAT	**19**
SUN	**20**
MON	**21**
TUES	**22**
WED	**23**
THUR	**24**
FRI	**25**
SAT	**26**
SUN	**27**
MON	**28**
TUES	**29**
WED	**30**
THUR	**31**

Chan claims the body, sends it to the Walter Cooke Memorial Home on 72nd Street, and makes arrangements for Charlie to be buried next to his daughter Pree at Mount Hope Cemetery in New York. However, Doris, Charlie's last legal wife, has other plans and the body is removed to the Unity Funeral Home and services arranged at the Abyssinian Baptist Church prior to burial in Kansas City.

MONDAY 21 MARCH 1955
Charlie's funeral takes place at the Abyssinian Baptist Church on 138th Street. The pallbearers include Leonard Feather, Teddy Reig, Dizzy Gillespie, Sonny Stitt, Lennie Tristano, Louis Bellson and Charlie Shavers. Later the body is flown to Kansas City for burial.

No More Agony
Parker Finally Finds Peace

By Leonc

... many times afterward that he forgot.
... the times that he re-
... Doris left

The agony of Charlie (Yardbir... agony he had be... to face during t... us who were for... Bird as a frien... rience of watch... knowing that... him because h... helped or to he

Those who the great yea... and heard onl... his horn. Kn... ward struggl... talked carele... tle too loud,... cotics addict... and the le... him.

Behind t... heard wa... and inten... was when...

Jazz World Mourns Loss Of Charlie Parker

Petrillo Seeks UN Orchestra

Washington — James C. Petrillo, President of the American Federation of Musicians of the United States and Canada, in a recent visit with President Eisenhower at the White House, discussed the possibilities of "a United Nations Orchestra to bring the universal language of music to this multilingual but vital organization." Petrillo also spoke about "relief from the wartime amusement tax which is a severe employment deterrent for musicians and others, and which has now become a source of declining federal revenue.

"The United Nations," said Petrillo, "should possess and make generous use of the finest symphonic orchestra it is possible to recruit. Such an orchestra would be the rallying point for the diverse elements that comprise the U. N., for it alone would speak a universal language known and appreciated by all . . . I am well a... the U...

Charlie Parker

Betty Clooney

New York—Charles Christopher Parker Jr., acknowledged by most of his contemporaries as the greatest jazzman of modern times, is dead.

The alto sax king died of an acute heart seizure at 8:45 p.m. Saturday, March 12. An autopsy revealed that he had lobar pneumonia; he had also been suffering from ulcers and cirrhosis of the liver.

Parker died at the Fifth Avenue apartment of Baroness Nica Rothschild de Koenigswarter. The Baroness, an avid jazz fan and an old friend, told reporters that he had stopped off there the previous Wednesday. That day he complained of difficulty in breathing. A physician summoned by the Baroness recommended immediate hospitalization, but Parker refused to leave. "I did not have the heart to force him to go," she added.

On Saturday evening Parker was watching the Dorsey Brothers' TV show when he began to laugh, then collapsed, and died in a few minutes. His body was sent to Bellevue, where it remained unclaimed...

51350

EDELSTEIN BROS.

14TH ST. PAWNBROKERS, INC.

★LICENSED★

★PAWN BROKERS★

233 EAST 14th STREET

NEAR 2nd AVENUE   NEW YORK

1955

Saxaphone & case

100—

Amount Loaned

This article is protected against
damage by moths or breakage,
for which extra service we   *50*

charge as agreed

READ BOTH SIDES OF THIS TICKET

Office Hours: 9 A.M. to 6 P.M.